MAKING YOUR CHARACTER
COME TO LIFE

The playwright has given you the lines the character speaks and some of his or her actions. You must decide what kind of person would speak those lines and take those actions. Think of who you have known that might say and do the things your character says and does. In a sense, you are casting the role with the people you have known in your life. When a director of a play or film casts a role and sees a lot of different actors, he or she usually comes up with a clearer idea of what the essential characteristics of that role are. The same thing will happen to you as you think about who you have known in your life who seems like the character in the play. All your years of observing people will now help you define your character.

THE ACTOR'S SCENEBOOK
Volume II

Scenes and Monologues from Contemporary Plays

Edited by
Michael Schulman and Eva Mekler

BANTAM BOOKS
NEW YORK · TORONTO · LONDON · SYDNEY · AUCKLAND

THE ACTOR'S SCENEBOOK, VOLUME II
A Bantam Book / July 1987

ISBN 0-553-26581-4

ACKNOWLEDGMENTS

Published simultaneously in the United States and Canada

Bantam Books are published by Bantam Books, Inc. Its trademark, consisting of the words "Bantam Books" and the portrayal of a rooster, is Registered in U.S. Patent and Trademark Office and in other countries. Marca Registrada. Bantam Books, Inc., 666 Fifth Avenue, New York, New York 10103.

PRINTED IN THE UNITED STATES OF AMERICA

O   0 9 8 7 6 5 4 3

BOOK DESIGNED BY MIERRE

NOTICE: The scenes and monologues in this anthology are intended to acquaint the student of acting with a wide variety of new plays and playwrights. These scenes and monologues are not ends in themselves. In order to play them fully it is essential that actors read the entire play from which they are excerpted and become familiar with the background and circumstances of the character they are playing. Character work in particular can only be accomplished through a thorough study of the entire text.

Contents

Scenes for Two Women

Scenes for Two Men

Monologues for Women

Monologues for Men

CREATING A CHARACTER
by Michael Schulman

We can think of actors as falling into two categories: character actors and personalities. To illustrate, imagine both George C. Scott and Marlon Brando playing Richard III. Both are fine actors and anyone would love to see either of them play the part. But if your impression of these two actors is similar to mine, you already have quite a good picture of how Scott's performance would look and sound—much like almost all of his other roles. But there is no way to know what Brando's version of Richard III would be like, because in most of Brando's roles he has sought to create a unique character, one unlike any he has played before. He is, as I am using the term here, a *character actor*. In contrast, Scott's characters are all shaped to fit much the same mold—his own impressive personality (or at least the personality he displays in his film and stage work; it may not really be what he is like in his private life).

Many of our most successful film stars fall into the personality category. Katharine Hepburn and Jimmy Stewart are two extraordinarily fine actors of this type. Among the best known "character actors" are Laurence Olivier, Meryl Streep, Dustin Hoffman, Swoosie Kurtz, and Robert DeNiro (which does not necessarily mean that they have sought to create a unique and particular character for every role).

All actors must master certain aspects of their craft, regardless of whether they approach a role by trying to create a unique character or by attempting to express their own personalities. For instance, all actors must learn how to create what I call "basic realities," whatever their personal performing styles or the style and period of the play or film. *All* characters take actions in pursuit of objectives and all characters react to stimuli. Actions and reactions are two essential aspects of all human beings, on stage and off.

Hamlet, for example, takes the action of asking the visiting players to enact a play about murder as a way to resolve his doubts about whether his uncle killed his father. In order to play the reality of Hamlet's action, the actor, regardless of whether he is a character or personality actor, must know how to create the anguish that those doubts have inflicted on Hamlet, the anguish that drives his action. Otherwise he will make empty sounds and gestures.

Similarly, whenever Hamlet talks of his father, the actor playing him must bring to mind actual images and remembrances of a father. These may be of a father he has created in his imagination, or memories of his own father. He may even use another person as a substitute father, or he may use a combination of all three approaches, but he *must* have a father-stimulus and he must have those images of his father in mind *on stage* as he speaks Hamlet's lines; otherwise, he can not authentically experience the life of Hamlet. (Try talking about your own father without images of him; you'll find that it is impossible).

So all actors must learn how to create realities that lead to authentic physical and verbal actions and reactions, but only some actors are concerned with the question of how to create unique characters.

There are three main ingredients for creating authentic characters. The first is commitment. Most actors don't think about how to make their portrayals unique and specific to each role they play, but great actors do. Olivier spoke of this attitude in an interview some years ago. He was discussing the important influence Clare Eames had on his approach to acting and he said, "I used to talk about a straight part or a character part and she said, 'What's the difference? Don't tell me there's such a thing as a straight part. There isn't a part in the world that isn't a character part.' And it was she who gave me that attitude."[1]

---

[1] Hal Burton, ed., *Great Acting* (New York: Bonanza Books, 1967), p. 16.

In another part of the interview, Olivier revealed that initially he wasn't enthusiastic about playing Richard III—a role for which he received great acclaim—because he felt he had nothing unique to offer in the role. As he put it, "One thing that may lead an actor to be successful in a part, not always, but it may, is to try to be unlike somebody else in it."[2] Marlon Brando appears to have the same attitude. In an interview on his work in the western film *Missouri Breaks*, he described his interest in creating a cowboy unlike any he had ever created before and unlike any he had seen other actors portray. In general, character actors are committed to creating unique and authentic lives.

Perhaps the strongest statements about character acting were written by Constantin Stanislavski:

> I claim that all actors must be character actors. . . . This does not mean [the actor] must lose his own individuality and his personality; it means that in each role he must find his individuality and his personality, but nevertheless be different in every role.
>
> Any role that does not include a real characterization will be poor, not lifelike, and the actor who cannot convey the character of the roles he plays is a poor and monotonous actor. As a matter of fact, there is no person on earth who does not possess his own individual character. . . . That is why I propose for actors a complete inner and external metamorphosis.
>
> There are actors and especially actresses who do not feel the need of preparing characterizations or transforming themselves into other characters because they adapt all roles to their own personal appeal.
>
> Characterization, when accompanied by a real transposition, a sort of re-incarnation, is a great thing. . . . In other words all actors who are artists should make use of characterization. A capacity to

transform himself, body and soul, is the prime requirement for an actor.[3]

The second ingredient for successful character acting is to base your characters on real people. Olivier finally realized that he could bring something special to the role of Richard III by basing his character on Jed Harris, the American producer (the same person that Disney modeled the Big Bad Wolf after). Another of Olivier's major roles, Archie Rice in *The Entertainer*, was, it has been said, based on the English vaudevillian Vic Oliver.

Most character actors, when they talk about their work process, talk about spending lots of time observing other people, and either base a character on one particular individual or piece a character together by drawing various aspects from different people. Meryl Streep once commented that one of her problems in becoming a star was that it became difficult to watch people since now everyone was watching her. Olivier put it this way:

> You've got to find, in the actor, a man who will not be too proud to scavenge the tiniest little bit of human circumstance; observe it, find it, use it some time or another. I've frequently observed things, and thank God, if I haven't got a very good memory for anything else, I've got a memory for little details. I've had things in the back of my mind for as long as eighteen years before I've used them. And it works sometimes that, out of one little thing you've seen somebody do, something causes you to store it up. In the years that follow you wonder what it was that made them do it, and, ultimately, you find in that the illuminating key to a whole bit of characterization.[4]

There has been a lot of confusion among acting teachers about using people as character models. I believe that most of this confusion stems from Lee Strasberg's dictum to his stu-

---

[3]Constantin Stanislavski, *An Actor's Handbook*, ed. Elizabeth Reynolds Hapgood (New York: Theatre Arts Books, 1963), pp. 32–34.

[4]Burton, *loc. cit.*, p. 23.

dents that one never bases a character on people. I studied with Lee and then taught in his school for a number of years, and I must say that characterization was one of the areas he never really came to grips with. He almost never dealt with it in his classes, either in his own school or at The Actors Studio, at least not during the eight or so years that I saw his classes on a regular basis.

Indeed, at The Actors Studio, auditioners are discouraged from presenting anything but a role that is "close" to themselves, as if playing a role that is like you is a higher form of acting or reveals more of an actor's true ability than does creating a character. In actuality, many actors are not very good at playing parts that are close to themselves but are truly brilliant when they play characters. John Gielgud, who has done both with great success, described the "release" he found the first time he created a character that was very different from himself:

> It was when I played Trofimov, the student in *The Cherry Orchard* . . . and suddenly having to put on a bald wig and glasses and a shambling walk, I found a kind of impersonating release from my own personality that seemed to give me a freedom of expression which I had never found before . . . and I was able to lose myself completely in the role. I was relaxed for the first time.[5]

Lee Strasberg was a powerful influence on many of today's teachers and, unfortunately, many have blindly accepted his rule against using people as models. He did have one character exercise and it did involve observation—the observation of animals. Actors certainly have found animals useful as character models, but such study is a much slower and more difficult process than using people and more likely to lead to conventional, "archetypal" choices. People, with all their quirks and idiosyncracies, provide much more varied and individualized models. The question of using people as models should never have become a theoretical issue at all, not when great actors tell us that they are constantly observing

---

[5]Lewis Funke and John E. Booth, eds., *Actors Talk About Acting* (New York: Avon, 1963), p. 15.

people and basing their characters on what they've observed. The only sensible question for the acting student to ask is how to do it, not whether the process fits into his or her teacher's theory. (One recent actor's manual goes so far as to say that there is no such thing as character acting, as if all it takes to get acting students to deny what they see with their own eyes is to make a nonsensical assertion boldly.)

Character Exercises

The best way I've found to describe the process of creating a character is with the phrase, "getting possessed by a life." That is what the actor who strives to create characters must learn to do. There is a standard character exercise I do with students to help them learn this process of "getting possessed." It provides a structured procedure for learning and practicing the craft of character acting.

Start by thinking of five people you know who are very different from each other. To help select individuals who are very contrasting, pick one person who is easily irritated, one who is funny, one who is shy, one who appears very confident, and one who is overtly sexual. The people must be real and be recalled with a fair degree of clarity. The character labels (irritable, funny, shy, etc.) are only used to prompt thought. You must never merely play the general quality of irritability or shyness or any other personality label. If you do, your portrayal will rarely rise above the most obvious and conventional character choices. It is also important not to base a character on other actors' portrayals. For example, you should not choose Jackie Gleason's Ralph Cramden as a character model. If you do, your character will be two steps removed from life and almost certainly will be a caricature.

After selecting your five models, choose an "ongoing activity," something like painting a wall or vacuuming the house—an activity that involves your whole body and that can continue for a fairly long time. You will also need to memorize a monologue to use when working on the character's voice.

Start the exercise as yourself, engaging in the ongoing activity. Give yourself a good reason for doing it. Walls, carpets, paintbrushes, and the rest will all be created "sensorially"— through your imagination. It is important to provide yourself with obstacles to the task (the paint drips, the wall cracks, the paintbrush leaves hairs in the paint, the carpet has gum in it, and so on). These obstacles will intensify your sense of reality as you pantomime the activity. Obstacles will also allow you to experience the differences in temperament of each of your characters, because each will react to the obstacles in his or her own very particular way. After working on the activity for about three minutes, begin to recite your monologue as you work, speaking it as if you were practicing it in a fairly casual way.

After another couple of minutes it will be time to "get possessed" by the first character, say the irritable one. Stop the activity and feel the character "take over" your body. In class I will say, "Feel the character move right inside you and take over your body. Feel how the distribution of your weight changes, and how your posture and stance change. Feel the change in the rhythm in your body. Now let the character take over your eyes. You are seeing the room and the people in it through his or her eyes now. Feel the character take over your lips and face muscles, then your arms and fingers. Begin to walk around as the character. Feel how different your stride is. Feel what that stride is saying."

If there are odd aspects of a character or apparent infirmities, try to understand the physical or emotional causes that lie behind those behaviors. For example, a particular stride or posture may be a compensation for a physical infirmity or for a feeling of insecurity.

As the exercise continues, check all parts of the body and try to find which elements (eyes? stride?) seem most effective in triggering your sense of becoming the character. Then start your activity again, but now *as the character*. When working on a character, never ask yourself "How would my character do this (paint or vacuum or any other activity)?" You will usually have no idea and begin to worry about whether you are getting it right. Don't be concerned about getting it right; your only goal is to *feel* as if you are the character as you do it. Simply take your character into the situation and discover how he or she wants to behave. It doesn't matter whether your character model would actually carry out the task in the same way.

There is, though, one important way in which you must be true to your character. You must be faithful to your character's reactions, whatever they are, and not to the label you have applied to him or her. For example, you may find in working on your "funny" character, that he or she may not react with any humor to a paintbrush that falls. That's fine. Just express what seems true for your character at that moment.

After awhile, try to find the voice of the character, using the memorized monologue. Find the areas of resonance, the rhythms of the voice, and the way consonants are hit and vowels held. You are likely to find that the very meanings of the words change when you speak them while you are possessed by someone whose temperament and self-image are very different from your own.

Work on a character for about ten minutes, then switch to a second character and repeat the process. Do the same for all five. In class, after we go through all the characters, I will have students do a group improvisation in which each participates as one of his or her characters. Some will work on their funny character, others will do their irritable one, etc., so that all five types are represented in the improvisation. Sometimes I will strand them all in a bus station during a snowstorm or put them in a barn that they are converting to a summer theater. After a few minutes I will ask them to switch to a second character. They switch every five minutes or so until each student has tried all his or her characters in the improvisation. As they improvise, if I see a character slipping or becoming too general, I will remind the actor to go back to the "triggers" that will help him or her get possessed again.

Consider the exercise a success even if you experienced only a few seconds when you felt that you were taken over by another life. Once you know the experience of reacting spontaneously as another authentic human being, you can sort out the elements that worked for you and apply them more systematically the next time you practice the exercise.

You are likely to discover that you were more comfortable with some characters than others. Some people, for example, have trouble being assertive or expressing anger. Sometimes when they work on the irritable character, their own fears about anger conflict with their attempts to express the impulses rising up in them as the character. If you do experience a conflict between your own personality and the character's, you can overcome your fears and inhibitions by using some of the concentration and confidence-building techniques that I describe in my chapter, "Overcoming Stage Fright," in the first volume of *The Actor's Scenebook.*

While some actors experience discomfort playing certain kinds of characters, others find it liberating to play a character who is very different from themselves; in the guise of the character they feel free to express passions that they ordinarily inhibit in life.

The last phase of the character exercise teaches the actor how to use incidents, relationships, and objects from his own life (I call them "personal stimuli") in combination with character work. Many actors use personal stimuli to arouse strong emotions in themselves and have done so throughout the history of theater. Perhaps the most powerful example of this process is the story of the ancient Greek actor Polus, who, when playing Electra's mourning scene over the ashes of her brother, carried onstage the urn and ashes of his own recently deceased child.[6] (Students who have a misconception of British acting technique are usually surprised when they learn that John Gielgud uses personal stimuli.)[7]

When playing a character, you can use personal stimuli, but your reactions should be expressed in a form appropriate for your character. Start by imagining yourself in an emotionally arousing situation, for example, talking with someone who makes you very angry. Express your feelings to that person. Use words or even gibberish (random sounds), or put the feeling into the words of a memorized monologue. After a few minutes "get possessed" by one of your characters and repeat the exercise, again expressing your anger. The emotional stimuli will come from your own experience, but its expression should now be the character's. Try this exercise with all five characters. The form of your anger should be different for each.

When using the process of character creation in a play, there will be times when you want to create a fairly close facsimile of your character model, incorporating all the details of the person's voice and movements, all of his or her mannerisms

---

[6]Aulus Gellius, "Attic Nights," in *Actors on Acting*, ed. by Toby Cole and Helen Krich Chinoy (New York: Crown, 1970), pp. 14–15.

[7]Funke and Booth, *op. cit.*, p. 26.

and gestures. To accomplish this you'll need to observe the person very carefully. (Don't confuse this process with what nightclub impersonators do; they are caricaturists and are only concerned with copying—and usually magnifying—the externals of a character, not the feelings and thoughts that lie behind a person's particular style of expression.) For some roles you will only want to incorporate a more global sense of your character model, such as aspects of temperament or just stance and stride, but not particular mannerisms. Sometimes you may wish to capture aspects of a model's voice such as its resonance or rhythm without incorporating the accent or melody. And sometimes you will want to combine elements from two or more character models. In his autobiography, Olivier notes that "by the alteration of one major characteristic, not hitherto associated with you, you can become another person with a different personality."[8]

The third ingredient for successful character acting is finding aspects of yourself that are similar to the character you are playing. Even when playing a character who experiences and expresses emotions very differently from the way you do, you can still draw on your own feelings and behavior. Your character may be easily aroused to violence while you may be a pacifist who tries to handle conflicts reasonably. Yet you will still have had strong feelings of anger and have imagined yourself engaging in acts that are far more aggressive than any you've actually carried out. Also, you can probably imagine circumstances in which you would act violently, even if just to protect yourself or someone else. By using situations from your own life that have angered you—both real and imagined—and incorporating them as personal stimuli into your onstage thoughts and images and by allowing your body and voice to express the violent behavior that you have imagined yourself engaging in, you will be putting your personal experiences in the service of your character.

The lesson here is that you create convincing characters by combining a character model and appropriate aspects of yourself. Say you are playing someone who is more suave than you are, and you pick a suave character model. It will help if you also find the suave aspects of yourself. The suave person

---

[8]Laurence Olivier, *Confessions of An Actor: An Autobiography* (New York: Simon and Schuster, 1982), p. 165.

is comfortable in his environment; he knows the social rules and what to talk about and what words to use.

Now you may not be suave in the usual sense of the term, which generally refers to polished and polite behavior in sophisticated circles. But there may be environments where you do, in fact, display many of the essential ingredients—where you are comfortable, know the social rules, and make good conversation. Perhaps you experience all these elements when you are in a locker room. Even though your character's suavity is expressed in very different ways and in very different surroundings—in elegant salons and restaurants—you can use your own experiences *(in conjunction with your character model)* to help you achieve the proper behavior and feelings. A useful way to do this is to place onstage, via your imagination, objects from your own life that will help give you the proper reactions. For example, you might imagine a part of the locker room in a corner of the stage set, or a particular locker room buddy seated among the patrons of the elegant restaurant.

How Do You Choose a Character Model for a Role You Are Playing?

The playwright has given you the lines the character speaks and some of his or her actions. You must decide what kind of person would speak those lines and take those actions. Think of who you have known that might say and do the things your character says and does. Consider more than one person: different people will highlight different aspects of the character, and you may discover interesting facets of the person you are playing that you hadn't thought of before.

In a sense, you are casting the role with the people you have known in your life. When a director of a play or film casts a role and sees a lot of different actors, he or she usually comes up with a clearer idea of what the essential characteristics of that role are. The same thing will happen to you as you think about who you have known in your life who seems like the character in the play. All your years of observing people will now help you define who this person you are playing really is.

To illustrate, let's say you are playing Shakespeare's Coriolanus. Most actors simply play his haughtiness and disdain for the populace in a very general way, shouting from beginning to end, never revealing the human nature that lies behind all this anger (in a recent highly touted TV version from the BBC, the actor just brayed for three hours). But perhaps as you read the play you find yourself focusing on the side of Coriolanus' character that is extremely uncomfortable with being a public figure. In thinking about who you know that is uncomfortable like that, perhaps someone will come to mind. This will help you root the character in a real life. For instance, when I think of who I know that has that kind of discomfort, someone comes to mind who is somewhat of a cross between Robert Stack (who played Eliot Ness in *The Untouchables* series) and Gary Cooper—a man whose system seems to recoil when he is the center of attention and who will rarely engage in any kind of superficial social exchanges. By having a specific character model, a whole personality begins to take shape. Then begin to explore what you, in your own life, have experienced that is similar to what you have chosen for your character (such as discomfort that you have felt when public attention is focused on you).

In searching for a character model you may find that someone you know has many of the characteristics that are perfect for the character, but others that don't fit—someone who perhaps has the temperamental aspects that seem right for Coriolanus, but who uses his body in ways that seem inappropriate for a great warrior. The solution is to combine elements from different models.

Thinking of a role in terms of actual people will ground you in the realities of the events your character goes through and help you define the psychological attributes that lie behind his or her actions. In his autobiography, Olivier describes Jed Harris (his character model for his Richard III) as sadistic, arrogant, and charming. Those characteristics are all evident in Olivier's Richard. Any actor playing Richard will play the sadistic and arrogant qualities. But it is the charming side of Olivier's Richard that makes his rendering so unique and fascinating. That is the aspect that was brought to life by his choice of Jed Harris as a character model.

One doesn't *always* need a specific character model to create a fully defined character. Many times as you read a script a very specific life will emerge from the dialogue without any conscious effort on your part to define the character. You will simply know intuitively how that person moves and talks and feels. Sometimes you may realize that your intuition about this character comes from having known someone in your past who is like the person the author has described. At other times you won't have any idea where your sense of the character comes from. If, as you play the character, he or she feels like a real person to you, then you may not have to use a specific character model at all.

Sometimes, though, a character can feel real, while in actuality you will be playing a "type" (for example, a "southern belle" or a "tough guy") that is based on what you have seen other actors do. It's a pretty good sign that you are playing a type and not a person when your emotional reactions are missing their normal bodily component, as when you express anger but don't experience the physiological sensations that accompany real feelings of anger. If you find yourself playing a type, it is time to do your character work in a more conscious and systematic way.

Some teachers mistakenly refer to physical character work as an "external" process, in contrast to the "internal" process of working on a character's stimuli and motivation. But physical character work, properly done, does not only deal with the externals of a character. One chooses the particular walk or voice or facial features of a character only because one has some sense of the character's inner life—of his or her temperament and needs and vulnerabilities—and because those physical characteristics help one experience and reveal that inner life more fully.

Creating a character takes a lot more thought than simply playing one's personality. Finding just the right character to fit what a playwright has written is no easy task. It is an act of creativity. I have favorite personality actors and I see most of what they do because I enjoy spending a few hours with them and they always do a fine job. But I don't rush to see their latest efforts with the same enthusiasm and excitement as I do when one of my favorite character actors is in a new production or film. Then I rush to see the mind of an actor at work, trying to create a life that reveals what is essential about the particular human experience of a specific character.

Characters in Shakespeare and Other Period Plays

When creating a character for a period play, you will need to understand the behavioral conventions that prevailed at that period, or at least the conventions as they have been handed down to us through theatrical tradition. We can learn something about how people behaved in other periods from the painting and literature of the time, but to a large degree what is considered acceptable period playing is based on a tradition that is passed down from one generation of actors to the next.

Sometimes what is passed down goes through sizable changes from the original. For example, if you see films or hear tapes of Noël Coward's original productions, the actors— including Coward himself—were much more naturalistic and less eccentric than the performers you are likely to see in a current production of a Coward script. Today's Coward players work so hard trying to be ever and ever more arch, whereas the original players had an ease and effortless quality and bore a closer resemblance to actual human beings.

Similarly, many of Shaw's plays are about men pursuing women, and in his notes on directing, Shaw wrote that he wanted his actors to play his characters as real people ("[make] the audience believe that real things [are] happening to real people").[9] But in many contemporary productions of Shaw in both the U.S. and London, masculine sexuality is in short supply and the actors are working so hard at being eccentric Englishmen and women that nothing Shaw would have recognized as a real person is to be seen. Here, too, if one watches some of the fine old film versions of Shaw plays, such as *Pygmalion* with Leslie Howard and *Major Barbara* with Wendy Hiller, one sees acting that is far less ornate than contemporary versions and much closer to what Shaw described.

Perhaps the greatest alterations from what appear to be the playwright's original intention are found in contemporary productions of Molière. Molière praised the actor who played "in the most natural manner he could," and he derided the use of artificial emphases for theatrical effect.[10] Yet it is rare to see characterizations that resemble human beings in Molière's plays. Unfortunately we have no films to show us what "natural" meant to Molière.

Regardless of the particular behavioral conventions you

---

[9] George Bernard Shaw, *The Art of Rehearsal* (New York: Samuel French, 1928), p. 5.

[10] Cole and Chinoy, *op. cit.*, pp. 156–57.

adopt to represent a period, and regardless of whether the author intended the play to be naturalistic (for its time) or stylized (as, say, Goethe did), you must still play your character's basic realities; that is, every character in every play in every period and style takes actions in pursuit of objectives and reacts to stimuli. And even in period plays you can still develop a character through observation. It is not hard to find characteristics in people you meet today that are useful for fleshing out characters from other periods.

Basing your character in a period play on a real person will help root the character's "period" behavior in a human reality. It's important to keep in mind that the behavioral conventions of any period have a psychological basis. For example, Restoration male characters walked and held their arms in distinctive ways, often with a hand held up. Many acting students feel awkward and artificial trying to use their bodies this way. The reason may be that the only reason they are usually given for why Restoration characters held their hands up was because they wore large shirt sleeves that would get soiled if they lowered their arms. This is nonsensical and totally useless to the actor. If you hold your arms up simply to keep your sleeves clean, rest assured that you will not look anything like a Restoration character.

No one in any period would let a fashion designer give him overflowing sleeves or any other uncomfortable clothing *unless* that style helped the person express something he or she wanted to express. The Restoration male held his hands and body in particular ways in order to express his virility and his elegance. He was a peacock and his flowing sleeves helped him convey that image. The only way an actor will impart the distinctive and unusual Restoration style of movement is by playing the intentions that lay behind that style. Most actors today find it much easier to adopt the characteristic swagger of a ghetto youth, even though this walk is just as distinctive and unusual as the Restoration walk. But the contemporary actor is likely to understand, at least intuitively, what that walk is saying, that its message is, "I'm tough. I'm cool. I know my way around." By playing that message, the walk makes sense.

One of the problems in developing characters for Shakespeare's plays is that it is hard to locate his characters in a particular period and place. Many other English "period" playwrights wrote about their own times, often satirizing the style and manners of their contemporaries. So when we do their plays, we do our best to convey the behavior of those times. But none of Shakespeare's plays takes place in Elizabethan England and none are primarily social satires. So when an actor plays Mercutio in *Romeo and Juliet*, does he play him as a fourteenth century Veronese, a seventeenth century Elizabethan, or as a modern young man? There are no right or wrong answers. Audiences would be startled to hear Mercutio's lines spoken with a modern Brooklyn dialect, but perhaps less because of the particular speech sounds than because one doesn't associate the brilliance and complexity of Mercutio's words with a youth who speaks in a typical Brooklyn dialect.

Most contemporary American actors use a "standard" American dialect when playing Shakespeare, except when portraying his rustics and certain other regional characters. For these they use one or another British regional dialect. There is a danger in using a "standard" dialect, whether it is standard American or English: you may sound like everybody else, with no individuality to your voice. In most Shakespeare productions the stars (Laurence Olivier, John Gielgud, Derek Jacobi, Ralph Richardson, Richard Burton) all have very distinctive speaking styles. The rustics and regional characters, like the gravedigger in *Hamlet*, speak with various regional dialects. And then there are the assortment of dukes, messengers, and courtiers who all sound alike, fresh from their voice and speech classes. Even worse, they often all behave alike too, adopting a kind of "standard" Shakespearean demeanor—which "neither having the accent of Christians nor the gait of Christian, pagan, nor man" would not likely have pleased the author. Even when using a standard American or English dialect, you should give your characters their own personal voices and their own distinctive *human* qualities.

Some of our finest Shakespearean actors, like Richard Burton, pretty much play their own personalities from role to role. Others, like Olivier, apply their process of characterization to Shakespeare's characters just as they do when playing any other characters. They look for the unique physical, vocal, and temperamental attributes of the life they are creating. Some actors may be so appealing as personalities that audiences forgive the fact that their Hamlet, Macbeth, and Benedick are identical, but most actors are not that compelling. A couple of years ago I rushed with great enthusiasm to Stratford, England, to see a production of *Macbeth* starring an actor I'd seen in the Royal Shakespeare Company's *Nicholas Nickleby*. In *Nicholas* he played two characters that were so distinctive that most members of the audience didn't realize they were played by the same man. Both performances were brilliant.

But it was apparent that this actor had not used the same process of characterization for his Macbeth (perhaps because he did not have the precision and clarity of Dickens's character descriptions to guide him). Unfortunately his Macbeth had not been formed into a particular person with a distinctive manner and temperament. He played the *moments* that Macbeth lives through, but not the *life* that lives those moments in a particular way. This is a common problem in Shakespearean productions, even with fine actors.

When I say look for the unique attributes of your character, I don't mean that there is any single correct solution to this search—and don't believe any teachers who say otherwise, no matter how distinguished their credentials or authoritative their tone. There is no one correct way to play a Shakespearean character or to speak his or her lines. If you see both Laurence Olivier's and Orson Welles's film versions of *Othello* you will get a wonderful demonstration of how differently Shakespeare's characters can be played. Olivier's Othello is a powerful, confident, and warm "negro." When he finally succumbs to suspicion—after some resistance—it is like a giant oak falling. Welles's Othello is more "Moorish" in physiognomy and more mistrusting from the start. He is a man who knew all the time that he should never have trusted any of these Venetians. But he let his guard down with Desdemona and when he believes she has betrayed him, it confirms his worst fears. Virtually every line in the play is spoken differently by these two actors.

When creating a Shakespearean character, use all the same basic acting elements that you would use for any character, such as objectives, obstacles, and imagery (see my chapter "How to Approach a Scene," for a discussion of these).[11] But also pay attention to physical behavior and language in a more systematic way than you usually need to in contemporary plays. We know how people behave in the kitchens and living rooms in which today's authors place their characters. But how does one behave in a castle?

One of the great challenges in playing Shakespeare is to find behavior that illuminates the actions and personalities in the play. On one side one can err by overwhelming the events of the play with a flood of mundane behavior that may be authentic but is totally extraneous to the scene as written (and tends to make productions intolerably long). On the other side, in many productions the actors just rush on, take their positions, and recite their lines. The goal is to find actions that clarify the human events of the play. In *Richard II*, Bolingbroke launches a rebellion against Richard while the king is in Ireland. In "a camp in Wales" the Welsh Captain tells a duke who is still aligned with Richard that he and his army will not wait any longer for Richard to return to lead them against Bolingbroke:

> My Lord of Salisbury, we have stay'd ten days,
> And hardly kept our countrymen together,
> And yet we hear no tidings from the king;
> Therefore we will disperse ourselves: farewell.
>
> (Act II, iv, 1–4)

How might the actor playing the captain convey why he is leaving? What does waiting in the field for ten days actually mean to him and his men? If, before he speaks, the captain—seated perhaps with his shirt open—makes some gesture indicating heat, then swats a mosquito on his forehead, and finally reaches for a water skin and finds it empty, the audience will get a sense of what the waiting has come to. Then if he says his lines as he rises and gathers his belongings to leave, they will understand his motivation more fully than if the actor simply entered and said his lines.

---

[11]Michael Schulman, "How to Approach a Scene" in *Contemporary Scenes for Student Actors*, ed. by Michael Schulman and Eva Mekler (New York: Penguin, 1980).

* * *

The best way to deal with Shakespeare's language is not through any external devices, but by realizing that the language is *intrinsic* to the character you are playing. You need to create a life that is totally at home with the words you speak. Shakespeare's plays are stylized. His characters have real feelings and desires, but do not express them in naturalistic ways. You must accept that you are playing people who express their passions in language that has a richness far beyond ordinary speech. They are clearer about their feelings and describe them in more detail than people in everyday life. To "own" the language, your characters need to experience that clarity. And if your characters say things that are brilliant and perceptive, then, as in any play, they must be played as people who have the intelligence that allows them to make those statements.

I have seen a number of fine American actors (and recently some English ones too) fall on their faces when doing Shakespeare by trying to make their characters sound "natural," like ordinary people. In so doing they produce a totally unnatural effect. They are so afraid to sound artificial that they overly constrict the melody of their voices and stress virtually no words or phrases. They are so busy trying not to sound phony that they forget to apply their basic acting craft to the role. They forget that a particular image or stimulus *does* make one stress or isolate particular words. And they forget that we use words as actions and in so doing we (even we moderns) use emphasis, melody, pauses, and all sorts of vocal dynamics.

Richard II says, "What must the king do now? Must he submit?" If, in playing Richard, the actor experiences shame or disbelief at hearing himself use the word "submit," perhaps wanting to take the word back as it is spoken, then the actor should convey that experience by how he speaks that word. If, however, he is preoccupied with how Shakespeare's words should be spoken (Do they sound natural enough? Do they sound "Shakespearean" enough?), then he will never engage his acting process fully enough to discover and experience his Richard's particular relationship to the word "submit."

Whether you are playing in a Shakespeare play or any other play, never ask yourself how to say the words. In life, how our words come out depends on what we are reacting to and why we are saying them. The same principle should hold in theater. Focusing on trying to speak "naturally" is as useful to an actor as focusing on trying to walk "naturally." Both are guaranteed to produce artificial behavior.

Benedick, in a soliloquy in *Much Ado About Nothing*, says,

> I do much wonder that one man, seeing how much another man is a fool when he dedicates his behaviors to love, will, after he hath laughed at such shallow follies in others, become the argument of his own scorn by falling in love: and such a man is Claudio.   (Act II, iii, 7–12)

The only *natural* way to speak these nested clauses with clarity is by isolating each clause through melody, emphasis, and pauses. An actor who, in the hope of sounding natural, runs the phrases together will sound highly unnatural. He won't sound as if he owns the character's speech and thoughts, and no one will know what he is talking about.

Moreover, if the actor playing Benedick actually remembers Claudio laughing in mockery at another companion who had fallen in love, then when he gets to the word "laughed" the actor will do something specific with it, or, to put it more correctly, the image of Claudio laughing will do something to the actor's voice (and body) as he speaks that part of the speech.

In addition, *all* of Benedick's words must reflect the particular motivation that lies behind his criticism of Claudio. In other words, an actor plays an *event*, not words or lines. Perhaps right now Benedick is feeling especially irritated as he speaks because he's lost his last pal and must spend his afternoons alone (he's just sent for a book to read in his garden—not the most exciting afternoon's activity for a man of action). If that's what the actor chooses to play, then all his words must reflect this condition.

Shakespearean and other stylized plays often call for a character to speak directly to the audience. Many actors find this difficult, primarily because they don't establish a relationship to the audience. Perhaps they have had a teacher who advised them to speak to the exit sign or doorway or some other spot that has nothing to do with their character's life. If you address the audience, establish what your relationship is to them and what you want from them, just as you would for anyone else your character speaks to. In other words, you must know why you are speaking to them. Do you need their support or want to justify your behavior to them? Do you want to charm them or perhaps teach them something? Do they start out on your side, or do you have to win them over?

Talk *to* them, not just toward them. Even if the stage lights prevent you from seeing their faces, you must sense their reactions to what you are saying.

Olivier's film of *Richard III* provides an extraordinary example of an actor thoroughly defining his character's relationship to the audience. His Richard makes us his confidants. He mocks the gullibility of the other characters to us, as if he is baiting them for our entertainment. He lets us know he has exciting plans and that if we stick with him we will have an exciting time. At times he frightens us, perhaps to let us experience directly what we are about to witness him doing to others. That he manages to create this level of intimacy with an audience *in a film* is quite an achievement.

Sometimes it is obvious that a monologue is intended to be directed to the audience, as in the opening speech of *Richard III* ("Now is the winter of our discontent . . ."). Sometimes you will have a choice as to whether to direct a monologue to the audience or speak it as a private airing of your thoughts. Some soliloquies, such as Hamlet's "To be, or not to be" speech, can be spoken all to oneself, all to the audience, or a combination of both.

If you decide that a soliloquy is private, create your environment very fully and include the fourth wall between you and the audience. If your character truly inhabits an environment while speaking his or her innermost thoughts, there is a good chance that interesting behavior will emerge from you quite spontaneously. I once saw an actor produce a marvelous effect by shrinking back toward a wall as he began to speak a soliloquy. Although he spoke only for himself, he was so troubled by where his thoughts were leading him that it appeared as if he wished to find a crevice in the wall in which to hide. Without a clear sense of his environment the actor could not have come upon this interesting physical expression of his feelings.

* * *

Some Shakespeare teachers will consider my next point heretical: Do not pay any attention to the iambic pentameter. When we read any other poet, there is no footnote to tell us what meter to use. If we read the lines sensibly, the meter is there automatically. Only with Shakespeare are we supposed to do something special with the meter. It makes no sense and it stifles the actor. Many of Shakespeare's lines break the iambic pentameter. How do we know which lines keep the meter and which break it? Simply by speaking them sensibly. Nothing else need be done.

You will hear some teachers say that by scanning the meter, special meanings that Shakespeare intended are revealed. I've heard many of their examples and found that the "hidden" meanings were usually obvious, without any special attention to the meter, or that they had come up with some bizarre interpretations that made no sense in the context of the play. Normal English speech is, on average, stressed on every other syllable; that is, it naturally falls into an iambic pattern. So, when playing Shakespeare, if you make sense of what your character is saying, you will have no trouble with the meter and will be speaking in a rhythm quite close to your natural speech.

I've also heard teachers tell students that in Shakespeare emotions are conveyed by long vowels and intellectual ideas by consonants, and they have their students stretch the vowels during emotional moments and smash the consonants when conveying ideas. This leads to highly artificial playing and puts the actor's focus in precisely the wrong place—on how the lines should sound. Even if the formula about vowels and consonants made sense (and I don't believe it does), if your emotions are properly aroused and authentic and you are expressing your character's ideas for a purpose, then your voice will handle the vowels and consonants appropriately.

As you study a Shakespeare part, you'll find that your character's experiences won't divide neatly into such discrete entities as the "emotional" and the "intellectual." People are emotional about ideas and have ideas while in the throes of emotion. Besides, one can find endless counter-examples to the formula, such as the line from *Richard II* quoted above: "What must the king do now? Must he submit?" These words are said at a highly emotional moment yet are filled with short vowels and strong consonants.

Every so often I come across an actor who refuses to experience real feelings while doing Shakespeare. "What, cry during a Shakespeare speech? That ruins the poetry," is their attitude. Sometimes merely letting them listen to John Gielgud's highly poetic, tear-filled, and exquisite rendering of Richard II's soliloquies from his *Ages of Man* production is enough to change their minds. Shakespeare himself had something to say on the subject of real emotions in acting. Hamlet refers to the high esteem in which the players who come to Elsinore are held and he immediately asks to hear a favorite speech that he has heard the First Player do before. The player's eyes fill with tears as he delivers the speech. As Polonius puts it, "Look, whether he has not turned his color and has tears in's eyes." This upsets Polonius who Hamlet has mocked as "for a jig or a tale of bawdry, or he sleeps."

Polonius stops the speech, but Hamlet is impressed and says "'Tis well; I'll have thee speak out the rest of this soon." Later Hamlet will puzzle over the actor's ability to arouse real emotions in himself. Assuming that Hamlet was speaking for Shakespeare, we have a good idea of the kind of "organic," emotional acting that Shakespeare wanted for his plays.

Another caution: Be wary of what nowadays passes for what the English call "text analysis." Too often a teacher or director will go through the text of a Shakespeare play making isolated associations to words and phrases. One teacher in a well-known academy insisted that a student play Hamlet's "O, what a rogue and peasant slave am I" soliloquy with a wry chuckle because the word "rogue," he said, connotes "a likeable though slightly naughty chap." His argument was that if Hamlet has chosen that word then he must be giving himself a fairly lighthearted reprimand.

Of course the actor must decide why the character speaks precisely the words the playwright has given him. But the connotation of most words has a good deal of latitude and should be determined by the overall events that the character is experiencing. Given the moment in the play that Hamlet speaks that soliloquy, an actor could make a pretty good case for interpreting those lines as filled with self-loathing (besides, a "peasant slave" is a pretty severe condemnation).

A "good" example of the kind of harmful text analysis I am talking about was provided by the English actor Ian McKellen in a television presentation called *Ian McKellen Acting Shakespeare*. Phrase by phrase, McKellen went through Macbeth's speech that begins:

> Tomorrow, and tomorrow, and tomorrow,
> Creeps in this petty pace from day to day,
> To the last syllable of recorded time . . .
> (Act V, v, 19–21)

For each phrase the actor had a specific association that led to a particular reading. Some of the associations led to odd deliveries (particularly, his idiot-like intonation of the phrases following "It is a tale told by an idiot") that, I believe, would not have been understood by an audience that didn't have the actor's running commentary as a guide to his substitutions. Not one of the actor's associations had anything to do with the context of that moment in the life of Macbeth. The speech comes right after Macbeth learns that his wife has died. McKellen's phrase by phrase substitutions did not deal with that fact at all. Surely it should have some bearing on how this speech comes out.

By doing this kind of text analysis you will find that all you are playing is a series of disconnected ideas based on your personal associations to Shakespeare's lines. You certainly won't find it any easier to play these associations than to play what the lines mean in the context of the character's life. When the great British actors of an earlier generation discussed their approaches to Shakespeare, they didn't talk about anything resembling this kind of text analysis.

For example, when Olivier described his approach to playing Macbeth, he mentioned that a key choice for him was that from the moment Macbeth encounters the first witch he knows what will befall him,[12] and then finds himself powerless to alter his fate, though he continues to try. This kind of choice provides an overall context for the events of the play, and every line is affected by it. No line should find its meaning through isolated and arbitrary associations.

* * *

---

[12]Burton, *op. cit.*, p. 21.

In playing plays from other periods it is useful to research the period, to read about it in histories and novels, to look at paintings and sculpture of the time, and to familiarize yourself with the clothes, furnishings, and artifacts of the time. But don't let what you read lead you to distort what the playwright has written. Shakespeare was a sixteenth century Englishman, and his Joan of Arc (LaPucelle in *Henry VI, Part 1*) is a vicious young woman. It would violate his writing to turn her into the saintly heroine depicted by modern writers. Similarly, contemporary historians view Richard III in a much more flattering way than Shakespeare did. If you are doing his play, do *his* Richard. Otherwise, the dialogue will make no sense.

Sometimes academicians get caught up in historical details that have little bearing on an audience's response to a play. One expert argued that Hamlet should always wear a hat because a young man in his day would never have appeared in court hatless; indeed Ophelia even describes her fright when Hamlet came into her chamber with disheveled clothes and "no hat upon his head." Contemporary audiences don't know these kinds of details. For centuries audiences have gone to Shakespeare plays for the power of his imagination, for his language, and for his insight into what is universal about mankind. It is questionable that complete faithfulness to historical details adds to the experience of a contemporary audience.

Remember, remember, remember: There is no one correct way to say a Shakespeare line. I come back to this because I have seen so many Shakespeare teachers force readings on their students. When Hamlet says, "Now I am alone," he might mean, "Now I am *finally* alone," if he had been impatient for the players to leave so he could vent his rage at himself. On the other hand, he might mean, "Oh God, I'm left alone now," if he had been enjoying himself with the players, but then found himself thrust back into his agony as soon as they left. Each of these interpretations (and these are only two out of many possible ones) will lead to very different deliveries.

It is a useful classroom exercise to give students this single line to act and to ask each student to work out a context that motivates Hamlet to speak it. Each context should produce its own particular rendering.

Scenes for One Man
and
One Woman

THE REAL THING
by Tom Stoppard

SCENE 9

Annie and Henry have been married for two and a half years. He's an established playwright and screenwriter, very skilled and very traditional. She's a famous actress with an interest in radical politics. One day, on the way to an anti-missile rally, she encounters a young soldier, Brodie, who joins the protest and is arrested and jailed. In jail, Brodie writes a play about his experiences and Annie wants Henry to polish it and help to have it produced. Henry considers the script shallow and self-serving and wants nothing to do with it.

When Henry and Annie met both were married. They had a torrid love affair that was discovered by Annie's husband. Now Henry suspects Annie of having an on-going affair with a fellow actor, Billy. She and Billy have been co-starring in an out-of-town production in Glasgow. The play has just completed its run and Henry expects Annie back in London this morning, but she's late. Henry waits in their living room "alone, sitting in a chair, doing nothing."

(ANNIE *is heard letting herself in through the front door. Then she comes in from the hall.*

ANNIE *enters wearing a topcoat and carrying a suitcase and a small travelling bag.*)

Annie: Hello, I'm back.

(*She puts down the suitcase and the bag and goes to kiss* HENRY.)

3

Henry: Hello.

(*She starts taking off her coat.*)

How was it?

Annie: We had a good finish—a woman in the audience was sick. Billy came on with my heart skewered on his dagger and—ugh—whoops!

(*She takes her coat out into the hall, reappears and goes to the travelling bag.*)

Henry: I thought you were coming back overnight.

(*From the travelling bag* ANNIE *takes a small, smart-looking carrier bag with handles, a purchase from a boutique.*)

Annie: What have you been doing? How's the film?

(*She gives the present to* HENRY, *kissing him lightly.*)

Henry: I thought you were on the sleeper.
Annie: What's the matter?
Henry: I was wondering what happened to you.
Annie: Nothing happened to me. Have you had lunch?
Henry: No. Did you catch the early train this morning, then?
Annie: Yes. Scratch lunch, all right?

(*She goes into the kitchen and returns after a moment.*)

My God, it's all gone downhill since Sunday. Hasn't Mrs. Chamberlain been?

Henry: I phoned the hotel.
Annie: When?
Henry: Last night. They said you'd checked out.
Annie: Did they?

(*She picks up her suitcase and goes out into the bedroom.* HENRY *doesn't move. A few moments later* ANNIE *reappears, without the suitcase and almost walking backwards.*)

Oh, God, Hen. Have we had burglars? What were you doing?

Henry: Where were you?
Annie: On the sleeper. I don't know why I said I came down

this morning. It just seemed easier. I wasn't there last night because I caught the train straight from the theatre.

Henry: Was the train late arriving?

Annie: Do you want to see my ticket?

Henry: Well, have you been to the zoo?

(*She meets his look expressionlessly.*)

Who were you with?

Annie: Don't be like this, Hen. You're not like this.

Henry: Yes, I am.

Annie: I don't want you to. It's humiliating.

Henry: I really am not trying to humiliate you.

Annie: For you, I mean. It's humiliating for you. (*Pause*) I travelled down with one of the company. We had breakfast at Euston Station. He was waiting for a train. I stayed talking. Then I came home, not thinking that suddenly after two and a half years I'd be asked to account for my movements.

Henry: You got off the sleeper and spent the morning sitting at Euston Station?

Annie: Yes.

Henry: You and this actor.

Annie: Yes. Can I go now?

(*She turns away.*)

Henry: How did you sleep?

(*She turns to look at him blankly.*)

Well, did you?

Annie: Did I what?

What's the point? You'd only wonder if I was lying.

Henry: Would you lie?

Annie: I might.

Henry: Did you?

Annie: No. You see? I'm going to tidy up and put everything back.

Henry: Do you want to know what I was looking for?

Annie: No. Did you find it?

Henry: No.

(*She turns towards the bedroom.*)

Henry: Was it Billy?

(*She turns back.*)

Annie: Why Billy?

Henry: I know it's him. Billy, Billy, Billy, the name keeps dropping, each time without significance, but it can't help itself. Hapless as a secret in a computer. Blip, blip. Billy, Billy. Talk to me.

I'm sorry about the bedroom.

Annie: You should have put everything back. Everything would be the way it was.

Henry: You can't put things back. They won't go back. Talk to me.

I'm your chap. I know about this. We start off like one of those caterpillars designed for a particular leaf. The exclusive voracity of love. And then not. How strange that the way of things is not suspended to meet our special case. But it never is. I don't want anyone else but sometimes, surprisingly, there's someone, not the prettiest or the most available, but you know that in another life it would be her. Or him, don't you find? A small quickening. The room responds slightly to being entered. Like a raised blind. Nothing intended, and a long way from doing anything, but you catch the glint of being someone else's possibility, and it's a sort of politeness to show you haven't missed it, so you push it a little, well within safety, but there's that sense of a promise almost being made in the touching and kissing without which no one can seem to say good morning in this poncy business and one more push would do it. Billy. Right?

Annie: Yes.

Henry: I love you.

Annie: And I you. I wouldn't be here if I didn't.

Henry: Tell me, then.

Annie: I love you.

Henry: Not that.

Annie: Yes, that. That's all I'd need to know.

Henry: You'd need more.

Annie: No.

Henry: I need it. I can manage knowing if you did but I can't manage not knowing if you did or not. I won't be able to work.

Annie: Don't blackmail.

Henry: You'd ask me.

Annie: I never have.

Henry: There's never *been* anything.

Annie: Dozens.

Henry: In your head.

Annie: What's the difference? For the first year at least, every halfway decent looking woman under fifty you were ever going to meet.

Henry: But you learned better.

Annie: No, I just learned not to care. There was nothing to keep you here so I assumed you wanted to stay. I stopped caring about the rest of it.

Henry: I care. Tell me.

Annie: (*Hardening*) I did tell you. I spent the morning talking to Billy in a station cafeteria instead of coming straight home to you and I fibbed about the train because *that* seemed like infidelity—but all you want to know is did I sleep with him first?

Henry: Yes. Did you?

Annie: No.

Henry: Did you want to?

Annie: Oh, for God's sake!

Henry: You can ask me.

Annie: I prefer to respect your privacy.

Henry: I have none. I disclaim it. Did you?

Annie: What about your dignity, then?

Henry: Yes, you'd behave better than me. I don't believe in behaving well. I don't believe in debonair relationships. 'How's your lover today, Amanda?' 'In the pink, Charles. How's yours?' I believe in mess, tears, pain, self-abasement, loss of self-respect, nakedness. Not caring doesn't seem much different from not loving. Did you? You did, didn't you?

Annie: This isn't caring. If I had an affair, it would be out of need. Care about that. You won't play on my guilt or my remorse. I'd have none.

Henry: Need?
What did you talk about?

Annie: Brodie mostly.

Henry: Yes. I had it coming.

Annie: Billy wants to do Brodie's play.

Henry: When are you going to see Billy again?

Annie: He's going straight into another show. I promised to see him. I want to see him.

Henry: Fine, when should we go? It's all right to come with you, is it?

Annie: Why not? Don't let me out of your sight, eh, Hen?

Henry: When were you thinking of going?

Annie: I thought the weekend.

Henry: And where is it?

Annie: Well, Glasgow.

Henry: Billy travelled down with you from Glasgow and then took a train back?

Annie: Yes.

Henry: And I'm supposed to score points for dignity. I don't think I can. It'll become my only thought. It'll replace thinking.

Annie: You mustn't do that. You have to find a part of yourself where I'm not important or you won't be worth loving. It's awful what you did to my clothes and everything. I mean what you did to yourself. It's not you. And it's you I love.

Henry: Actually I don't think I can manage the weekend. I hope it goes well.

Annie: Thank you. (*She moves towards the bedroom.*)

Henry: What does Billy think of Brodie's play?

Annie: He says he can't write.

(*She leaves.* HENRY *takes his present out of its bag. It is a tartan scarf.*)

HURLYBURLY
by David Rabe

ACT III, SCENE 1

Eddie lives in a house in the Hollywood Hills. He is a scriptwriter whose career hasn't been going well lately. He is angry about the course his life has taken and the state of the world. He spends a good part of his day ingesting an assortment of drugs and alcoholic beverages. Most of the time he argues with anyone he comes in contact with. Among the people he does regular battle with are his ex-wife (she has their daughter), his roommate, Mickey, his friend Phil (who is upset because his wife, who recently had a baby girl, won't take him back), and his girlfriend, Darlene. Darlene is a photojournalist, and she spends a great deal of time out of town on assignments—which Eddie interprets as a sign that she doesn't love him.

As the scene opens, Eddie tells Mickey that he's worried about Phil. Phil left some frantic messages for Eddie earlier in the day, but now he can't be found. When Mickey leaves, Eddie and Darlene are alone.

Eddie: Let's just hang around a little in case he calls.

Darlene: I'm tired anyway.

Eddie: It's the kid thing, you know, that's the thing. He could walk in a second it wasn't for the kid.

Darlene: He should have then.

Eddie: Exactly. But he couldn't. (*Heading for the stairs, beginning to take off his jacket.*) So what am I talking about? It's just a guy like Phil, for all his appearances, this is what can make him nuts. You don't ever forget about 'em if you're a guy like Phil. I mean, my little girl is a factor in every calculation I make—big or small—she's a constant. You can imagine, right?

Darlene: Sure. I had a, you know—and that was—well, rough, so I have some sense of it, really, in a very funny way.

Eddie: (*As he goes into his bedroom*) What?

Darlene: My abortion. I got pregnant. I wasn't sure exactly which guy—I wasn't going crazy or anything with a different guy every night or anything, and I knew them both very well, but I was just not emotionally involved with either one of them, seriously. (*Emerging from the bedroom, he freezes, staring down at her, his shirt half off.*) Though I liked them both. A lot. Which in a way made the whole thing even more confusing on a personal level, and you know, in terms of trying to figure out the morality of the whole thing, so I finally had this abortion completely on my own without telling anybody, not even my girlfriends. I kept thinking in my mind that it wasn't a complete baby, which it wasn't, not a fully developed person, but a fetus which it was, and that I would have what I would term a real child later, but nevertheless, I had these nightmares and totally unexpected feelings in which in my dreams I imagined the baby as this teenager, a handsome boy of real spiritual consequences, which now the world would have to do without, and he was always like a refugee, full of regret, like this treasure that had been lost in some uncalled-for way, like when a person of great potential is hit by a car. I felt I had no one to blame but myself, and I went sort of out of my mind for a while, so my parents sent me to Puerto Rico for a vacation, and I got myself back together there enough to come home with my head on my shoulders at least semi-straight. I was functional, anyway. Semi-functional, anyway. But then I told everybody what had happened. I went from telling nobody to everybody.

Eddie: This was . . .

Darlene: What?

Eddie: When?

Darlene: Seven and a half years ago.

Eddie: That's what I mean, though; those feelings.

Darlene: I know. I understood, see, that was what you meant, which was my reason for trying to make the effort to bring it up, because I don't talk about it all that much at all anymore, but I wanted you to know that when you said that about your daughter, I, in fact, in a visceral sense, knew what you were talking about.

Eddie: (*Moving down the stairs toward her, as it seems they agree on everything.*) I mean, everybody has this baggage, and you can't ignore it or what are you doing?

Darlene: You're just ignoring it.

Eddie: You're just ignoring the person then, that's all. But at the same time your own feelings are—it's overwhelming or at least it can be. You can't take it all on.

Darlene: No.

Eddie: (*Holding her hand, he pats her in consolation.*) There's nothing I can do about all that, you know, that happened to you.

Darlene: No.

Eddie: It really messed you up, though.

Darlene: For a while. But I learned certain things from it, too, you know.

Eddie: (*Still holding her hand.*) Sure.

Darlene: It was painful, but I learned these things that have been a help ever since, so something came out of it good.

Eddie: So . . . these two guys . . . . Where are they?

Darlene: Oh, I have no idea. This was in Cincinnati.

Eddie: Right. (*Now he rises and begins mixing drinks for them both.*)

Darlene: I don't know what happened to them. I think one got married and I have this vague sense that—I don't know what EXACTLY—but . . . No. I can't remember. But I have this sense that SOMETHING happened to him. I don't know what. Anyway, I rarely think about it anymore. I'm a very different person.

Eddie: Did . . . they know each other?

Darlene: The two guys?

Eddie: Yeah.

Darlene: No. I mean, not that I know of. Why?

Eddie: Just wondering.

Darlene: What?

Eddie: Nothing. Just . . . you know.

Darlene: You must have been wondering something. People don't just wonder nothing.

Eddie: No, no. I was just wondering, you know, was it a pattern? That's all.

Darlene: No.

Eddie: I mean, don't get irritated. You asked me.

Darlene: You asked me. I mean, I was trying to tell you something else entirely.

Eddie: I know that.

Darlene: So what's the point?

Eddie: I'm aware absolutely of what you were trying to tell me. And I heard it. But am I just supposed to totally narrow down my whole set of perceptions, just filter out everything, just censor everything that doesn't support your intention? I made an association. And it was not an unreasonable association.

Darlene: It was totally off the wall, and hostile.

Eddie: Hostile?

Darlene: And you know it.

Eddie: Give me a break! What? I'm supposed to sit still for the most arcane association I ever heard in my life, that levitation leads to dogs? But should I come up with an equally—I mean, equally, shit—when I come up with a hundred percent more logical association, I'm supposed to accept your opinion that it isn't?

Darlene: No, no, no.

Eddie: Well, that's all it was. An association. That's all it was.

Darlene: Okay.

Eddie: I mean, for everybody's good, it appeared to me a thought worth some exploration, and if I was wrong, and I misjudged, then I'm sorry.

Darlene: It's just something I'm very, sometimes, sensitive about.

Eddie: Sure. What? The abortion.

Darlene: Yeah.

Eddie: (*Handing her the drink, he pats her hand.*) Sure. Okay, though? You okay now? You feel okay?

Darlene: I'm hungry. You hungry?

Eddie: I mean, if we don't talk these things out, we'll just end up with all this, you know, unspoken shit, following us around. You wanna go out and eat? Let's go out. What are you hungry for? How about Chinese?

Darlene: Sure.

Eddie: (*Grabbing up the phone and starting to dial.*) We could go to Mr. Chou's. Treat ourselves right.

Darlene: That's great. I love the seaweed.

Eddie: I mean, you want Chinese?

Darlene: I love Mr. Chou's.

Eddie: We could go some other place. How about Ma Maison?

Darlene: Sure.

Eddie: (*Hanging up the phone.*) You like that better than Mr. Chou's?

Darlene: I don't like it better, but it's great. Which one is your preference?

Eddie: Well, I want—you know—this should be—I'd like this to be your choice.

Darlene: It doesn't matter to me.

Eddie: Which one should I call?

Darlene: Surprise me.

Eddie: I don't want to surprise you. I want to, you know, do whatever you say.

Darlene: Then just pick one. Call one. Either.

Eddie: I mean, why should I have to guess? I don't want to guess. Just tell me. I mean, what if I pick the wrong one?

Darlene: You can't pick the wrong one. Honestly, Eddie, I like them both the same. I like them both exactly the same.

Eddie: Exactly?

Darlene: Yes. I like them both.

Eddie: I mean, how can you possibly think you like them both the same? One is French and one is Chinese. They're different. They're as different as—I mean, what is the world, one big blur to you out there in which everything that bears some resemblance to something else is just automatically put at the same level in your hierarchy, for chrissake, Darlene, the only thing they have in common is that they're both restaurants!

Darlene: Are you aware that you're yelling?

Eddie: My voice is raised for emphasis, which is a perfectly legitimate use of volume. Particularly when, in addition, I evidently have to break through this goddamn cloud in which you are obviously enveloped in which everything is just this blur totally void of the most rudimentary sort of distinction.

Darlene: Just call the restaurant, why don't you?

Eddie: Why are you doing this?

Darlene: I'm hungry. I'm just trying to get something to eat before I faint.

Eddie: The fuck you are. You're up to something.

Darlene: What do you mean, what am I up to? You're telling me I don't know if I'm hungry or not? I'm hungry!

Eddie: Bullshit!

Darlene: (*Leaping up from her chair, she strides across the room.*) "Up to?" Paranoia, Eddie. Para-fucking-noia. Be alert. Your tendencies are coming out all over the place.

Eddie: I'm fine.

Darlene: (*Pacing near the base of the stairs.*) I mean, to stand there screeching at me about what-am-I-up-to is paranoid.

Eddie: Not if you're up to something, it's not.

Darlene: I'm not. Take my word for it, you're acting a little nuts.

Eddie: I'm supposed to trust your judgment of my mental stability? I'm supposed to trust your evaluation of the nuances of my sanity? You can't even tell the difference between a French and a Chinese restaurant!

Darlene: I like them both.

Eddie: But they're different. One is French, and the other is Chinese. They are totally fucking different.

Darlene: Not in my inner, subjective, emotional experience of them.

Eddie: The tastes, the decors, the waiters, the accents. The fucking accents. The little phrases the waiters say. And they yell at each other in these whole totally different languages, does none of this make an impression on you?

Darlene: It impresses me that I like them both.

Eddie: Your total inner emotional subjective experience must be THIS EPIC FUCKING FOG! I mean, what are you on, some sort of dualistic trip and everything is in twos and you just can't tell which is which so you're just pulled taut between them on this goddamn high wire between people who might like to have some kind of definitive reaction from you in order to know!

Darlene: Fuck you!

Eddie: What's wrong with that?

Darlene: Is that what this is all about? Those two guys. I happened to mention two guys!

Eddie: I just want to know if this is a pattern. Chinese restaurants and you can't tell the difference between people. (*They stand, staring at each other.*)

Darlene: Oh, Eddie. Oh, Eddie, Eddie.

Eddie: What?

Darlene: Oh, Eddie, Eddie. (*Moving to the couch, she slumps down, sits there.*)

Eddie: What?

Darlene: I just really feel awful. This is really depressing. I really like you. I really do.

Eddie: I mean . . .

Darlene: What?

Eddie: Well, don't feel too bad, okay?

Darlene: I do, I feel bad. I feel bad.

Eddie: (*Moving now, he sits down on the edge of the arm-chair, and leans toward her.*) But, I mean, just—we have to talk about these things, right? That's all. This is okay.

Darlene: No, no.

Eddie: Just don't—you know, on the basis of this, make any sort of grand, kind of overwhelming, comprehensive, kind of, you know, totally conclusive assessment here. That would be absurd, you know. I mean, this is an isolated, individual thing here, and—

Darlene: No.

Eddie: (*Moving to the couch, he tries to get close to her, settles on his knees on the floor beside the couch.*) Sure. I mean, sometimes what is it? It's stuff, other stuff; stuff under stuff, you're doing one thing you think it's something else. I mean, it's always there, the family thing, the childhood thing, it's—sometimes it comes up. I go off. I'm not even where I seem anymore. I'm not there.

Darlene: Eddie, I think I should go.

Eddie: I'm trying to explain.

Darlene: (*Sliding away from him.*) I know all about it.

Eddie: Whata you know all about?

Darlene: Your fucking childhood, Eddie. You tol' me.

Eddie: Whata you know?

Darlene: I know all I—what is this, a test? I mean, I know: Your parents were these religious lunatics, these pious frauds, who periodically beat the shit out of you.

Eddie: They weren't just religious, and they didn't just—

Darlene: Your father was a minister, I know.

Eddie: What denomination?

Darlene: Fuck you. (*She bolts away, starts gathering up her things: She's going to leave.*)

Eddie: You said you knew.

Darlene: I don't think there's a lot more we ought to, with any, you know, honesty, allow ourselves in the way of bullshit about our backgrounds to exonerate what is our just plain mean behavior to one another.

Eddie: That's not what I'm doing.

Darlene: So, what are you doing?

Eddie: (*Following her.*) They took me in the woods; they prayed and then they beat the shit out of me; they prayed and beat me with sticks. He talked in tongues.

Darlene: She broke your nose and blacked your eyes, I know.

Eddie: Because I wanted to watch *Range Rider* on TV, and she considered it a violent program. (*Phone rings.*) So she broke my nose. That's insane.

Darlene: But I don't care, Eddie. I don't care. (*She's really ready to go now.*)

Eddie: Whata you mean?

Darlene: I mean, it doesn't matter. (*She steps for the door.*)

Eddie: It doesn't matter? What are you talking about? (*Grabbing her by the arm to detain her.*)

Darlene: It doesn't.

Eddie: No, no, no. (*As he grabs up the phone and yells into it.*) Hold on. (*Clutching* DARLENE *in one hand and the phone in the other, he turns to her.*) No, no; it matters, and you care. What you mean is, it doesn't make any difference. (*Releasing her, he speaks into the phone.*) Hello.

Darlene: I can't stand this goddamn semantic insanity anymore, Eddie—I can't be that specific about my feelings—I can't. Will you get off the phone!

Eddie: (*Into the phone.*) What? Oh, no. No, no. Oh, no.

Darlene: What?

Eddie: (*Into phone.*) Wait there. There. I'll come over. (*He hangs up and stands.*)

Darlene: Eddie, what? You look terrible. What? (*He starts toward the front door.*) Eddie, who was that? What happened? Eddie!

Eddie: Phil's dead.

Darlene: What?

Eddie: Car. Car.

Darlene: Oh, Eddie, Eddie.

Eddie: What?

Darlene: I'm so sorry.

(EDDIE gives her a look and goes.)

FOOL FOR LOVE
by Sam Shepard

The play opens with May sitting on the edge of a bed in a "low-rent motel room on the edge of the Mojave Desert." She stares at the floor. She is in her early thirties and wears a denim skirt and T-shirt. Eddie, her half brother and sometimes lover, sits in a chair. Eddie works with horses. He wears "broken-down cowboy boots" and "faded, dirty jeans that smell like horse sweat." He is a few years older than May, but "aged long before his time."

"On the floor, between his feet, is a leather bucking strap like bronc riders use. He wears a bucking glove on his right hand and works resin into the glove from a small white bag. He stares at May . . . (then) he leans over, sticks his gloved hand into the handle of the bucking strap and twists it so that it makes a weird stretching sound from the friction of resin and leather. . . . He pulls his hand out and removes gloves."

(For more information on this play, see other scenes in other sections of this book.)

Eddie: *(Seated, tossing glove on the table.)* *(Short pause.)* May, look. May? I'm not goin' anywhere. See? I'm right here. I'm not gone. Look *(She won't.)* I don't know why you won't just look at me. You know it's me. Who else do you think it is. *(Pause.)* You want some water or somethin'? Huh? *(He gets up slowly, goes cautiously to her, strokes her head softly, she stays still.)* May? Come on. You can't just sit around here like this. How long you been sittin' here anyway? You want me to go outside and get you something? Some potato chips or something? *(She suddenly grabs his closest leg with both arms and holds tight burying her head between his knees.)* I'm not gonna' leave. Don't worry. I'm not gonna' leave. I'm stayin' right here. I already told ya' that. (*She squeezes tighter to his leg, he just stands there, strokes her head softly.*) May? Let go, okay? Honey? I'll put you back in bed. Okay? (*She grabs his other leg and holds on tight to both.*) Come on. I'll put you in bed and make you some hot tea or somethin'. You want some tea? (*She shakes her head violently, keeps holding on.*) With lemon? Some Ovaltine? May, you gotta' let go of me now, okay? (*Pause, then she pushes him away and returns to her original position.*) Now just lay back and try to relax. (*He starts to try to push her back gently on the bed as he pulls back the blankets. She erupts furiously, leaping off bed and lashing out at him with her fists. He backs off. She returns to bed and stares at him wild-eyed and angry, faces him squarely.*)

Eddie: (*After pause.*) You want me to go? (*She shakes her head.*)

May: No!

Eddie: Well, what do you want then?

May: You smell.

Eddie: I smell.

May: You do.

Eddie: I been drivin' for days.

May: Your fingers smell.

Eddie: Horses.

May: Pussy.

Eddie: Come on, May.

May: They smell like metal.

Eddie: I'm not gonna' start this shit.

May: Rich pussy. Very clean.

Eddie: Yeah, sure.

May: You know it's true.

Eddie: I came to see if you were all right.

May: I don't need you!

Eddie: Okay. (*Turns to go, collects his glove and bucking strap.*) Fine.

May: Don't go!

Eddie: I'm goin'.

(*He exits stage left door, slamming it behind him; the door booms.*)

May: (*Agonized scream.*) Don't go!!!

(*She grabs pillow, clutching it to her chest then throws herself face down on bed, moaning and moving from one end of bed to the other on her elbows and knees.* EDDIE *is heard returning to stage left door outside. She leaps off bed clutching pillow, stands upstage right of bed, facing stage left door.* EDDIE *enters stage left door, banging it behind him. He's left the glove and bucking strap off stage. They stand there facing each other for a second. He makes a move toward her.* MAY *retreats to extreme upstage right corner of room clutching pillow to her chest.* EDDIE *stays against left wall, facing her.*)

Eddie: What am I gonna' do? Huh? What am I supposed to do?

May: You know.

Eddie: What.

May: You're gonna' erase me.

Eddie: What're you talkin' about?

May: You're either gonna' erase me or have me erased.

Eddie: Why would I want that? Are you kidding?

May: Because I'm in the way.

Eddie: Don't be stupid.

May: I'm smarter than you are and you know it. I can smell your thoughts before you even think 'em.

(EDDIE *moves along wall to upstage left corner.* MAY *holds her ground in opposite corner.*)

Eddie: May, I'm tryin' to take care of you. All right?

May: No, you're not. You're just guilty. Gutless and guilty.

Eddie: Great.

(*He moves down left to table, sticking close to wall.*) (*Pause*)

May: (*Quietly, staying in corner.*) I'm gonna' kill her ya' know.

Eddie: Who?

May: Who.

Eddie: Don't talk like that.

(MAY *slowly begins to move down stage right as* EDDIE *simultaneously moves up left. Both of them press the walls as they move.*)

May: I am. I'm gonna' kill her and then I'm gonna' kill you. Systematically. With sharp knives. Two separate knives. One for her and one for you. (*She slams wall with her elbow. Wall resonates.*) So the blood doesn't mix. I'm gonna' torture her first though. Not you. I'm just gonna' let you have it. Probably in the midst of a kiss. Right when you think everything's been healed up. Right in the moment when you're sure you've got me buffaloed. That's when you'll die.

(*She arrives extreme down right at the very limits of the set.* EDDIE *in the extreme up left corner. Pause.*)

Eddie: You know how many miles I went outa' my way just to come here and see you? You got any idea?

May: Nobody asked you to come.

Eddie: Two thousand, four hundred and eighty.

May: Yeah? Where were you, Katmandu or something?

Eddie: Two thousand, four hundred and eighty miles.

May: So what!

(*He drops his head, stares at floor. Pause. She stares at him. He begins to move slowly down left, sticking close to wall as he speaks.*)

Eddie: I missed you. I did. I missed you more than anything I ever missed in my whole life. I kept thinkin' about you the whole time I was driving. Kept seeing you. Sometimes just a part of you.

May: Which part?

Eddie: Your neck.

May: My neck?

Eddie: Yeah.

May: You missed my neck?

Eddie: I missed all of you but your neck kept coming up for some reason. I kept crying about your neck.

May: Crying?

Eddie: (*He stops by stage left door. She stays down right.*) Yeah. Weeping. Like a little baby. Uncontrollable. It would just start up and stop and then start up all over again. For miles. I couldn't stop it. Cars would pass me on the road. People would stare at me. My face was all twisted up. I couldn't stop my face.

May: Was this before or after your little fling with the Countess?

Eddie: (*He bangs his head into wall. Wall booms.*) There wasn't any fling with any Countess!

May: You're a liar.

Eddie: I took her out to dinner once, okay?

May: Ha!

(*She moves upstage right wall.*)

Eddie: Twice.

May: You were bumping her on a regular basis! Don't gimme that shit.

Eddie: You can believe whatever you want.

May: (*She stops by bathroom door, opposite* EDDIE.) I'll believe the truth! It's less confusing.

(*Pause.*)

Eddie: I'm takin' you back, May.

(*She tosses pillow on bed and moves to upstage right corner.*)

May: I'm not going back to that idiot trailer if that's what you think.

Eddie: I'm movin' it. I got a piece of ground up in Wyoming.

May: Wyoming? Are you crazy? I'm not moving to Wyoming. What's up there? Marlboro Men?

Eddie: You can't stay here.

May: Why not? I got a job. I'm a regular citizen here now.

Eddie: You got a job?

May: (*She moves back down to head of bed.*) Yeah. What'd you think, I was helpless?

Eddie: No. I mean—it's been a long time since you had a job.

May: I'm a cook.

Eddie: A cook? You can't even flip an egg, can you?

May: I'm not talkin' to you anymore!

(*She turns away from him, runs into bathroom, slams door behind her.* EDDIE *goes after her, tries door but she's locked it.*)

Eddie: (*At bathroom door.*) May, I got everything worked out. I been thinkin' about this for weeks. I'm gonna' move the trailer. Build a little pipe corral to keep the horses. Have a big vegetable garden. Some chickens maybe.

May's Voice: (*Unseen, behind bathroom door.*) I hate chickens! I hate horses! I hate all that shit! You know that. You got me confused with somebody else. You keep comin' up here with this lame country dream life with chickens and vegetables and I can't stand any of it. It makes me puke to even think about it.

Eddie: (EDDIE *has crossed stage left during this, stops at table.*) You'll get used to it.

May: (*Enters from bathroom.*) You're unbelievable!

(*She slams bathroom door, crosses upstage to window.*)

Eddie: I'm not lettin' go of you this time, May.

(*He sits in chair upstage of table.*)

May: You never had a hold of me to begin with. (*Pause.*) How many times have you done this to me?

Eddie: What.

May: Suckered me into some dumb little fantasy and then dropped me like a hot rock. How many times has that happened?

Eddie: It's no fantasy.

May: It's all a fantasy.

Eddie: And I never dropped you either.

May: No, you just disappeared!

Eddie: I'm here now aren't I?

May: Well, praise Jesus God!

Eddie: I'm gonna take care of you, May. I am. I'm gonna' stick with you no matter what. I promise.

May: Get outa' here.

(*Pause.*)

Eddie: What'd you have to go and run off for anyway.

May: Run off? Me?

Eddie: Yeah. Why couldn't you just stay put. You knew I was comin' back to get you.

May: (*Crossing down to head of bed.*) What do you think it's like sittin' in a tin trailer for weeks on end with the wind ripping through it? Waitin' around for the Butane to arrive. Hiking down to the laundromat in the rain. Do you think that's thrilling or somethin'?

Eddie: (*Still sitting.*) I bought you all those magazines.

May: What magazines?

Eddie: I bought you a whole stack of those fashion magazines before I left. I thought you liked those. Those French kind.

May: Yeah, I especially liked the one with the Countess on the cover. That was real cute.

(*Pause.*)

Eddie: All right.

(*He stands.*)

May: All right, what.

(*He turns to go out stage left door.*)

May: Where are you going?

Eddie: Just to get my stuff outa' the truck. I'll be right back.

May: What're you movin' in now or something?

Eddie: Well, I thought I'd spend the night if that's okay.

May: Are you kidding?

Eddie: (*Opens door.*) Then I'll just leave, I guess.

May: (*She stands.*) Wait.

(*He closes door. They stand there facing each other for a while. She crosses slowly to him. She stops. He takes a few steps toward her. Stops. They both move closer. Stop. Pause as they look at each other. They embrace. Long, tender kiss. They are very soft with each other. She pulls away from him slightly. Smiles. She looks him straight in the eyes, then suddenly knees him in the groin with tremendous force. EDDIE doubles over and drops like a rock. She stands over him. Pause.*)

May: You can take it, right. You're a stuntman.

(*She exits into bathroom, stage right, slams the door behind her.*)

PLENTY
by David Hare

SCENE 5

All of Susan's experiences after World War II pale in comparison to her recollections of her wartime activities as an English courier stationed in Nazi-occupied France. As she describes her feelings in one scene, "I think of France more than I tell you. I was seventeen and I was thrown into the war. I often think of it. . . . The most unlikely people. People I met only for an hour or two. Astonishing kindnesses. Bravery. The fact you could meet someone for an hour or two and see the very best of them and then move on."

Since the war Susan has found all her jobs dull and all the men she has met weak and uninteresting. The following scene takes place in May 1951. Susan now works for the Festival of Britain. She has asked Mick, a young man she met through her friend Alice, to meet her secretly at the Embankment, overlooking the Thames River. Mick is from the East End, a working-class district in London. He sells kitchenware and has sold Susan spoons for the Festival.

As the scene opens it is evening. Susan waits for Mick while eating hot chestnuts and looking across the river at a "barrage balloon" that she has commissioned for the Festival. Mick enters, unseen by her.

Mick: Five hundred cheese-graters.

Susan: Oh no.

Mick: I got five hundred cheese-graters parked round the side. Are you interested?

Susan: I'm afraid you're too late. We took a consignment weeks ago. (SUSAN *laughs.* MICK *moves down beside her.*)

Mick: Where we looking?

Susan: Across the river. Over there.

Mick: Where?

Susan: South Bank. That's where the fireworks are going to be. And there's my barrage balloon.

Mick: Oh yeah. What does it say?

Susan: Don't say that, that's the worst thing you can say.

Mick: It's dark.

Susan: It says Bovril.

Mick: Oh Bovril.

Susan: Yes. It's meant to blaze out over London.

Mick: Surprised it hasn't got your name on.

Susan: What do you mean?

Mick: Everywhere I go. (*Pause. They look at each other.* SUSAN *smiles and removes a napkin from her coat pocket, and unfolds its bundle.*)

Susan: I managed to steal some supper from the Festival Hall. There's a reception for its opening night. They're using your cutlery, I'm happy to say.

Mick: I wish I could see it.

Susan: Yes, yes, I wish you could too. (*She smiles.*) I've actually decided to leave the Festival now. Having worked so hard to get the wretched thing on. I'm thinking of going into advertising.

Mick: Ah very good.

Susan: I met some people on the Bovril side. It's . . . well I doubt if it'll stretch me, but it would be a way of having some fun. (*Pause.*) Would you like a canapé?

Mick: How's Alice?

Susan: She's very well.

Mick: Haven't seen her lately.

Susan: No.

Mick: She went mainstream you see. I stayed revivalist. Different religion. For me it all dies with Dixie. (*He takes a canapé.*) So how can I help?

Susan: I'm looking for a father. I want to have a child. (*Pause.*) Look it really is much easier than it sounds. I mean marriage is not involved. Or even looking after it. You don't even have to see the pregnancy through. I mean conception will be the end of the job. (MICK *smiles.*)

Mick: Ah.

Susan: You don't want to?

Mick: No, no-I'm delighted, I'm lucky to be asked . . .

Susan: Not at all.

Mick: But it's just . . . your own people. I mean friends, you must have friends . . .

Susan: It's . . .

Mick: I mean . . .

Susan: Sorry.

Mick: No, go on, say.

Susan: The men I know at work, at the Festival, or even friends I've known for years, they just aren't the kind of people I would want to marry.

Mick: Ah.

Susan: I'm afraid I'm rather strongminded as you know, and so with them I usually feel I'm holding myself in for fear of literally blowing them out the room. They are kind, they are able, but I don't see . . . why I should have to compromise, why I should have to make some sad and decorous marriage just to have a child. I don't see why any woman should have to do that.

Mick: But you don't have to marry . . .

Susan: Ah well . . .

Mick: Just go off with them.

Susan: No that's really the problem you see. These same men, these kind and likeable men, they do have another side to their nature and that is they are very limited in their ideas, they are frightened of the unknown, they want a quiet life where sex is either sport or duty but absolutely nothing in between, and they simply wouldn't agree to sleep with me if they knew it was a child I was after.

Mick: But you wouldn't have to tell them . . .

Susan: I did think that. And then I thought it would be dishonest. And so I had the idea of asking a person whom I barely knew. (*Pause.*)

Mick: What about the kid?

Susan: What?

Mick: Doesn't sound a very good deal. Never to see his dad . . .

Susan: It's not . . .

Mick: I take it that is what you mean.

Susan: I think it's what I mean.

Mick: Well?

Susan: The child will manage.

Mick: How do you know?

Susan: Being a bastard won't always be so bad . . .

Mick: I wouldn't bet on it.

Susan: England can't be like this for ever. (MICK *looks at her.*)

Mick: I would like to know . . .

Susan: Yes?

Mick: I would like to know. Why you chose me. I mean, how often have you met me?

Susan: Yes, but that's the whole point . . .

Mick: With Alice a few times . . .

Susan: And you sold me some spoons.

Mick: They were good spoons.

Susan: I'm not denying it. (MICK *smiles.*)

Mick: And Alice says what? That I'm clean and obedient and don't have any cretins in the family . . .

Susan: It's not as calculated as that.

Mick: Not calculated? Several hundred of us, was there, all got notes . . .

Susan: No.

Mick: Saying come and watch the Festival fireworks, tell no one, bring no friends. All the secrecy, I thought you must at least be after nylons . . .

Susan: I'll buy nylons. If that's what you want. (*They stare at each other.*)

Mick: So why me?

Susan: I like you.

Mick: And?

Susan: 'I love you'? (*Pause.*) I chose you because . . . I don't see you very much. I barely ever see you. We live at opposite ends of town. Different worlds.

Mick: Different class.

Susan: That comes into it. (*There is a pause.* MICK *looks at her. Then moves away. Turns back. Smiles.*)

Mick: Oh dear.

Susan: Then laugh. (*Pause.*) I never met the man who I wanted to marry. (*They smile.*)

Mick: It can't be what you want. Not deep down.

Susan: No.

Mick: I didn't think so.

Susan: Deep down I'd do the whole damn thing by myself. But there we are. You're second best. (*They smile again.*)

Mick: Five hundred cheese-graters.

Susan: How much?

Mick: Something over the odds. A bit over the odds. Not much.

Susan: Done. (*Pause.*) Don't worry. The Festival will pay. (SUSAN *moves across to* MICK. *They kiss. They look at each other. He smiles. Then they turn and look at the night. He is barely audible.*)

Mick: Fireworks. If you . . .

Susan: What?

Mick: Stay for the fireworks.

Susan: If you like. (*Pause.*)

Mick: Great sky.

Susan: Yes.

Mick: The light. Those dots.

Susan: A mackerel sky.

Mick: What?

Susan: That's what they call it. A mackerel sky.

FOOLS
by Neil Simon

Act I

Leon Tolchinsky, an idealistic young man, arrives in Kulyenchikov, a remote Ukranian village, to begin his career as a school teacher. "I like it!" he says. "It's exactly as I pictured: a quite pleasant village, not too large . . . the perfect place for a new school teacher to begin his career." But he quickly learns that the village is filled with fools. As he enters the town he meets a shepherd who tells him the town has had thousands of teachers, "but not one of them lasted through the first night." Leon, in disbelief, replies, "You've had thousands of teachers?" "More," says the shepherd. "Hundreds! We're unteachable. We're all stupid. . . . All good people, mind you, but not a decent brain among them."

Leon soon learns that there is a two-hundred-year-old curse on the village that keeps everyone stupid, and he vows to apply his powers as a teacher to help them break the curse. When he is introduced to Sophia, whom he was hired to teach, he immediately falls in love with her. She is beautiful, but, unfortunately, just as dumb as the other villagers. She's nineteen years old and just recently learned to sit down, and the language she would like to study is *Rabbit*. "Hardly anyone speaks it anymore," she says.

The following scene begins just as Leon is considering leaving the village. Sophia calls him from her balcony. She is very excited that her lessons will begin "tomorrow."

Sophia's Voice: Schoolmaster!

Leon: Sophia? Where are you?

(She appears on the balcony.)

Sophia: Down here. I had to see you once more.

Leon: Without a wrap? In the cold night air, you'll come down with a chill.

Sophia: Oh, I never catch colds.

Leon: You don't?

Sophia: I've tried. I've just never learned how to do it.

Leon: Be grateful . . . Some things are not worth knowing.

Sophia: I know that something has happened a long time ago that prevents me from knowing what happened a long time ago. If only you knew me the way I might have been instead of the way I am.

Leon: But if you were not the way you are, then I would not have come here to help you to become the way you might have been. *(Aside, quickly.)* Careful! You're beginning to think like her.

Sophia: Could you—could you ever care for someone who never became the way I might have been?

Leon: Could I ever care for someone who never became—I see what you mean. I see what you're getting at. Yes. Yes, I could. I would. I shall. I will. I have. I do.

Sophia: Is that rabbit you're speaking? It's hard to follow.

Leon: If it sounds like gibberish it's because you do that to me, Sophia. When thoughts come from the heart they sometimes trip over the tongue.

Sophia: Then I must watch where I walk when you speak . . . I must go. Everything depends upon tomorrow.

Leon: And if not tomorrow, then the tomorrow after tomorrow. And all the tomorrows for the rest of my life, if that's what it takes.

Sophia: No. It all rests on tomorrow. If we fail, we shall never see each other again.

Leon: Never see each other? What do you mean?

Sophia: I never know what I mean. I do have thoughts but they seem to disappear when they reach my lips.

Leon: If I ever reached your lips, I would never disappear.

Sophia: Would you like to kiss me?

Leon: With all my heart.

Sophia: No. I meant with your lips.

Leon: An even better suggestion.

Sophia: Hurry. Hurry.

(He climbs up to the balcony.)

Leon: I'm climbing as fast as I can.

(She disappears.)

Leon: *(Arrives on the balcony.)* Where are you?

Sophia: *(Appears below.)* Up here.

Leon: *(To the audience.)* If only she were ugly, I'd be halfway home by now. *(To* SOPHIA.*)* Stay where you are. I'll come to you.

Sophia: All right.

(But he doesn't move.)

Leon: *(To the audience.)* After a while you get the hang of it.

Sophia: *(Reappears on the balcony.)* Here I am.

Leon: My kiss, sweet Sophia.

(They kiss.)

Sophia: As we kissed I felt a strange flutter in my heart.

Leon: So did I.

Sophia: You felt a flutter in my heart as well? How alike we are. And yet your hair is so much shorter . . . I must go. I'm about to fall asleep and I want to get to bed in time.

(She leaves.)

Leon: (*To the audience.*) I know the dangers of loving such a simple soul. It would mean a lifetime of sweet, blissful passion—and very short conversations at breakfast. (*There is a clap of thunder.*) I'd best find some comfortable lodgings.

BURIED CHILD
by Sam Shepard

ACT II

Vince and Shelly arrive at the old farmhouse of Vince's family. Vince, in his early twenties, hasn't been home in six years and wants to see his family. Shelly, his girlfriend, is about nineteen and very beautiful. They shake the rain off as they enter the porch through the screen door. Vince is carrying a saxophone case. He is eager to make a good impression on his family. He will soon learn that the family members are a very strange lot, not at all as he remembers them.

Shelly: (*Laughing, gesturing to house.*) This is it? I don't believe this is it!

Vince: This is it.

Shelly: This is the house?

Vince: This is the house.

Shelly: I don't believe it!

Vince: How come?

Shelly: It's like a Norman Rockwell cover or something.

Vince: What's a' matter with that? It's American.

Shelly: Where's the milkman and the little dog? What's the little dog's name? Spot. Spot and Jane. Dick and Jane and Spot.

Vince: Knock it off.

Shelly: Dick and Jane and Spot and Mom and Dad and Junior and Sissy!

(*She laughs. Slaps her knee.*)

Vince: Come on! It's my heritage. What dya' expect?

(*She laughs more hysterically, out of control.*)

Shelly: "And Tuffy and Toto and Dooda and Bonzo all went down one day to the corner grocery store to buy a big bag of licorice for Mr. Marshall's pussy cat!"

(*She laughs so hard she falls to her knees holding her stomach.* VINCE *stands there looking at her.*)

Vince: Shelly will you get up!

(*She keeps laughing. Staggers to her feet. Turning in circles holding her stomach.*)

Shelly: (*Continuing her story in kid's voice.*) "Mr. Marshall was on vacation. He had no idea that the four little boys had taken such a liking to his little kitty cat."
Vince: Have some respect would ya'!
Shelly: (*Trying to control herself.*) I'm sorry.
Vince: Pull yourself together.
Shelly: (*Salutes him.*) Yes sir.

(*She giggles.*)

Vince: Jesus Christ, Shelly.
Shelly: (*Pause, smiling.*) And Mr. Marshall—
Vince: Cut it out.

(*She stops. Stands there staring at him. Stifles a giggle.*)

Vince: (*After pause.*) Are you finished?
Shelly: Oh brother!
Vince: I don't wanna go in there with you acting like an idiot.
Shelly: Thanks.
Vince: Well, I don't.
Shelly: I won't embarrass you. Don't worry.
Vince: I'm not worried.
Shelly: You are too.
Vince: Shelly look, I just don't wanna go in there with you giggling your head off. They might think something's wrong with you.
Shelly: There is.
Vince: There is not!

Shelly: Something's definitely wrong with me.
Vince: There is not!
Shelly: There's something wrong with you too.
Vince: There's nothing wrong with me either!
Shelly: You wanna know what's wrong with you?
Vince: What?

(SHELLY *laughs.*)

Vince: (*Crosses back left toward screen door.*) I'm leaving!
Shelly: (*Stops laughing.*) Wait! Stop. Stop! (VINCE *stops.*)
What's wrong with you is that you take the situation too
seriously.
Vince: I just don't want to have them think that I've sud-
denly arrived out of the middle of nowhere completely
deranged.
Shelly: What do you want them to think then?
Vince: (*Pause.*) Nothing. Let's go in.

(*He crosses porch toward stage right interior door.*
SHELLY *follows him. The stage right door opens slowly.*
VINCE *sticks his head in, doesn't notice* DODGE *sleeping.*
Calls out toward staircase.)

Vince: Grandma!

(SHELLY *breaks into laughter, unseen behind* VINCE.
VINCE *pulls his head back outside and pulls door shut.*
We hear their voices again without seeing them.)

Shelly's Voice: (*Stops laughing.*) I'm sorry. I'm sorry, Vince.
I really am. I really am sorry. I won't do it again. I
couldn't help it.
Vince's Voice: It's not all that funny.
Shelly's Voice: I know it's not. I'm sorry.
Vince's Voice: I mean this is a tense situation for me! I
haven't seen them for over six years. I don't know what to
expect.
Shelly's Voice: I know. I won't do it again.
Vince's Voice: Can't you bite your tongue or something?
Shelly's Voice: Just don't say "Grandma," okay? (*She giggles,*
stops.) I mean if you say "Grandma" I don't know if I can
stop myself.
Vince's Voice: Well try!
Shelly's Voice: Okay. Sorry.

EDUCATING RITA
by Willy Russell

ACT I, SCENE 1

Frank teaches English literature at a university in the North of England. He is unhappy with his career, his marriage, and himself. His only solace these days is alcohol, which he hides on his bookshelves behind his volumes of Dickens and Eliot. He has taken an after school position as a tutor in the "Open University," a branch of the school that offers college entrance and special training to students who would not ordinarily go to college. "Oh God, why did I take this on?" he asks himself. "I suppose . . . to pay for the drink," he admits.

Rita is one of those students who wouldn't ordinarily seek out a university education. She is a hairdresser and has barely any education, but she is uncommonly bright and free-thinking and says she wants to know "everything." She explains that she came to college because "I wanna discover myself." As the play progresses, Frank and Rita have a profound effect on each other's lives.

As the scene below begins, Frank is in his office on the phone with his wife. They are arguing about his drinking and his having forgotten to tell her he'd be working late (the meal she prepared has burned). There is a knock at the door.

(*For more information see other scenes from this play in "Monologues for Women" section of this book.*)

Frank: Look, I'll have to go. . . . There's someone at the door. . . . Yes, yes I promise. . . . Just a couple of pints. . . . Four. . . .

(*There is another knock at the door.*)

(*Calling in the direction of the door.*) Come in! (*He continues on the telephone.*) Yes. . . . All right . . . yes. . . . Bye, bye. . . . (*He replaces the receiver.*) Yes, that's it, you just pop off and put your head in the oven. (*Shouting*) Come in! Come in!

(*The door swings open revealing* RITA.)

Rita: (*From the doorway.*) I'm comin' in, aren't I? It's that stupid bleedin' handle on the door. You wanna get it fixed! (*She comes into the room.*)

Frank: (*Staring, slightly confused.*) Erm—yes, I suppose I always mean to . . .

Rita: (*Going to the chair by the desk and dumping her bag.*) Well that's no good, always meanin' to, is it? Y' should get on with it; one of these days you'll be shoutin' "Come in" an' it'll go on forever because the poor sod on the other side won't be *able* to get in. An' you won't be able to get out.

(FRANK *stares at* RITA *who stands by the desk.*)

Frank: You are?
Rita: What am I?
Frank: Pardon?
Rita: What?
Frank: (*Looking for the admission papers.*) Now you are?
Rita: I'm a what?

(FRANK *looks up and then returns to the papers as* RITA *goes to hang her coat on the door hooks.*)

(*Noticing the picture.*) That's a nice picture, isn't it? (*She goes up to it.*)

Frank: Erm—yes, I suppose it is—nice . . .
Rita: (*Studying the picture.*) It's very erotic.
Frank: (*Looking up.*) Actually I don't think I've looked at it for about ten years, but yes, I suppose it is.
Rita: There's no suppose about it. Look at those tits.

(*He coughs and goes back to looking for the admission paper.*)

Is it supposed to be erotic? I mean when he painted it do y' think he wanted to turn people on?

Frank: Erm—probably.

Rita: I'll bet he did y' know. Y' don't paint pictures like that just so that people can admire the brush strokes, do y'?

Frank: (*Giving a short laugh.*) No—no—you're probably right.

Rita: This was the pornography of its day, wasn't it? It's sort of like *Men Only*, isn't it? But in those days they had to pretend it wasn't erotic so they made it religious, didn't they? Do *you* think it's erotic?

Frank: (*Taking a look.*) I think it's very beautiful.

Rita: I didn't ask y' if it was beautiful.

Frank: But the term "beautiful" covers the many feelings I have about that picture, including the feeling that, yes, it is erotic.

Rita: (*Coming back to the desk.*) D' y' get a lot like me?

Frank: Pardon?

Rita: Do you get a lot of students like me?

Frank: Not exactly, no . . .

Rita: I was dead surprised when they took me. I don't suppose they would have done if it'd been a proper university. The Open University's different though, isn't it?

Frank: I've—erm—not had much more experience of it than you. This is the first O.U. work I've done.

Rita: D' y' need the money?

Frank: I do as a matter of fact.

Rita: It's terrible these days, the money, isn't it? With the inflation an' that. You work for the ordinary university, don't y'? With the real students. The Open University's different, isn't it?

Frank: It's supposed to embrace a more comprehensive studentship, yes.

Rita: (*Inspecting a bookcase.*) Degrees for dishwashers.

Frank: Would you—erm—would you like to sit down?

Rita: No! Can I smoke? (*She goes to her bag and rummages in it.*)

Frank: Tobacco?

Rita: Yeh. (*She half-laughs.*) Was that a joke? (*She takes out a packet of cigarettes and a lighter.*) Here—d' y' want one? (*She takes out two cigarettes and dumps the packet on the desk.*)

Frank: (*After a pause.*) Ah—I'd love one.

Rita: Well, have one.

Frank: (*After a pause.*) I—don't smoke—I made a promise not to smoke.

Rita: Well, I won't tell anyone.

Frank: Promise?

(*As* FRANK *goes to take the cigarette* RITA *whips it from his reach.*)

Rita: (*Doing a Brownie salute.*) On my oath as an ex Brownie. (*She gives him the cigarette.*) I hate smokin' on me own. An' everyone seems to have packed up these days. (*She lights the cigarettes.*) They're all afraid of gettin' cancer.

(FRANK *looks dubiously at his cigarette.*)

But they're all cowards.

Frank: Are they?

Rita: You've got to challenge death an' disease. I read this poem about fightin' death . . .

Frank: Ah—Dylan Thomas . . .

Rita: No. Roger McGough. It was about this old man who runs away from hospital an' goes out on the ale. He gets pissed an' stands in the street shoutin' an' challengin' death to come out an' fight. It's dead good.

Frank: Yes. I don't think I know the actual piece you mean . . .

Rita: I'll bring y' the book—it's great.

Frank: Thank you.

Rita: You probably won't think it's any good.

Frank: Why?

Rita: It's the sort of poetry you can understand.

Frank: Ah. I see.

(RITA *begins looking idly round the room.*)

Can I offer you a drink?

Rita: What of?

Frank: Scotch?

Rita: (*Going to the bookcase U.R.*) Y' wanna be careful with that stuff, it kills y' brain cells.

Frank: But you'll have one? (*He gets up and goes to the small table.*)

Rita: All right. It'll probably have a job findin' my brain.

Frank: (*Pouring the drinks.*) Water?

Rita: (*Looking at the bookcase.*) Yeh, all right. (*She takes a copy of "Howards End" from the shelf.*) What's this like?

(FRANK *goes over to* RITA, *looks at the title of the book and then goes back to the drinks.*)

Frank: *Howards End?*

Rita: Yeh. It sounds filthy, doesn't it? E. M. Foster.

Frank: Forster.

Rita: Oh yeh. What's it like?

Frank: Borrow it. Read it.

Rita: Ta. I'll look after it. (*She moves back towards the desk.*) If I pack the course in I'll post it to y'.

(FRANK *comes to the desk with the drinks.*)

Frank: (*Handing her the mug.*) Pack it in? Why should you do that?

(RITA *puts her drink down on the desk and puts the copy of "Howards End" in her bag.*)

Rita: I just might. I might decide it was a soft idea.

Frank: (*Looking at her.*) Mm. Cheers. If—erm—if you're already contemplating "packing it in," why did you enroll in the first place?

Rita: Because I wanna know.

Frank: What do you want to know?

Rita: Everything.

Frank: Everything? That's rather a lot, isn't it? Where would you like to start?

Rita: Well, I'm a student now, aren't I? I'll have to do exams, won't I?

Frank: Yes. Eventually.

Rita: I'll have to learn about it all, won' I? Yeh. It's like y' sit there, don't y', watchin' the ballet or the opera on the telly an'—an' y' call it rubbish cos that's what it looks like? Cos y' don't understand. So y' switch it off an' say, that's fuckin' rubbish.

Frank: Do you?

Rita: I do. But I don't want to. I wanna see. Y' don't mind me swearin', do y'?

Frank: Not at all.

Rita: Do you swear?

Frank: Never stop.

Rita: See, the educated classes know it's only words, don't they? It's only the masses who don't understand. I do it to shock them sometimes. Y' know when I'm in the hairdresser's—that's where I work—I'll say somethin' like, "Oh, I'm really fucked," y' know, dead loud. It doesn't half cause a fuss.

Frank: Yes—I'm sure . . .

Rita: But it doesn't cause any sort of fuss with educated people, does it? Cos they know it's only words and they don't worry. But these stuck-up idiots I meet, they think they're royalty just cos they don't swear; an' I wouldn't mind but it's the aristocracy that swears more than anyone, isn't it? They're effin' an' blindin' all day long. It's all "Pass me the fackin' grouse" with them, isn't it? But y' can't tell them that round our way. It's not their fault; they can't help it. (*She goes to the window and looks out.*) But sometimes I hate them. God, what's it like to be free?

Frank: Ah. Now there's a question. Will you have another drink? (*He goes to the small table.*)

Rita: (*Shaking her head.*) If I'd got some other tutor I wouldn't have stayed.

Frank: (*Pouring himself a drink.*) What sort of other tutor?

Rita: Y' know, someone who objected to swearin'.

Frank: How did you know I wouldn't object?

Rita: I didn't. I was just testin' y'.

Frank: (*Coming back to the desk and looking at her.*) Yes. You're doing rather a lot of that, aren't you?

Rita: That's what I do. Y' know, when I'm nervous.

Frank: (*Sitting in the swivel chair.*) And how am I scoring so far?

Rita: Very good, ten out of ten go to the top of the class an' collect a gold star. I love this room. I love that window. Do you like it?

Frank: What?

Rita: The window.

Frank: I don't often consider it actually. I sometimes get an urge to throw something through it.

Rita: What?

Frank: A student usually.

Rita: (*Smiling.*) You're bleedin' mad you, aren't y'?

Frank: Probably.

(*Pause.*)

Rita: Aren't you supposed to be interviewin' me?

Frank: (*Looking at the drink.*) Do I need to?

Rita: I talk too much, don't I? I know I talk a lot. I don't at home. I hardly ever talk when I'm there. But I don't often get the chance to talk to someone like you; to talk at you. D' y' mind?

Frank: Would you be at all bothered if I did?

(*She shakes her head and then turns it into a nod.*)

I don't mind. (*He takes a sip of his drink.*)

Rita: What does assonance mean?

Frank: (*Half-spluttering.*) What? (*He gives a short laugh.*)

Rita: Don't laugh at me.

Frank: No. Erm—assonance. Well, it's a form of rhyme. What's a—what's an example—erm—? Do you know Yeats?

Rita: The wine lodge?

Frank: Yeats the poet.

Rita: No.

Frank: Oh. Well—there's a Yeats poem, called *The Wild Swans at Coole*. In it he rhymes the word "swan" with the word "stone." There, you see, an example of assonance.

Rita: Oh. It means gettin' the rhyme wrong.

Frank: (*Looking at her and laughing.*) I've never really looked at it like that. But yes, yes you could say it means getting the rhyme wrong; but purposefully, in order to achieve a certain effect.

Rita: Oh. (*There is a pause and she wanders round.*) There's loads I don't know.

Frank: And you want to know everything?

Rita: Yeh.

(FRANK *nods and then takes her admission paper from his desk and looks at it.*)

Frank: What's your name?

Rita: (*Moving towards the bookcase.*) Rita.

Frank: (*Looking at the paper.*) Rita. Mm. It says here Mrs. S. White.

(RITA *goes to the right of* FRANK, *takes a pencil, leans over and scratches out the initial "S."*)

Rita: That's "S" for Susan. It's just me real name. I've changed it to Rita, though. I'm not a Susan anymore. I've called meself Rita—y' know, after Rita Mae Brown.

Frank: Who?

Rita: Y' know, Rita Mae Brown who wrote *Rubyfruit Jungle*? Haven't y' read it? It's a fantastic book. D' y' wanna lend it?

Frank: I'd—erm—I'd be very interested.

Rita: All right.

(RITA *gets a copy of "Rubyfruit Jungle" from her bag and gives it to* FRANK. *He turns it over and reads the blurb on the back cover.*)

What's your name?

Frank: Frank.

Rita: Oh. Not after Frank Harris?

Frank: Not after Frank anyone.

Rita: Maybe y' parents named y' after the quality. (*She sits in the chair by the desk.*)

(FRANK *puts down "Rubyfruit Jungle."*)

Y' know Frank, Frank Ness. Elliot's brother.

Frank: What?

Rita: I'm sorry—it was a joke. Y' know, Frank Ness, Elliot's brother.

Frank: (*Bemused.*) Ah.

Rita: You've still not got it, have y'? Elliot Ness—y' know, the famous Chicago copper who caught Al Capone.

Frank: Ah. When you said Elliot I assumed you meant T. S. Eliot.

Rita: Have you read his stuff?

Frank: Yes.

Rita: All of it?

Frank: Every last syllable.

Rita: (*Impressed.*) Honest? I couldn't even get through one poem. I tried to read this thing he wrote called *J. Arthur Prufrock*; I couldn't finish it.

Frank: *J. Alfred.*

Rita: What?

Frank: I think you'll find it was *J. Alfred Prufrock*, Rita. J. Arthur is something else altogether.

Rita: Oh yeh. I never thought of that. I've not half got a lot
to learn, haven't I?

Frank: (*Looking at her paper.*) You're a ladies' hairdresser?

Rita: Yeh.

Frank: Are you good at it?

Rita: (*Getting up and wandering around.*) I am when I
wanna be. Most of the time I don't want to though. They
get on me nerves.

Frank: Who?

Rita: The women. They never tell y' things that matter.
Like, y' know, doin' a perm, well y' can't use a strong
perm lotion on a head that's been bleached with certain
sorts of cheap bleach. It makes all the hair break off. But
at least once a month I'll get a customer in for a perm
who'll swear to God that she's not had any bleach on; an'
I can tell, I mean I can see it. So y'go ahead an' do the
perm an' she comes out the drier with half an inch of
stubble.

Frank: And what do you do about it?

Rita: Try and sell them a wig.

Frank: My God.

Rita: Women who want their hair doin', they won't stop at
anythin', y' know. Even the pensioners are like that, y'
know; a pensioner'll come in an' she won't tell y' that she's
got a hearin' aid: so y' start cuttin' don't y'? Next thing—
snip—another granny deaf for a fortnight. I'm always
cuttin' hearin' aid cords. An' ear lobes.

Frank: You sound like something of a liability.

Rita: I am. But they expect too much. They walk in the hairdresser's an' an hour later they wanna walk out a different person. I tell them I'm a hairdresser, not a plastic
surgeon. It's worse when there's a fad on, y' know like
Farrah Fawcett Majors.

Frank: Who?

Rita: Far-rah Fawcett Majors. Y' know, she used to be with
Charlie's Angels.

(FRANK *remains blank.*)

It's a telly programme on ITV.

Frank: Ah.

Rita: (*Wandering towards the door.*) You wouldn't watch
ITV though, would y'? It's all BBC with you, isn't it?

Frank: Well, I must confess . . .

Rita: It's all right, I know. Soon as I walked in here I said to meself, "Y' can tell he's a *Flora* man."

Frank: A what?

Rita: A *Flora* man.

Frank: Flora? Flowers?

Rita: (*Coming back to the desk.*) No, *Flora,* the bleedin' margarine, no cholesterol; it's for people like you who eat pebble-dashed bread, y' know the bread, with little hard bits in it, just like pebble-dashin'.

Frank: (*Realizing and smiling.*) Ah—pebble-dashed bread.

Rita: Quick? He's like lightenin'. But these women, you see, they come to the hairdresser's cos they wanna be changed. But if you want to change y' have to do it from the inside, don't y'? Know like I'm doin'. Do y' think I'll be able to do it?

Frank: Well, it really depends on you, on how committed you are. Are you sure that you're absolutely serious about wanting to learn?

Rita: I'm dead serious. Look, I know I take the piss an' that but I'm dead serious really. I take the piss because I'm not, y' know, confident like, but I wanna be, honest.

(*He nods and looks at her. She becomes uncomfortable and moves away a little.*)

Tch. What y' lookin' at me for?

Frank: Because—I think you're marvellous. Do you know, I think you're the first breath of air that's been in this room for years.

Rita: (*Wandering around.*) Tch. Now who's taking the piss?

Frank: Don't you recognize a compliment?

Rita: Go way . . .

Frank: Where to?

Rita: Don't be soft. Y' know what I mean.

Frank: What I want to know is what is it that's suddenly led you to this?

Rita: What? Comin' here?

Frank: Yes.

Rita: It's not sudden.

Frank: Ah.

Rita: I've been realizin' for ages that I was, y' know, slightly out of step. I'm twenty-six. I should have had a baby by now; everyone expects it. I'm sure me husband thinks I'm sterile. He was moanin' all the time, y' know, "Come off the pill, let's have a baby." I told him I'd come off it, just to shut him up. But I'm still on it. (*She moves round to Frank.*) See, I don't wanna baby yet. See, I wanna discover meself first. Do you understand that?

Frank: Yes.

Rita: (*Moving to the chair U. of the desk and fiddling with it.*) Yeh. They wouldn't round our way. They'd think I was mental. I've tried to explain it to me husband but between you an' me I think he's thick. No, he's not thick, he's blind, he doesn't want to see. You know if I'm readin', or watchin' somethin' different on the telly he gets dead narked. I used to just tell him to piss off but then I realized that it was no good doin' that, that I had to explain to him. I tried to explain that I wanted a better way of livin' me life. An' he listened to me. But he didn't understand because when I'd finished he said he agreed with me and that we should start savin' the money to move off our estate an' get a house out in Formby. Even if it was a new house I wanted I wouldn't go an' live in Formby. I hate that hole, don't you?

Frank: Yes.

Rita: Where do you live?

Frank: Formby.

Rita: (*Sitting.*) Oh.

Frank: (*Getting up and going to the small table.*) Another drink?

(*She shakes her head.*)

You don't mind if I do? (*He pours himself a drink.*)

Rita: No. It's your brain cells y' killin'.

Frank: (*Smiling.*) All dead long ago I'm afraid. (*He drinks.*)

(RITA *gets up and goes to* FRANK's *chair. She plays with the swivel and then leans on it.*)

Rita: When d' y' actually, y' know, start teaching me?

Frank: (*Looking at her.*) What can I teach you?

Rita: Everything.

(FRANK *leans on the filing cabinet, drinks, shakes his head and looks at her.*)

Frank: I'll make a bargain with you. Yes? I'll tell you everything I know—but if I do that you must promise never to
come back here . . . You see I never—I didn't actually
want to take this course in the first place. I allowed myself to be talked into it. I knew it was wrong. Seeing you
only confirms my suspicion. My dear, it's not your fault,
just the luck of the draw that you got me; but get me you
did. And the thing is, between you, me and the walls, I'm
actually an appalling teacher. (*After a pause.*) Most of
the time, you see, it doesn't actually matter—appalling
teaching is quite in order for most of my appalling students. And the others manage to get by despite me. But
you're different. You want a lot, and I can't give it. (*He
moves towards her.*) Everything I know—and you must
listen to this—is that I know absolutely nothing. I don't
like the hours, you know. (*He goes to the swivel chair and
sits.*) Strange hours for this Open University thing. They
expect us to teach when the pubs are open. I can be a
good teacher when I'm in the pub, you know. Four pints
of weak *Guinness* and I can be as witty as Wilde. I'm
sorry—there are other tutors—I'll arrange it for you . . .
post it on . . . (*He looks at her.*)

(RITA *slowly turns and goes towards the door. She goes
out and quietly closes the door behind her. Suddenly the
door bursts open and* RITA *flies in.*)

Rita: (*Going up to him.*) Wait a minute, listen to me. Listen: I'm on this course, you are my teacher—an' you're
gonna bleedin' well teach me.

Frank: There are other tutors—I've told you . . .

Rita: You're my tutor. I don't want another tutor.

Frank: For God's sake, woman—I've told you . . .

Rita: You're my tutor.

Frank: But I've told you—I don't want to do it. Why come to
me?

Rita: (*Looking at him.*) Because you're a crazy mad piss artist who wants to throw his students through the window,
an' I like you. (*After a pause.*) Don't you recognize a compliment?

Frank: Do you think I could have a cigarette?

Rita: (*Offering the packet of cigarettes.*) I'll bring me scissors next week and give y' a haircut.

Frank: You're not coming here next week.

Rita: (*Lighting his cigarette.*) I am. And you're gettin' y' hair cut.

Frank: I am not getting my hair cut.

Rita: (*Getting her bag.*) I suppose y' wanna walk round like that, do y'? (*She goes towards the door.*)

Frank: Like what?

Rita: (*Getting her coat.*) Like a geriatric hippie.

(*Black-out*)

BEYOND THERAPY
by Christopher Durang

SCENE 2

Bruce and Prudence are both about thirty years old and single. Will they ever find love and romance? Clearly their only chance is if they can get "beyond therapy"—if they can get out from under the influence of their totally wacky psychotherapists. Bruce's therapist urges him to find a woman by placing a personal ad in *The New York Review of Books*. Prudence answers the ad, but their encounter turns out terrible for both of them. Bruce is very strange, to say the least.

The scene that follows takes place after their encounter. Prudence is at the office of her psychotherapist, Dr. Stuart Framingham, and she has a lot to tell him about her date. As it turns out, Dr. Framingham has a lot on his mind also.

(*Psychiatrist's office.* DR. STUART FRAMINGHAM. *Very masculine, a bit of a bully, wears boots, jeans, a tweed sports jacket, open sports shirt. Maybe has a beard.*)

Stuart: (*Speaking into intercom.*) You can send the next patient in now, Betty. (*Enter* PRUDENCE. *She sits. After a moment.*) So, what's on your mind this week?

Prudence: Oh I don't know. I had that Catherine the Great dream again.

Stuart: Yeah?

Prudence: Oh I don't know. Maybe it isn't Catherine the Great. It's really more like National Velvet.

Stuart: What do you associate to National Velvet?

Prudence: Oh I don't know. Childhood.

Stuart: Yes?

Prudence: I guess I miss childhood where one could look to a horse for emotional satisfaction rather than a person. I mean, a horse never disappointed me.

Stuart: You feel disappointed in people?

Prudence: Well every man I try to have a relationship with turns out to be crazy. And the ones that aren't crazy are dull. But maybe it's me. Maybe I'm really looking for faults just so I won't ever have a successful relationship. Like Michael last year. Maybe he was just fine, and I made up faults that he didn't have. Maybe I do it to myself. What do you think?

Stuart: What I think doesn't matter. What do you think?

Prudence: But what do *you* think?

Stuart: It's not my place to say.

Prudence: (*Irritated.*) Oh never mind. I don't want to talk about it.

Stuart: I see. (*Makes a note.*)

Prudence: (*Noticing he's making notes; to make up.*) I did answer one of those ads.

Stuart: Oh?

Prudence: Yes.

Stuart: How did it work out?

Prudence: Very badly. The guy was a jerk. He talked about my breasts, he has a male lover, and he wept at the table. It was really ridiculous. I should have known better.

Stuart: Well, you can always come back to me, babe. I'll light your fire for you anytime.

Prudence: Stuart, I've told you you can't talk to me that way if I'm to stay in therapy with you.

Stuart: You're mighty attractive when you're angry.

Prudence: Stuart . . . Dr. Framingham, many women who have been seduced by their psychiatrists take them to court . . .

Stuart: Yeah, but you wanted it, baby . . .

Prudence: How could I have "wanted" it? One of our topics has been that I don't know what I want.

Stuart: Yeah, but you wanted that, baby.

Prudence: Stop calling me baby. Really, I must be out of my mind to keep seeing you. (*Pause.*) Obviously you can't be my therapist after we've had an affair.

Stuart: Two lousy nights aren't an affair.

Prudence: You never said they were lousy.

Stuart: They were great. You were great. I was great. Wasn't I, baby? It was the fact that it was only two nights that was lousy.

Prudence: Dr. Framingham, it's the common belief that it is wrong for therapists and their patients to have sex together.

Stuart: Not in California.

Prudence: We are not in California.

Stuart: We could move there. Buy a house, get a Jacuzzi.

Prudence: Stuart . . . Dr. Framingham, we're not right for one another. I feel you have masculinity problems. I hate your belt buckle. I didn't really even like you in bed.

Stuart: I'm great in bed.

Prudence: (*With some hesitation.*) You have problems with premature ejaculation.

Stuart: Listen, honey, there's nothing premature about it. Our society is paced quickly, we all have a lot of things to do. I ejaculate quickly on purpose.

Prudence: I don't believe you.

Stuart: Fuck you, cunt.

Prudence: (*Stands.*) Obviously I need to find a new therapist.

Stuart: Okay, okay. I lost my temper. I'm sorry. But I'm human. Prudence, that's what you have to learn. People *are* human. You keep looking for perfection, you need to learn to accept imperfection. I can help you with that.

Prudence: Maybe I really should sue you. I mean, I don't think you should have a license.

Stuart: Prudence, you're avoiding the issue. The issue is you, not me. You're unhappy, you can't find a relationship you like, you don't like your job, you don't like the world. You *need* my help. I mean, don't get hung up on who should have a license. The issue is I can help you fit into the world. (*Very sincerely, sensitively.*) Really I can. Don't run away.

Prudence: (*Sits.*) I don't think I believe you.

Stuart: That's okay. We can work on that.

Prudence: I don't know. I really don't think you're a good therapist. But the others are probably worse, I'm afraid.

Stuart: They are. They're much worse. Really I'm very nice. I *like* women. Most men don't.

Prudence: I'm getting one of my headaches again. (*Holds her forehead.*)

Stuart: Do you want me to massage your neck?

Prudence: Please don't touch me.

Stuart: Okay, okay. (*Pause.*) Any other dreams?

Prudence: No.

Stuart: Perhaps we should analyze why you didn't like the man you met through the personal ad.

Prudence: I . . . I . . . don't want to talk anymore today. I want to go home.

Stuart: "You can never go home again."

Prudence: Perhaps not. But I can return to my apartment. You're making my headache worse.

Stuart: I think we should finish the session. I think it's important.

Prudence: I just can't talk anymore.

Stuart: We don't have to talk. But we have to stay in the room.

Prudence: How much longer?

Stuart: (*Looks at watch.*) Thirty minutes.

Prudence: Alright. But I'm not going to talk anymore.

Stuart: Okay. (*Pause. They stare at one another.*) You're very beautiful when you're upset.

Prudence: Please don't you talk either. (*They stare at each other; lights dim.*)

MONDAY AFTER THE MIRACLE
by William Gibson

ACT II

The scene is between Annie Sullivan and her husband,
John Macy. But the strongest presence in the scene, although
she has left the room, is Helen Keller. The play describes
events seventeen years after those in the author's earlier play,
The Miracle Worker, when Annie Sullivan first became Helen
Keller's teacher. Now Helen is a young woman, studying at
Radcliffe and off to a promising career as a writer. Annie is
still her teacher and she and Helen live together, along with
Annie's husband, John.

The scene below occurs six years after John first came to
Annie and Helen's house to work as an editor for Helen. He
and Annie fell in love and they married. But Annie's round-
the-clock devotion to Helen left little time for companionship
or tenderness. Nor has John's professional life flourished as he
had hoped. He has not had the career as a writer that he
sought, and he still works as an editor at *Youth's Companion*
magazine.

As Helen matures into a young woman she discovers that
she has all the physical and emotional needs of any woman,
despite being deaf and blind. One lonely night while Annie is
out, Helen and John embrace and kiss. When Annie returns
she discovers that Helen, filled with guilt, is very upset. John
tells her what has happened, and Annie grabs her coat and
storms off in a rage, with John chasing after her. Helen becomes frantic and accidentally knocks over a lamp, starting a
fire. John and Annie rush back in and put the fire out. After
Helen is reassured that Annie will not leave, she goes off, leaving John and Annie alone. Annie pours herself some brandy
and wipes a tear from her eye.

John: Kissed the girls and made them cry.

Annie: You haven't even the grace to be embarrassed.

John: I am, very; that's when I joke.

Annie: It's not comic.

John: It's not tragic. You should cry oftener, it's very attractive.

Annie: Give me a reason. Not pregnant, work fifteen hours a day, find you kissing a younger woman, and you tell me you're dying in this house, what have I to cry about?

John: I'm not dying.

Annie: I didn't think so from *her* story. (*She drinks.*)

John: (*Watches.*) You shouldn't drink alone. (*He reaches; she edges away.*)

Annie: Get your own glass.

John: (*Hand out.*) I dont' want to leave you.

Annie: I wonder.

John: Ever.

Annie: Why not?

John: I love you, idiot.

Annie: Is that love?

John: What else?

Annie: Inertia.

John: All right, I'll drink out of your shoe, damnit— (*He picks up a shoe.*) —that's a classic proof.

Annie: Of which?

John: What's this?

Annie: Love me, love my foot powder.

John: I'll get my own glass.

Annie: Here. Do you make love to others too?

John: No.

Annie: At the office?

John: No.

Annie: Would you tell me if you did?

John: No.

Annie: You do.

John: Yes, all day long, they line up at my desk.

Annie: Give me my drink.

John: I don't want others; it's you I want to love. I said dying—

Annie: Want to?

John: —because loving is the juice that keeps us alive, and I feel it—draining out of me. (ANNIE *shuts her eyes.*) And

I'm frightened. Thirty-one is no longer a—Look at me, I want to be in focus.

Annie: (*Does.*) Go on.

John: *Some*where—

Annie: Why draining?

John: —I'm a cog here and in that office—

Annie: Why draining?

John: Because I'm married to a pair of Siamese twins, every time I reach for you she's in the way!

Annie: You reached for her.

John: I'm human. But I don't seduce helpless deaf-blind virgins—

Annie: She's not helpless.

John: —and I wasn't going to.

Annie: If she's helpless, my whole life has been a waste—

John: Whole life is right, give *me* some of that devotion—

Annie: (*Fierce.*) I'm trying to hold it together! I do love you, I do have her on my hands every waking hour, and I expect you to feel for me when day after day I'm yanked back and forth between the two of you.

John: I do.

Annie: No—you feel neglected, is that what you mean by loving, I'm to spoon-feed you the way I do her? I need some looking after too—

John: Can I make an appointment?

Annie: I have a round-the-clock duty in this house!—it was never a secret—

John: I didn't marry a duty!

Annie: Oh yes you did!—

John: Then get her mother in here!

Annie: —it was to see Helen with my eyes, and that's what *I* mean by loving, she's our ward, and in this house we both watch over her or I don't know what you're doing in it.

John: (*Taken aback.*) Heyy—

Annie: Did you or did you not promise that?

John: You want me out?

Annie: I put my life in the hands of the one man who saw me as a woman, not a doormat to Helen, and then find him in her arms—

John: Now stop it—

Annie: —and if that's what this marriage is for I do want you out!

John: Stop *ranting*! —you know you don't—

Annie: I don't know it! —not tonight—

John: Then why didn't you leave?

Annie: Because I leave her to you for one minute and she's in flames!

John: Sonofabitch, I—

Annie: You don't look after me *or* her!

John: You win, you win, satisfied?

Annie: You look after yourself, you darling boy—

John: And who else does? —all week long that office is hell by daylight, companioning youth, shrinks my brain, and what little of it's left I bring home to companion you two in a house where I don't have a wife, don't have a child—

Annie: Ohhh—

John: —which would change everything—

Annie: —be careful!—

John: —give us both a focus—

Annie: —or I'll humiliate you too, me bucko, I don't have a child you go see a doctor!

John: I'll tell you one thing, the strength you've fed Helen for twenty years I find a pain in the ass as a daily diet. You're a tough morsel to digest! And if for half an hour I turn to *that* child because she needs cuddling it's the fall of the house of Usher?

Annie: Because it's her—can't you get that through your skull—

John: She lets me feel tender! You don't. (ANNIE *sits rigid. And covers her face; now she really cries, is wracked by it.* JOHN *after a time touches her.*) Hey— (*She rolls away from him, and flees upstairs.*)

GENIUSES
by Jonathan Reynolds

ACT II

The characters in *Geniuses* are trying to finish making a film. It's called *Parabola of Death*, and it is not going well, to say the least. Their location is a small village in the Philippines, "200 miles north of Manila," and now all work is stopped because a typhoon has blown up. The rain and wind have been "ferocious" and the crew has been trapped inside for four days. Among this cooped up collection of oddballs are Jocko and Skye. Jocko is the most recent of a series of screenwriters, each of whom has been fired. He is a thirty-three-year-old novelist from New York who puts down everything Hollywood (but doesn't want to be fired). He also puts down Skye as much as possible. Skye is a former *Playboy* Playmate who has been flown in for a brief nude scene. She is "very blond, very gorgeous," and very Hollywood. She has also had bouts of nausea since the day she arrived about a week ago. Since they met, Jocko has done his best to appear immune to Skye's incredibly good looks—which he is not immune to at all.

The following scene comes right after another of their verbal encounters. Skye has just asked everyone to leave the room so she can be alone with Jocko.

Skye: You win. Let's go.
Jocko: What? Where?
Skye: To bed.
Jocko: (*Amazed.*) What?
Skye: I can't stand to be ridiculed. You really made me believe you hated me.
Jocko: I did, huh.

Skye: At first I thought it was a new approach, and real obvious—remember when you told me off about being a stew and a Playmate? My take was, hey is he coming on to me! But now after these four days or whatever it is, you're not kidding. You may really hate me!

Jocko: More than life itself.

Skye: I don't believe you, but it's very seductive. Let's go.

Jocko: No.

Skye: No? Why not?

Jocko: I don't want to.

Skye: My God, you like little boys, don't you?

Jocko: That's it, that's it, whenever you don't want to go to bed with a woman, suddenly you're homosexual.

Skye: Then how come you won't go to bed with me?

Jocko: Going to bed with you is not the only alternative to homosexuality.

Skye: I am prime meat! Do you know how many men out there would kill for a piece of this pie? Guys hump their pillows thinking of me! Just because you get depressed more doesn't mean you're smarter.

Jocko: You see the whole world in terms of a pass, don't you?

Skye: What?

Jocko: Somebody likes you, you think it's a pass; somebody hates you, you think *that's* a pass. You're way beyond being a sex object—you're a sex subject! Your life is defined by sex—and not by its pleasure, but by its power. Right this minute, you don't care about me, you just want to make peace in case we're stuck here for three months! Yes, you are prime meat, but no I'm not homosexual, and no I'm not going to bed with you.

Skye: Well, why did you come on to me like that? All night, all yesterday, the day before—

Jocko: Who said I was coming on to you?

Skye: Oh, don't kid me, bub—I know a tour de force when I see one. All that putting me down, all that passion. Your eyes were blazing with the excitement of the kill. Flattery by insult. Where do you think I've been? You *do* want me, don't you? Come on, come on . . .

Jocko: (*Struggling with himself.*) Maybe.

Skye: Then why won't you go to bed with me!

Jocko: You're . . . sick.

Skye: What?

Jocko: You're sick. You've got diarrhea, your breath is bad, your skin's clammy. There'd be . . . stuff on the bed.

Skye: (*Dejected.*) I don't believe it.

Jocko: I'm sorry, but the lifelong fantasy of a one-night stand with the Playmate of the Year doesn't include her having amoebic dysentery. (*He starts for the door, turns.*) Oh, but hey—what's your phone number? Y'know, in case we ever get back to L.A.

Skye: 213-851-7986. (*He writes it down.*)

Jocko: And your address?

Skye: 8979 and ¼, Wonderland Avenue, Hollywood, California, 90048.

Jocko: There really is a Wonderland Avenue?

Skye: It's in the hills. Jocko—do I really look that bad?

Jocko: No, no, you're very attractive, really. You're the most beautiful creature I've ever seen. It's just that you're . . . so . . . sick . . .

Skye: Don't say it again, okay? (JOCKO *drinks an enormous amount from a bottle of vodka.*) Hey, take it easy.

Jocko: Just a little nightcap. Good night and so forth.

(*He drunkenly exits into his room.*)

NINE
Book by Arthur Kopit
Music and Lyrics by Maury Yeston
Adaptation from the Italian by Mario Fratti

ACT II

Nine is adapted from Federico Fellini's film *8½*. It is about the life and loves of Guido Contini, a famous Italian film director. Guido is now middle-aged and finds himself assessing his past and concerned about his future. Claudia Nordi has starred in most of Guido's successful movies. Their careers were linked for many years and they were lovers, but they haven't worked together for some time.

Claudia is now a major actress in her own right and Guido has asked her to star in his new movie. She wants to see the script before making a decision, but Guido has asked her to meet him in Venice so he can explain her role to her himself. They are on a beach.

Claudia: Guido, I've just flown in from Paris. I am extremely tired, hungry, cold. Why have you brought me to this beach?

Guido: (*Abstracted.*) What?

Claudia: Guido, where is my hotel? (OTHERS *begin slowly to exit.*)

Guido: Oh. I'll drive you there in a minute. But first I thought you'd like to see this beach. An extraordinary woman once danced for me on a beach like this.

Claudia: Is that the woman I'm supposed to play in your film?

Guido: No. No-no!

Claudia: Then why'd you think I'd want to see this beach?

Guido: Well I just thought you'd be interested. God, I love it when it's cold like this! The wind whipping in off the Adriatic! You really feel it! Right down to the bone!

Claudia: (*Shivering.*) Yes. It's a wonderful feeling. Guido, who do I play in this film?

Guido: A woman who heals.

Claudia: (*Disappointed.*) You mean like a nurse?

Guido: No, nothing like a nurse! Nurses heal the flesh! You . . . you . . .

Claudia: I know. I heal the *spirit*.

Guido: Yes, that's it!

Claudia: And how do I do this?

Guido: Well with, with . . .

Claudia: Sorcery!

Guido: Exactly! God, I can't believe how suited you are for this role! I can see you in it now!

Claudia: Guido, this is the part I played in "The Garden of Earthly Delights."

Guido: Yes, well, that was a long time ago. And let me remind you, it was a very big hit! Visconti never had a hit like that!

Claudia: It's also the role I played in "Cathedral of Dreams."

Guido: An even bigger hit.

Claudia: And in "Via Veneto."

Guido: Biggest hit of all! You see? This role is made for you!

Claudia: I don't want to play it anymore.

Guido: But you've got to! I haven't had a hit like those in years!

Claudia: Of course you have.

Guido: No-no, not really. My last three have been outright flops. Producers are not exactly knocking down my door. I've lost something, I don't know what. But I know you can help me find it.

Claudia: Inspiration.

Guido: Yes!

Claudia: Guido, I was never your inspiration. That's what you imagine, but it was always you. I can't play this role for you anymore.

Guido: This role made you a star!

Claudia: Guido, I am not a spirit. I am real. I have a life you know nothing about. And have never shown the slightest interest in. I shouldn't have come here.

Guido: So why did you? . . . You came because I understand you like no other person does.

Claudia: You don't understand me at all!

Guido: That just shows how much you know about yourself.

Claudia: Guido, you have invented me! No such person exists!

Guido: In my mind, she exists! On the screen, she exists! And now, everywhere, in people's dreams, *she exists.*

Claudia: I came because Luisa asked me to come.

Guido: . . . What?

Claudia: Luisa. She called me in Paris. She said she didn't think she could help you anymore. She thought maybe I could. Well, I can't.

Guido: Look, I'll change the role. You'll play a different role.

Claudia: It wouldn't work.

Guido: Why not?

Claudia: Because I can't go through this kind of relationship with you again. It takes too much out of me. And Luisa is your wife. Excuse me, I'm going back to the car. (*She starts off.*)

Guido: Claudia, I love you!

Claudia: (*Stopping; to herself.*) Oh my God.

Guido: It's true. And you know it's true. Why are you laughing?

Claudia: I'm not laughing.

Guido: I can see your back moving up and down. Of course you're laughing! My life's falling apart, my career is crumbling, I tell you that I love you, and you're standing there laughing. . . !

A MAP OF THE WORLD
by David Hare

ACT II, SCENE 6

The play weaves two stories together. One takes place in a hotel in Bombay, India, during an international conference on world poverty. The other takes place some time later at a film studio in England where a movie is being made about the dramatic events that took place at that conference. The story at the conference revolves around three characters: Victor Mehta, an urbane, cynical, and highly successful Indian novelist who lives in England and who, to the chagrin of the more left-leaning participants of the conference, has been invited to give the opening address; Stephen Andrews, an impassioned young journalist who resents everything that Victor stands for; and Peggy Whitton, a beautiful and bright American actress who is in Bombay making a picture and who happens to be staying at the hotel where the conference is being held.

Both men are interested in Peggy, and she quickly becomes embroiled in their endless political arguments. (Having majored in philosophy, she holds her own during these debates.) She finds Stephen "charming," but is put off by his self-righteousness. She spends the night with Victor, who she describes as a "man of great gracefulness. Difficult, of course, like the best of men. And very proud."

Peggy challenges both her suitors to debate each other publicly before a neutral judge. "Whoever wins," she says, "wins me." Now, she points out, they argue about poverty from privileged positions: their own lives will not be affected by the outcome of their debates. But with her as the prize, they will have something to lose.

Victor and Stephen take up the challenge. The scene below takes place during the filming of the story. The actors playing Victor and Peggy are enacting what happened just before the debate. The film set is arranged to look like Peggy's hotel room in Bombay. The actor playing Victor is at the desk writing out his speech. The actress playing Peggy is on the bed wearing a dressing gown.

(For scene-study purposes the scene may be edited to omit the sequences with the waiter.)

Peggy: How do you write a book?

Mehta: *(Without looking up.)* Mmm?

Peggy: I mean, when you start out, do you know what you think?

Mehta: No.

Peggy: I don't mean the plot. I'm sure the plot's easy . . .

Mehta: No, the plot's very hard.

Peggy: Well, all right, the plot's hard. But what you *think* . . . do you know what you think?

Mehta: No.

(He turns from writing in his notebook and looks at her.)

The act of writing is the act of discovering what you believe.

(He turns back to his work, smiling slightly.)

How do you act?

Peggy: *(Smiles at once.)* Oh, lord . . .

Mehta: Well?

Peggy: I mean, I don't. Not really. I'm not an actress. I'm too conscious. I'm too self-aware. I stand aside.

Mehta: Does that mean you plan to give it up?

(PEGGY *does not answer. She has already picked up a booklet which is beside her on the bed.*)

Peggy: Don't you love this country?

Mehta: Why?

Peggy: An airline timetable, I was looking . . .

Mehta: Were you thinking of leaving?

Peggy: No, listen, what I love about India, the only country in the world where they'd print poetry—here, look, at the bottom of the Kuwait–Delhi airline schedule. A poem. 'Some come to India to find themselves, some come to lose themselves . . .' In an *airline schedule*? Isn't that a pretty frightening admission?

(*He is about to speak seriously but she interrupts.*)

Mehta: Peggy . . .

Peggy: No, I wasn't leaving. How could I be leaving? I'm here to make a film.

Mehta: But?

(*A pause. Then she looks away.*)

Peggy: But at lunchtime I did something so stupid that the thought of going down those steps . . .

Mehta: I see.

Peggy: . . . into that lobby, along that corridor, past those delegates, into that deserted conference hall, for this appalling contest . . .

Mehta: Yes.

Peggy: . . . when all I want is to spend my time with you.

(*A pause.* MEHTA *sets aside his notebook.*)

Mehta: American women, they make me laugh. I am at home.

Peggy: Well, good.

Mehta: It is like they pick you up in their lovemaking from wherever they last left off. At once, bang! and they're away. No matter with whom it was last time, if it was someone else, no matter, nevertheless, it is go at once. The passion again. Making love to an American woman, it is like climbing aboard an already moving train.

(PEGGY *smiles and gets off the bed to go to the bathroom.*)

Peggy: We have needs.

Mehta: I am sure.

Peggy: (*Calling as she goes out.*) We have no guilt. Americans are unashamed about their needs.

Mehta: (*Smiles.*) Yes.

Peggy: (*Off.*) When an Englishman has an emotion, his first instinct is to repress it. When an American has an emotion, his first instinct . . .

Mehta: Ah well, yes . . .

Peggy: (*Off.*) They express it!

Mehta: Usually at length.

Peggy: (*Off.*) Why not?

(MEHTA *sits smiling, contented, happy with* PEGGY *and able to show it clearly now she is out of the room.*)

Mehta: Always examining their own reactions . . .

Peggy: (*Off.*) Yes.

Mehta: Always analysing, always telling you what they feel—*I* think, *I* feel, let me tell you what *I* feel . . .

Peggy: Sure.

Mehta: The endless drama of it all.

(PEGGY *reappears at the bathroom door. She has taken off her dressing-gown and has changed into another loose cotton suit.*)

Peggy: And which is better, tell me, Victor, next to the English? Which is healthier, eh?

(*He looks at her with great affection.*)

Mehta: You make love like a wounded panther. You are like a paintshop on fire.

(*She looks at him. Then raises her eyebrows.*)

Peggy: Well, goodness.

Mehta: Yes.

Peggy: Writer, eh?

(*He smiles. There is a knock at the door,* PEGGY *goes to answer it.*)

Mehta: It comes in handy.

Peggy: Is that what you say to all the girls? 'Thank you, that was wounded-panther-like.'

(*She opens the door. A* WAITER *is standing outside.*)

Yes?

Waiter: Mr. Andrews. He is waiting downstairs.

(PEGGY *looks at the* WAITER *a moment, then nods.*)

Peggy: Thank you.

(*She closes the door, stands a moment, her face turned away from* MEHTA. *Then she turns, walks across to the dressing-table and picks up her hairbrush. Then, casually:*)

What about you?

Mehta: What?

Peggy: When are you thinking of leaving?

Mehta: Oh . . . tomorrow.

Peggy: Really?

Mehta: Yes.

(*There is a pause. Then deliberately:*)

After I make my speech, I would hope.

(*There is a slight pause, then both of them speak at once.*)

Peggy . . .

Peggy: I don't know. I can't say which of the two of you makes more sense to me. I've never had to choose, you see. Like so many people, I've never made a choice.

(*She turns and smiles at him.*)

Sitting at nights with my professors, sure, it was great. Philosophy, that was my major . . . eight arguments as to whether God exists.

Mehta: Does he?

Peggy: We never decided.

Mehta: There you are.

Peggy: But the game was fun. No question. Great nights. What are those things called? 'Angel Bars' we ate. Gloppy cherries covered in chocolate in a candy bar. To me there isn't a philosophical idea that isn't to do with food. Toasted marshmallows, late at night, when I first read Wittgenstein. I can still remember the taste of 'The world is all that is the case.' It tasted good, it still tastes good, that moment of understanding something. But *applying* it? Well, that's different, the world not offering so many opportunities for that sort of thing. Arts and humanities! Philosophy! What's the point in America, where the only philosophy you'll ever encounter is the philosophy of making money. In my case by taking off T-shirts. In fact, not even taking them off—I'm too up-market for that. I have only to hint there are situations in which I *would* show my breasts to certain people, certain *rich* people, that they do indeed exist under there, but for now it's enough to suggest their shape, hint at their shape, in a T-shirt. Often it will have to be wet. By soaking my T-shirts in water I make my living. It's true. Little to do with the life of ideas.

(*She smiles.*)

Spoilt. Spoilt doesn't say it, though that's what people say about Americans, and spoilt, I suppose, is what I was till lunchtime, till I made this ridiculous offer. A young idiot's suicidal offer with which she is now going to have to learn to live.

(*She turns and looks at* MEHTA.)

Well, good luck to you. Debate well, Victor, for on your performance depends . . .
Mehta: (*Smiles.*) Don't tell me.
Peggy: . . . my future. Tonight.

(*They stand a moment at opposite sides of the room, looking at one another.*)

Mehta: It's your fault.
Peggy: Oh yes.
Mehta: You with your 'Oh, Stephen is not such a bad fellow.' He *is* a bad fellow. This you must learn.

(*The* WAITER *knocks on the door.* PEGGY *does not move, just calls out, looking at* VICTOR *all the time.*)

Peggy: Yes!
Waiter: Madam, Mr. Andrews is asking why you are not downstairs.
Peggy: Tell him . . . tell him we are coming. Just one minute. Mr. Mehta is preparing his case.

(MEHTA *smiles at her, the two of them still not moving as the* WAITER *is heard to go.*)

Mehta: Give me a kiss.
Peggy: No kisses. I am no longer yours. I belong now to the winner of an argument.

(MEHTA *takes his jacket from the back of the chair, as she waits. He puts it on. He puts his notebook in his pocket and turns to her.*)

Mehta: Fine.

TEIBELE AND HER DEMON
by Isaac Bashevis Singer and Eve Friedman

ACT I, SCENE 1

The setting is the Jewish village of Frampol, Poland, in 1880. In that village live Teibele and Alchonon. Teibele is an attractive young woman, and also an *aguna*. In traditional Jewish life this term refers to "a woman whose husband has abandoned her, leaving her in a kind of marital limbo. Unless his death is proved, she is unable to divorce him, unable to remarry." Alchonon is an impoverished young religious scholar who is madly in love with Teibele, though he is too shy to ever let her know. Even if he spoke his mind and if she were free to remarry, Teibele would never choose him.

One night Alchonon overhears Teibele telling a friend about her passionless marriage and about the demons who come to women in the night and force them into sexual acts. Alchonon immediately concocts a scheme, and later that night after Teibele has fallen asleep, he crawls into her bedroom disguised as a demon. He lifts an end of her bed off the ground and lets it drop to the floor. (The published script provides a glossary of Jewish terms.)

Alchonon: Don't scream, Teibele. If you cry out, I will destroy you. I am the demon Hurmizah, ruler over darkness, rain, hail, thunder, and wild beasts. I am the evil spirit who espoused the young woman you spoke about tonight. And because you told the story with such relish, I heard your words from the abyss, and I was filled with lust for your body. Do not try to resist! Those who refuse to do my will I drag away beyond the Mountains of Darkness—to Mount Sair, into a wilderness where men seek not, where beasts tread not, among adders and scorpions, until every bone of their body is ground to dust, and they are lost forever in the nether depths. But if you comply with my wish, not a hair of your head will be harmed, and I will grant you success in everything.

Teibele: What do you want of me? I am a married woman.

Alchonon: Your husband is dead.

Teibele: How? When?

Alchonon: It's already a year and seven months. He died in a cholera epidemic in the city of Leipzig, and I followed his hearse with a swarm of other demons.

Teibele: Demons!

Alchonon: Evil deeds give birth to demons. They are the offspring of transgression.

Teibele: Moishe Mattis was not a sinner. He was a pious man.

Alchonon: A man who deserts his wife is not pious. He danced around with his Chassidim, drank aqua vitae, and left you alone. He didn't seek you in the nights when you came from the mikvah. And when he did, he couldn't satisfy you. After he left you, he indulged in the deeds of Onan, and from each drop of semen a devil was born. When he died they flew after his body, called him father and disgraced him.

Teibele: What was he doing in Leipzig?

Alchonon: The rabbi of Turisk had learned that he was not a whole man and made him leave. He stole the rabbi's spice box and wandered to the fair of Leipzig.

Teibele: Why?

Alchonon: All the great fairs team with living corpses.

Teibele: Must I sit shiva for him?

Alchonon: Not after so long an interval.

Teibele: Will I be permitted to remarry?

Alchonon: Never! I cannot testify for you. The testimony of a demon is not valid. But I'm not lying. Your husband is dead. The worms have already gnawed away his nose.

Teibele: How do you know?

Alchonon: I know. I am the Rabbi of the demons.

Teibele: Oh, God in heaven!

Alchonon: Don't invoke God's name. He cannot help you now. The Messiah on a white donkey hasn't come yet. And until resurrection at least another 689,000 years will pass.

Teibele: Sh'ma Israel!

Alchonon: Hush! Quiet! If you try this again I'll rip the tongue out of your mouth. I'll pluck your eyes out and bite off your nipples.

Teibele: Pity! Have pity!

Alchonon: We don't know what pity is.

Teibele: I will die if you touch me.

Alchonon: You won't die. I've yearned for you for years. I know all your innermost secrets. When you still went faithfully to the mikvah I accompanied you. I lusted for your body. You need not be ashamed before me because I've seen you naked many many times. Your breasts are white and your nipples are red. Is this true or not?

Teibele: True!

Alchonon: I had no power over you then but I spoke to you without language and tickled your hidden places. My words became your thoughts.

Teibele: What do you want of me? I will lose the world to come.

Alchonon: You will lose nothing. Many pious females copulated with our kind and today they're sitting on golden chairs in paradise. I myself have lain in the laps of the most beautiful and pious daughters of men. With Hodl, the daughter of Baalshem and with Sarah, the daughter of Good.

Teibele: Sarah, the daughter of Good?

Alchonon: She conjured me with holy names to come to her bed. I lay with Bathsheba long before David took her away from Uriah, and with Queen Esther when Ashasuerus brought her to his palace. That is mentioned in the Talmud.

Teibele: I'm still fertile. I may get pregnant. And then . . .

Alchonon: No grief will come to you. I've taken the form of a man in order not to terrify you. You won't be disgraced. I will be your husband, your brother, your father. I could force you but I'd rather you open your lap to me of your own free will.

Teibele: I'm afraid, I'm afraid.

Alchonon: They were all afraid. But after I came to them they loved me with a great love, longed for me and called my name in the night.

Teibele: Why have you chosen me?

Alchonon: I loved you the first time I saw you.

Teibele: When? Where?

Alchonon: On your wedding night. Your husband, Moishe Mattis, came to you but he did not know how to unbind you. He buzzed like a bee and in his clumsiness he gushed semen on your thighs. I entered your bed and your body burned me like fire. My tongue brushed your ear and told you sweet secrets.

Teibele: (*Almost screaming.*) Don't!

Alchonon: You are mine.

(*He flings himself on her. Blackout. The lights dim up. A short interval has passed.*)

Alchonon: Are you still afraid of me?

Teibele: Yes, I am.

Alchonon: Did I make you suffer? Tell the truth!

Teibele: No.

Alchonon: Was it pleasant? (TEIBELE *is silent.*) Yes or no?

Teibele: (*Hesitating.*) Yes, but . . .

Alchonon: But what?

Teibele: It is a sin.

Alchonon: No sin. You're not married. I came to give you pleasure, not to frighten you. I heard you crying in the nights and I knew your longing.

Teibele: Yes. Yes. Yes.

Alchonon: Don't keep muttering yes. Talk to me like a woman to a man. Kiss me! (TEIBELE *doesn't stir.*) Kiss my lips. They thirst for you. (TEIBELE *kisses his cheek timidly.*) Kiss my mouth! (*Kisses her.*) How sweet your mouth is. I'm the happiest demon in Frampol. You're better than all my wives.

Teibele: Wives!

Alchonon: Yes, wives. Don't be jealous of them. They are she-demons and you are the daughter of man. You are the only human female I possess.

Teibele: If you have them, why do you need me?

Alchonon: They are shrill and vulgar, but you are quiet and modest. Their bodies are made of air and spider webs while yours is flesh and blood.

Teibele: How many have you?

Alchonon: Seven.

Teibele: Seven!

Alchonon: Seven she-demons. Let's see. There's Naamah, Machlath, and Af, Chaimah, Zluchah, Nafka and Chuldah.

Teibele: Such names!

Alchonon: I left their beds and came to you.

Teibele: Why?

Alchonon: Because you loved me even though you didn't know me. You uncovered yourself before me. You fondled my tail unawares and you even licked it. (*He laughs.*)

Teibele: I? How? (*Pause.*) Don't your wives do the same?

Alchonon: They fornicate with all of us but you give yourself only to me.

Teibele: They betray you? Why do you stay with such kind?

Alchonon: It's our nature. We pair off in the dark, not knowing who with whom. Every night is a black wedding to us. But since we stem from Adam's loins we crave his daughters.

Teibele: What is so good about us?

Alchonon: I'll speak only about you. She-demons are false but you are true. With all their masks and cunning there is no substance to them. They are shadows of toadstools. They have no wombs. Their breasts are foam and scum. When you touch them they dissolve, while you can be caressed and pinched. (*Pinches her.*)

Teibele: It hurts! (*Giggles.*)

Alchonon: They can bark but you can cry. (*He kisses her eyes.*)

Teibele: My tears are gone.

Alchonon: New ones will gather.

Teibele: Tell me more about these wives of yours. What is Naamah like?

(*During the description of the seven wives,* TEIBELE *grows more and more titillated.*)

Alchonon: Naamah is a terror. When we quarrel she spits venom and blows fire at me through her nostrils.

Teibele: How awful!

Alchonon: Machlath has the face of a leech and those whom she lashes with her tongue are branded forever.

Teibele: Are you branded?

Alchonon: She left a scar on my belly. Touch it.

Teibele: No, no. (*She twists away from him.*)

Alchonon: Af bedecks herself with emeralds, diamonds and silver. Her braids are spun of gold. On her ankles she wears bells and bracelets. When she dances naked before our lord Asmodeus, all the deserts ring out with their tinkling.

Teibele: Naked? Before Asmodeus?

Alchonon: She is my wife but his concubine.

Teibele: She lives with both of you?

Alchonon: With all of us.

Teibele: Shameless!

Alchonon: Chaimah is the only one I can talk to. But she's awake only one night a year—the midnight of the winter solstice. We've had some rollicking times in the graveyard feasting on the freshly buried infants.

Teibele: Don't tell me any more!

Alchonon: Zluchah is the enemy of brides. If a bride steps outside alone at night during the Seven Nuptial Benedictions, Zluchah wriggles up to her and the bride falls down in a fit unable to speak.

Teibele: Why keep a vicious devil like her?

Alchonon: In the nether world you take what you get. (*Pause.*) How many did I mention?

Teibele: Five.

Alchonon: Yes, now who's next?

Teibele: Nafka!

Alchonon: Nafka is the most lecherous of all of them! Her speech is the hissing of the primeval serpent. She hangs down from the Tree of Death like a bat and shrieks for semen.

Teibele: This is horrible.

Alchonon: Chuldah has the shape of a cat. Her eyes are as

green as gall. She chews on bear's liver while we copu-
late.

Teibele: Disgusting!

Alchonon: Therefore, Teibele, when I observed you on your
wretched wedding night—your breasts, your belly, your
hips, your thighs—I loved you and I kept a watch on you.
Tonight when you told your tale with such skill and
charm, I couldn't curb my desire for you any more. I entered your house, your bed and you . . .

Teibele: It must be a dream. I'll wake up and—

Alchonon: This is no dream. I am your spouse. Be thou dese-
crated unto me by the lawlessness of Esau and Samael . . .

Teibele: I'll be lost, lost forever.

Alchonon: Dance with me. This is our black wedding.

Teibele: Leave me! Leave me!

Alchonon: You will, Teibele. Dance with me. (*Whirling her
in the air.*)
In the beginning
All was dust
And then came Satan
The Father of Lust.
Chaos above
The abyss below
And Satan's bark
Let there be dark.

Teibele: Leave me!

Alchonon: Never. You are mine forever! (*He falls on her.*)

DANNY AND THE DEEP BLUE SEA
by John Patrick Shanley

SCENE 3

Danny and Roberta met in a bar last night—two troubled and lonely people in a lonely neighborhood bar in the
Bronx. He's a truck driver who constantly gets into fights (his

hands are severely bruised from his most recent altercations; at work, he says, they call him "the Beast"). She's divorced, has a thirteen-year-old boy (who she says is "all fucked up"), and lives with her parents in a small apartment in their house. Danny and Roberta talked, argued, and cursed at each other; she hit him and he almost choked her. But they also told each other their most intimate secrets: She seduced her father ("I could never make him do anything. That's why I did it. So I could make him do things"). He told her of his fear that he might have killed a man in a fight. Then they went back to her house and made love, and, somehow, managed to touch each other and become vulnerable to each other. They even talked about getting married.

It is the next morning. Roberta and Danny are still asleep in her room.

(*Lights up. The bedroom. It's late morning.* ROBERTA *and* DANNY *are asleep.* DANNY *is snoring.* ROBERTA *wakes up. She touches* DANNY's *face tenderly, then hits him with a pillow.*)

Roberta: Tag!
Danny: (*Snapping into a violent stance.*) What?!
Roberta: You're it. Good mornin!
Danny: Oh yeah. Good mornin.
Roberta: Keep it down a bit.
Danny: Why?
Roberta: My family.
Danny: Oh. Okay.
Roberta: They'll be gone inna minute. Then I'll cook you breakfast if you want.
Danny: Sure. Where they goin?
Roberta: The kid goes to school. At least he leaves here with books. My mother goes to work. My father goes to work.
Danny: What about you?
Roberta: I don't work. Not right now. I didn't like my last job so I quit.
Danny: What did you do?
Roberta: I was a secretary for a bunch a exterminators.
Danny: You're kiddin!
Roberta: Nope. They had this truck with a big dead roach on top, an they were real nasty to me, and at night. I used

to dream the truck was chasin me an the roach was movin. So I quit. I gotta get somethin else, but I ain't started lookin yet. What about your job? When you gotta be there?

Danny: They don't need me till Wednesday this week. It's a slow time.

Roberta: So how do I look in the daylight?

Danny: Good.

Roberta: You still like my nose?

Danny: Oh yeah.

Roberta: You don't have to, you know.

Danny: Whaddaya mean?

Roberta: You know.

Danny: No, I don't.

Roberta: You don't haveta stick to nothin you said last night. It was nice that you said it at all. I slept good last night for about the first time inna fuckin century.

Danny: Whaddaya think I am?

Roberta: I think you're real nice. An I like ya. That's why I'm sayin what I'm sayin. So you won't haveta. You like eggs for breakfast? I think there'll be some.

Danny: I meant last night. What I said.

Roberta: You don't haveta say that.

Danny: I did!

Roberta: Aw comon, Danny.

Danny: I asked ya ta marry me last night square business an you said yes an I meant it!

Roberta: All right then, I didn't!

Danny: What?

Roberta: You heard me!

Danny: What?

Roberta: I was lyin cause I wanted a nice thing. Get serious. No way are you an me gettin married. That was strictly make-believe.

Danny: Don't do this to me!

Roberta: I gotta kid, a fucked up kid, no job, crazy parents. I'm crazy myself. I told you. Last night. Wake up. Open your fuckin eyes. I ain't got no serious way possible I could get married to anybody. Not anybody. No less a guy like you.

Danny: Whaddaya mean, a guy like me?

Roberta: Nothin, all right?

Danny: Tell me what you mean!

Roberta: You know.

Danny: I don't know nothin!

Roberta: Look at your hands, Danny. Why do you wanna make me say it? You're all fucked up. If ya didn't kill somebody the other night, ya will sometime. If I married ya, it could be me. Yud haveta be retarded not to see it! You're a fuckin caveman! Yud be bouncin me off the walls . . .

Danny: NO!

Roberta: You grabbed me last night. See the mark?

Danny: I'm sorry I hurt your throat.

Roberta: I'll make you breakfast. Then you'll go back to Zerega.

Danny: No.

Roberta: Then you'll go wherever, but you'll go.

Danny: I don't buy this line a shit, Roberta. Not just cause it makes me feel bad. It don't sound true to me.

Roberta: It don't matter how it sounds.

Danny: Yeah, it matters! I heard the way you really are last night. It whadn't this. Ya wanted to show somebody how ya really was last night. Ya showed me.

Roberta: This is how I really am! Last night was just time out.

Danny: You're lyin!

Roberta: And you're still dreamin!

Danny: No I'm not.

Roberta: I don't wanna talk. I don't care.

Danny: I care. I gotta care.

Roberta: Well don't bother me with it.

Danny: You gotta be straight with me at least.

Roberta: I don't gotta do nothin.

Danny: You do too! You were gonna marry me last night.

Roberta: I can't marry ya!

Danny: Tell me why!

Roberta: I told ya!

Danny: I know I'm fucked up! But I got control! Don't do this to me, Roberta! Ya kissed my hands. Ya kissed my hands. It ain't right ta do this to me. I got a heart in my body and it's gonna break and it's gonna be you that did it. What can I tell you? What can I tell you that'll make you like you were to me?

Roberta: Danny.

Danny: Anything. Don't just . . . just don't say no.

Roberta: I can't, baby. I can't.

Danny: Why not?

Roberta: Just leave it.

Danny: I can't go back.

Roberta: I heard the bird sing that sings outside my window. This mornin. When I was just gone asleep. I heard ya talkin an the bird singin. An it was the first time I could sleep right . . . since I was a young girl. But I'm sorry I told ya yes, cause I can't marry ya, baby. Just take it outta ya mind. It wouldn't be right.

Danny: There's a way ta make it right, if ya know enough! Tell me what's the matter an we'll make it right! There's people we can go to if we don't know enough between us. There's people an a way if ya want it bad enough, but ya just don't know how. An I want it bad an I think you do too! Do ya wanna marry me, Roberta?

Roberta: Sure. I mean no. I mean I can't.

Danny: What's the thing?

Roberta: Nothin.

Danny: What's the thing?

Roberta: I told ya.

Danny: Told me what?

Roberta: About my father.

Danny: So ya told me.

Roberta: Ya can't do a horrible thing like that, Danny, an not be punished. It was me that did it.

Danny: Whaddaya talkin about?

Roberta: I did a bad thing.

Danny: All right! So ya did a bad thing. Ya told me.

Roberta: An . . . An . . . nobody punished me.

Danny: Good.

Roberta: No! No, it ain't good! I did a bad thing an nobody punished me, and so . . . it stayed with me.

Danny: I don't get you.

Roberta: I made my father inta garbage. I made myself that way, too. It's all wrong. My mother don't know what happened, but she knows. Cause it stinks so bad. I can hear her prayin all the time. Crazy whinin prayin like needles. An when she's not prayin, she's lookin around like she lost somethin but she ain't lookin for anythin an

SHE WON'T LOOK AT ME! At the floor the wall anythin but not me! An my kid. I did that an I got a kid. I had no right to do what I did! It was too bad a thing to do. There's no happy thing possible becausa me. It's my house. It's my garbage. I can't leave this house cause it's my crime.

Danny: That's crazy.

Roberta: So what? Just cause it's crazy don't mean it ain't true.

Danny: You can do whatever you want.

Roberta: I did whatever I wanted, an it killed my whole fuckin family! I don't mean ta spill my poison any further than I already have! Ya hear me? It's over. I'm through screwin everythin up. I went out last night cause I couldn't stand it in this room anymore. I couldn't stand bein by myself anymore, with myself anymore. I talked ta you cause I hadda talk to somebody, somebody, an there you were, so fucked up ya might listen.

Danny: Roberta . . .

Roberta: No. An ya did listen. An I thank ya for it. An I slept last night so sweet, for the first time inna hundred years. Cause you were good ta me an talked nice. But that's it, man. That is strictly fuckin it. Cause this is my house. My house. And I gotta live in it.

Danny: I'm takin you outta here.

Roberta: Forget it. It ain't gonna happen.

Danny: I have to!

Roberta: You can't!

Danny: I love you.

Roberta: You just need ta say that for your own private fuckin reasons! You don't know me. It ain't possible ta know somebody that fuckin quick. I told ya last night, an I'm tellin you now. I'm nuts! An I'll tell you what I didn't tell you then. I'm bad.

Danny: Oh comon, gimme a break.

Roberta: I gotta badness in me. I did what I did ta my father an my family cause there's a big mean bad feelin in me that likes ta break an hurt, an I'd break an hurt you just the same. Just the same as I did them.

Danny: Get serious. You would not.

Roberta: You ain't nothin ta me! You ain't dog shit on my shoes! Get outta here, freak! With yar crazy fights. Go back to the cave ya crawled out of! Go beat up a wall! Go watch yar dishrag mother puke her dishrag guts! Ya fuckin Beast! Ya fuckin Beast! Ya got to screw the pig, and if ya'd played yar cards right, ya mighta got a free breakfast! But ya blew it, so get the fuck out! Get out! Get out! Get out, ya moron clown! Get the fuck outta here an leave me, leave me alone! (*She collapses, sobbing. Quiets.*)

Danny: I ain't too good at people. But I gotta say somethin. A crazy thing. To you. An you gotta let me say it. (*Embarrassed.*) I . . . forgive you.

Roberta: What?

Danny: I forgive you. Everythin you done.

Roberta: You can't do that.

Danny: I gotta be able. You gotta let me be.

Roberta: I can't.

Danny: You gotta let go. Let go of it.

Roberta: You don't know what you're sayin.

Danny: I know. You told me . . . what you done. An I don't care. There ain't nobody else. An it's gotta happen. So I do it. I forgive you. You're forgiven.

Roberta: Whaddaya think you are, a priest?

Danny: I am whatever I gotta be. It's over now. You've felt bad long enough. You did a bad thing. An it's been bitin you in the head for a long time. It's a long enough time. You paid for what you done. That's why you got me last night. That's why you brought me here. You knew . . . you'd paid up. That's why you told me your bad thing.

Roberta: You can't forgive me.

Danny: Yes, I can.

Roberta: No! (*He pulls her to him, and over his knee. He spanks her.*)

Danny: That's for doin what you did. All right? That's the punishment.

Roberta: I'm sorry. I didn't mean it. It just happened. It was . . . I'm sorry, I'm sorry, I'm sorry. Please . . .

Danny: (*Putting a hand on her.*) I forgive you. It's done. I've done it. It's done.

Roberta: Yeah?

Danny: Yeah.

Roberta: Thank you.

Danny: You're welcome.

Roberta: Thank you.

Danny: We were bullshit last night. It was bullshit. I'm not too good. At tellin the difference. I ain't been too good at people. Ever. But what we were makin believe, other people got.

Roberta: That's other people.

Danny: But if we want, why can't we?

Roberta: I don't know.

Danny: It ain't a lot, what I want. I don't see why I can't get it. I know there ain't no way my whole life's gonna turn a corner an be the perfect thing. Yours neither. But I can get a day, can't I? To start with? That seems like somethin I could get.

Roberta: What day?

Danny: Weddin day.

Roberta: No . . .

Danny: Listen. We could have a weddin day. You be dressed in white. The flowers. Everythin we said. Pretty much. I gotta job. I'll get the money. If you get a job, that's good, too. We'll plan it out. There don't haveta be no hurry with it. It'd be somethin ta make happen.

Roberta: It don't make no sense ta do it.

Danny: Just cause it don't make no sense don't mean it ain't true. It could be true. If you want it. I ain't never planned no single fuckin thing in my life. I ain't never done nothin. Things happen to me. Me, you, what you did. We didn't do that stuff. It happened ta us. That's why you're sayin no, Roberta. It's cause ya think we can't do nothin. Like it's always been, right? But we can. We can plan a weddin, an the weddin'ill happen the way we plan. The only surprise will be that we knew.

Roberta: Yeah? You think so?

Danny: Yeah. I do. I definitely definitely think I do. (*The lights fade.*)

SEDUCED
by Sam Shepard

Act I

Henry Hackamore is very old. He may be the richest man in the world. He is certainly one of the most eccentric. He knows he is dying and he fears death, as he fears almost everything that he encounters in life. He has shut himself off from the world and lives in a room that is bare except for two palm trees and a black reclining chair. He is taken care of by Raul, who serves as both bodyguard and nurse. Henry can barely move now, yet he has invited a number of women from his past to visit him in his penthouse hotel room on a Caribbean island. He sent his fleet of private planes to bring the women to him.

This will be a rare human contact for Henry since his terror of microbes has turned him into a recluse. Although each of the women he has invited has been his lover in the past, he vows not to touch any of them during the current encounter (and makes Raul take the same vow).

Luna is the first to arrive. It's been fifteen years since she and Henry have seen each other. She is in her thirties now, very beautiful and spirited. She complies with Henry's request that she empty the contents of her purse. Henry, always suspecting that someone might try to harm him, orders Raul to destroy the bag's contents (via a highly elaborate procedure). He also asks Raul to bring in a chaise longue before he departs.

Henry: (*After pause.*) Don't be insulted. Everyone gets the same treatment. Some are even flattered.

Luna: Flattered?

Henry: Yes, flattered. The innocent crave to be guilty. There's a certain pride in having one's dormant criminal instincts beckoned up by suspicion. It's not even that I'm particularly suspicious.

Luna: Just cautious.

Henry: Just careful.

Luna: Just nuts. That was harmless stuff. A bunch of harmless makeup!

Henry: Nothing's harmless til it's squashed.

Luna: If you expect this meeting to go on for any length of time you might try lightening up your act, Henry.

Henry: I'm sorry but I don't even know you.

Luna: That's it!

(*She moves as if to go then stops when* HENRY *speaks.*)

Henry: No please! I thought I'd recognize you immediately but it's taking some time. You are beautiful though.

Luna: Thanks.

Henry: There'll be something for you to sit on in a minute. I don't like keeping anything extra in here. Just more surfaces for things to collect on. Microscopic things. That's the worst. What you can't see. I'd have you sit on my chair—(*Pauses.*) Just a minute.

(*He starts pulling off sections of paper towel and spreading them on the chair beside him.*)

Luna: Don't worry about it. I like standing.

Henry: (*Continuing with towels.*) Did you like the plane?

Luna: The plane?

Henry: The jet. I designed it from scratch. The very latest.

Luna: Yes, it's fine.

Henry: It's yours. You can take it back with you.

Luna: Thanks.

Henry: Were you expecting more?

Luna: Look, Henry. Just relax, all right? I'm here out of curiosity more than anything else. Don't jump to conclusions.

Henry: Sorry.

Luna: I have a life already. I don't need more.

Henry: Good. One of the satisfied. One of the few.

(RAUL *pushes on a green and white striped bamboo chaise longue from stage left. He pushes it across the stage behind* HENRY's *chair and places it down right facing left. He exits left again.*)

Henry: There we are. Just in the nick of time. Bamboo. My favorite, bamboo. (*To* LUNA.) Now you won't have to sit on my chair after all. You won't have to deposit unseen, invisible plant life.

(*He pushes all the paper towels onto the floor and slaps his hands together.* LUNA *smiles at the chaise longue then looks at* HENRY.)

Luna: (*Looking at chaise.*) If I sit does that mean I'm staying?

Henry: You want to stay, don't you? You wouldn't have come if you didn't want to stay.

Luna: You don't seem to have any trouble staying. How long have you been here anyway?

Henry: None of that stuff!

Luna: Too sticky, huh? Too filled with reverberations? I could be working for anyone now, right?

Henry: You're still on the payroll.

Luna: Are you kidding? You think I've been sitting there by the pool, waiting for your next whim all these years?

Henry: Don't tell me about it! Times have changed. I've lived through earthquakes, disasters, corruptions, fallout, wives, losses beyond belief.

Luna: Poor baby.

Henry: I don't need that! I'm not responsible now for your naive beliefs in what I was then. Anything I might have told you was a lie.

Luna: True.

Henry: So why needle me?

Luna: Then you do recognize me? You do remember?

Henry: I remember something. Parts of something.

Luna: You're lucky I still recognize *you*.

Henry: I'm sorry. I didn't have a chance to clean up. We lost track of the planes.

Luna: Planes? You mean there's other ones coming?

(HENRY *pauses.*)

Luna: There are, aren't there? Same old shit as it always was. All the "dollies."

Henry: I've been in the company of men for twenty-one years and in all that time I've never raised my voice so much as I have in the past ten minutes!

Luna: (*In sex-kitten voice.*) I'm sorry, Henry. Let me comply. Anything you want. Just tell me. Tell me once and it's yours.

Henry: Anything?

Luna: The world.

Henry: I have that.

Luna: Something else?

Henry: What else is there?

Luna: Heaven?

Henry: Oh, my God!

Luna: Heaven, Henry?

Henry: You're being sarcastic! It's uncanny how you lose touch with female elusiveness.

Luna: I'm not, Henry. I'm not now and I wasn't then.

Henry: Wasn't what! My mind's a jumble from all this.

Luna: Sarcastic.

Henry: Oh.

Luna: I'm not. Anything you want.

Henry: Don't confuse my body. My mind can take it but not the body.

Luna: Are you actually dying, Henry?

Henry: I suppose. I suppose I actually am. They tell me I'm actually not but actually I am. I know it. They wouldn't have moved me here if I wasn't. I look it, don't I?

Luna: You look like something from another world.

Henry: I am. That's true. I can't take the sun anymore.

Luna: Do you want me to rub you like I used to?

Henry: No! I have a man for that! Nothing from outside touches me! Go sit down!

(LUNA *goes down right and sits on the chaise, facing toward* HENRY. *She preens herself, pulls her dress up and crosses her legs.*)

Henry: (*Struggling to get up from chair.*) It's a mutual arrangement. I don't touch it, it doesn't touch me. That's what happens when you rape something, isn't it?

Luna: Rape?

Henry: Yes! Rape. After that you don't touch. There's a repulsion between both sides.

Luna: I wouldn't know.

Henry: Really? That clean, huh? That above it all?

Luna: Don't fall, Henry.

Henry: (*Still struggling to stand.*) I'm not falling! I'm standing! There's certain machinery at work that thinks I can't even move. Some even think I'm dead. Others don't know. Most others don't know. That's the best of all. Keeping them all in the dark. That's the best.

(LUNA *stretches herself out on the chaise as* HENRY *tries to walk inch by inch toward her.*)

Luna: Like me?

Henry: You're the least of it. Harmless. The worst is invisible. They know that. That's why they fear me. That's why they can't put a finger on me. A stab in the dark.

Luna: Are you coming toward me Henry?

(LUNA *stretches herself seductively for him.* HENRY *inches his way toward her.*)

Henry: (*Trying to walk.*) They comb the cities for me. Little American towns. Fortunes are spent on hired assassins. Presidents fear me. International Secret Agencies, Internal Revenues. Secretaries of Defense. Mobsters. Gang Lords, Dictators, Insurance Detectives. None of them can touch me. None of them.

Luna: (*Stretching, arms over her head.*) You're a master, Henry. A wizard!

Henry: I'm invisible!

Luna: (*Giggling.*) I can see you.

Henry: Untouchable!

Luna: (*Holding out her arms to him.*) Touch me.

(HENRY *tries painfully to get closer to her. Puts out his arm.*)

Henry: I can't.

Luna: Can you see me, Henry? Look.

(*She rolls herself from side to side.*)

Henry: Something. Something's there.

Luna: What do you see?

(*She rakes her fingers through her hair and lets it fall over the chaise.*)

Henry: I see you moving.
Luna: Keep watching.
Henry: I am.

(*She writhes on the chaise as* HENRY *keeps getting nearer.*)

Luna: Do you see me breathing?
Henry: Yes! I see your skin moving. It's incredible.

(*She arches her back and smiles at him*)

Luna: Do you see my teeth?
Henry: Yes! Your teeth. Your pearly gates.
Luna: What else?
Henry: Your femaleness. It's an awesome power.

(LUNA *squirms with delight.* HENRY *is getting closer to her.*)

Luna: Henry, it's only me.
Henry: It's not only you! It's a force. With men I was always a master. They'd lick my heels. Men become dogs in a second. It's the female that's dangerous. Uncontrollable. Cat-like.
Luna: Henry.

(*She runs her hands over her stomach and hip.*)

Henry: Your pearly gates. Look at them spreading for me. Shining. Calling me in. It's exactly how I pictured it. Exactly. The gates of heaven! You were right.
Luna: I was?

(*Her actions get more and more erotic*)

Henry: They never counted on this. My private salvation. My ultimate acquisition. No spy in the world could ever see what I really had my eyes on. Where my real hunger lay. My ravenous appetite. Beyond private holdings. My instincts were right. At the front door to death I needed women! Women more than anything! Women to fill me up. To ease me into the other world. To see me across. To bring me ecstacy and salvation! Don't let me fall! Don't ever let me fall!

(HENRY *collapses on top of* LUNA *and goes unconscious.*
LUNA *screams and tries to struggle out from under him
but he stays laying across her.*)

IT HAD TO BE YOU
by Renée Taylor and Joseph Bologna

ACT II

Theda Blau wants to fall in love and achieve success in
her acting career—today. She didn't get the commercial she
just auditioned for, so success in her career seems not to be in
today's cards. But when the producer, Vito Pignoli, came over
to tell her that he thought she has "a very nutty original tal-
ent," Theda fell in love at first sight. She managed to get Vito
to walk her to her apartment (he helped her with her packages), and she was determined to prevent him from leaving.
When it was clear he was about to walk out, she took all her
clothes off. That changed his mind.

A short while later Vito, still in bed, explains that while
he thinks that she came up with "a very novel way of showing
someone you're interested in him," there is "no way" he is "going to be serious" about her. She ignores all this and plunks a
bowl of spaghetti and meatballs on his lap. "Our first holiday
meal together," she explains (it is Christmas Eve). She proceeds to tell him in excruciating detail about a play she is writing about "a very brave Russian woman." When she finishes
Vito tries to get out of bed. Theda stops him.

*(For more information see other scene in "Monologues for
Women" section of this book.)*

Theda: You're not going to believe this, but the moment I
met you our whole life together flashed before me. I saw
you and I in a little house in the woods. And when you
come home from work I show you what I wrote and we

rewrite it together. I had hoped to find love and success in New York but I didn't realize that it would be with the same person. So, what do you think of my vision, pretty romantic, huh?

Vito: Well, I wouldn't exactly call that a vision, it's more along the lines of an hallucination. Don't you think you should wait just a little before you have visions about people? I mean, at least until you meet somebody who loves you.

Theda: No, that's the easy part. I don't care what the poets say. Love is no big deal. Anybody can love anybody if you're open. I'll prove it to you. Who's your all-time favorite movie star?

Vito: Brigitte Bardot.

Theda: Alright, who would you rather be here with right now. Brigitte Bardot or me?

Vito: Brigitte Bardot.

Theda: You can't have Brigitte Bardot! Now who would you rather be here with?

Vito: Let me get this one straight. Out of all the women in the world, that's my choice, you or you?

Theda: I don't see anybody else in this bed.

Vito: Your logic is fascinating. (VITO *takes a bite of the meatball.*) What the hell kind of meatball is this?

Theda: Tofu and flaxseed. You were going to find out sooner or later. I'm a strict lacto-vegetarian. It's the meat that's killing our men.

Vito: Are you sure it's not the women who cook for them. (VITO *tastes the coffee.*) What's in the coffee?

Theda: I made it myself. Barley, chicory, shredded beet roots, figs, acorns and wheat grass (*She goes to stove and pours herself coffee while* VITO *fishes out a piece of grass from his coffee.*) You may not know this but there are thousands of delicious gourmet vegetarian dishes that would win you over. Unfortunately I don't know any of them. I'm not into cooking as much as I'd like to be because of my career . . . are you?

Vito: Am I, what?

Theda: Into cooking?

Vito: Well . . . uh . . . no, I can't . . . uh . . . cook much . . . uh . . . I mean, better than this.

Theda: (*She throws out the food from the plate into garbage pail.*) Forget the food, we'll eat out alot.

Vito: . . . . Uh . . . look, I've got to be going. I'm all disoriented. I've got last minute Christmas shopping to do and the stores are going to close. (VITO *gets out of bed quickly and grabs his shirt.*)

Theda: I have a feeling you're trying to skip out on us.

Vito: (*Putting on his shirt.*) What do you mean, "us"? Will you do me a favor and stop grouping you and me together. Look, I've had a very interesting time tonight but I've really got to go now . . . (VITO *looks around for the rest of his clothes.*) Where are the rest of my clothes?

Theda: This is a very good sign, your needing to leave so strongly.

Vito: You're a fruitcake! Do you know that? You hid my clothes, didn't you? (THEDA *has hidden* VITO's *clothes. He looks for them, finds them in various places in the apartment and proceeds to get dressed.*)

Theda: It's a good sign because you're starting to feel for me. And it's scaring you and that's why you want to run. You evidently have a fear of intimacy with women. It's called breast envy.

Vito: There is no such thing. There's only penis envy. Which is probably what you have and are projecting on me.

Theda: Breast envy came way before penis envy . . . way before. Read Melanie Klein. They say Sigmund Freud is the father of psychoanalysis . . . Well, Melanie Klein is the mother.

Vito: And who are you, the cousin?

Theda: Look, why don't you just tell me the kind of woman you're holding out for and I'll be her. Is she thin-lipped or thick? I can give you either one. These aren't my regular looks. Does she have a big bust? I have a bust range of 22 to 44. I can give you playful. I can give you pensive. I can give you bubbly. You want a combination. I can give you two-thirds pensive and one-third bubbly. Tell me your fantasy and you'll have it Tuesday. This isn't even my natural hair color.

Vito: Do you mean you're not really a platinum blonde?

Theda: Oh, no. I'm much lighter than this. I'm a woman of a thousand different looks. I once had a job as the intermission singer in a strip joint. One night there were only two people on the bill, me and a female impersonator. And when I came out and sang, (*She sings.*) "Embrace me, my sweet embraceable you." Everybody thought that I was the impersonator. He was so gorgeous. Do you know that I was like a dog next to him . . . her . . . are you in love with me yet?

Vito: Let me give you a word of advice. I mean, with me it's all right because I have a kind of show business background. But I wouldn't tell that particular story if you were trying to impress some other guy.

Theda: Why, isn't it funny?

Vito: Well, in a way. But it's not much of a turn on to refer to yourself as a dog. Where are my pants?

Theda: You look much cuter without them. (VITO *finds his pants in the freezer.*)

Vito: A nice thing to do to my favorite suit.

Theda: It was just a joke.

Vito: (*He begins putting them on.*) Damn it, they're cold! I'm going to get pneumonia.

Theda: Let me put them in the oven for a second and warm them up.

Vito: Don't touch me! I'm getting out of here! Alright, where are my shoes?

Theda: Are you sure you had shoes when you came in?

Vito: I don't know if you can sense this, but you're starting to get on my nerves. (*He finds his shoes in the tub.*)

Theda: That's irrelevant.

Vito: It's irrelevant that you're getting on my nerves? You are a loony tune.

Theda: It's irrelevant because you're obviously crazy about me. That's why I don't take this attempt at rejection seriously.

Vito: Now listen to me. Miss Blue-Blau. Whatever your name is. This is no attempt at rejection. This is rejection. This is it. The real McCoy. The bronx cheer! (VITO *gives her a "Bronx Cheer."*)

Theda: Your mind is made up about this?

Vito: My mind is completely made up.

Theda: And you're actually going to leave?

Vito: I'm actually going to leave. Out the door. Out of your life forever and ever. In spades.

Theda: I see.

Vito: I'm sorry it worked out this way for you. And even though I'm leaving I'd like to still be friends or something. But I'm afraid that's going to be impossible because I don't have any friends that I've had good sex with. Can you understand that?

Theda: Sure, I understand.

Vito: Well, that's . . . uh . . . good that you're able to put this all in perspective and finally let me leave gracefully without either of us losing our dignity. Merry Christmas. (*He crosses to the door.*)

Theda: (*Sweetly.*) Oh, Vito . . . (*He turns back.*) Would you do me a small favor? When you get home later tonight, I'd like you to not go to sleep right away. I'd like you to sit up for a while, and I'd like you to just think about what took place between us. Would you do that?

Vito: Absolutely.

Theda: And then I'd like you to insert a large firecracker in your behind. And then light it.

Vito: Now that's hostile. Up to here you've just been goofy. But that was really hostile. But I'm glad you did it because it now allows me to leave and really feel like a good guy. So thank you for that. I'm leaving now. Goodbye. (VITO *tries to open the door. He keeps turning the locks but it won't open.*) The door seems to be stuck. Would you please open it?

Theda: I can't open it. It's locked from the outside.

Vito: What do you mean it's locked from the outside. How could it be locked from the outside? Come on, open it.

Theda: While you were napping after we made love I went outside and locked the door. I went up to the roof, came down a ladder, crawled along the ledge, and climbed in the window. And then I kicked the ladder into the alley.

Vito: (*Trying the locks again.*) Look, don't be ridiculous. They don't make doors that you can only lock from the outside. Come on, open it.

Theda: Well, I had a special lock made for my door. Because I knew someday I'd get a great catch like you up here and I wouldn't let you out. Ha. Ha. Ha.

Vito: Alright, now go open that door or I'm going to have to pick up the phone and call the cops and they're going to come and take you away with a net.

Theda: (*Maniacally.*) I cut the telephone cord. And you can scream all you want and no one will hear you. The apartment is soundproof. For centuries men have resisted loving good women. Now you're going to make it up to me for all the injustices that women have suffered at the hands of men throughout history.

Vito: Are you a lesbian? What is this, a political statement. Just let me in on the joke and I'll laugh too, okay? One of my friends told you to pull this on me. Didn't he. I know who. Little Dickie Wallburg, right? Because this is his kind of humor. Warped! Well, the joke's over. It's Christmas Eve. I've got a lot of things to do. Now go open that door. Do whatever you have to do. Go out the window. Go across the roof . . .

Theda: (*She opens the door. It had been unlocked.* VITO *assumed it was locked and in turning the lock, locked himself in.*) The door is open. It was open all the time. You locked yourself in. You actually thought that I had a special lock put on my door just to trap you. And then I climbed down from the roof and crawled in my window. You actually believed that? And you call me a fruitcake?

Vito: You know, I'm starting to get it now. Because things didn't work out for you, to get even, you've got yourself a little game going called, "Let's get Vito's goat." Right? Well, I've got a hot flash for you. I'm not going to give you the satisfaction of seeing me lose my cool. I'm just going to leave quietly. So the joke's over and the game's over and guess who loses?—you. (*He picks up his packages and turns to the door.* THEDA *puts her hand in her pocket and pokes* VITO *in the back.*)

Theda: I was hoping to stop you with reason or humor so I wouldn't have to use the gun.

Vito: (*He freezes.*) Gun? What gun?

Theda: This gun in my pocket . . . that looks like a finger. (THEDA *pulls her hand out of her pocket showing thumb and forefinger.*) I could get you to believe anything. You are one bona fide dummy. I don't know what I see in you.

Vito: You're going to see the toe of my shoe if you don't move away from the door.

Theda: Well, okay. But it's silly to leave now the way it's snowing. You'll never get a cab. There must be six inches out there. Didn't you hear it on the radio? (VITO *looks out the window*.)

Vito: Where the hell did that snow come from?

Theda: You mean it is snowing?

Vito: I've got to use your phone. (*It has been snowing.*)

Theda: (*She runs to the window.*) I was just making it up. But there's an actual blizzard. You're not going to be able to leave! It's a miracle! The whole universe wants me to win. You're a dead duck, Pignoli.

Vito: (VITO *puts down his things, picks up the phone and dials*.) Alright, I tried to leave here quietly without anybody getting hurt. But you wouldn't let me leave. So, now I'm going to tell you something. I don't like you, I don't need you, and I don't even want to know you . . . (*Into phone.*) Hello, Tommy? Vito Pignoli. I need a limousine right away . . . you don't have *any*? . . . No, never mind, Tommy. I can't wait.

THE DAY THEY SHOT JOHN LENNON
by James McLure

The date is December 9, 1980, the day John Lennon was shot. Shortly after the shooting was announced people began to gather across the street from his apartment house on Seventy-second Street in New York City. Some were fans; some were merely curious. They stood around for hours; they talked to strangers who stood near them; some cried.

One of those gathered that fateful day was Fran Lowenstein, whom the author describes as thirty-five years old, "a native New Yorker and all that implies. Tough, sensitive, a feminist and a member of the Woodstock generation who is also looking for a meaningful relationship." She works as a secretary.

Fran strikes up a conversation with Brian Murphy, who is

"in advertising." The author tells us he is "given to quick opinions and stances of self-confidence (though) he is basically a confused individual looking for love." He is thirty-three.

By the time the scene below begins, among the topics Fran and Brian have talked about are Lennon's music, their jobs, the bars they frequent, politics, and modern painting. Their conversation continues:

(*For more information see other scene from this play in "Monologues for Women" section of this book.*)

Fran: It's like spirals within spirals y'know. I mean I see images tumbling by. I see myself as a little girl on a visit to my grandmother's in Queens and we go to the park. And it's green and beautiful and my father's with me. Big, and young and strong. And whenever I think of that I think of "Penny Lane," it's like, that's the way it felt. (*Pause.*)

Brian: I know. It's like background music for our lives. I remember at my first high school dance and I was all sweaty and scared and I was gonna walk across the room to ask Richie Woodall to dance with me. And they started playing "Hey Jude" over the P.A. system. It was a Catholic dance. I think the nuns thought it was about St. Jude. The saint of lost causes.

Fran: (*Passionately.*) Maybe that's what all this is. A lost cause. The sixties. The peace movement. Look what's happenin' now in the Middle East. El Salvador. Are we any closer? Are we getting there? Take a look at the E.R.A.? Are we getting there? Three-Mile Island. Are we getting there? How can we say we're civilized when we continue to hold people back. Because of sex, because of race. Is that getting us anywhere? Increased military spending, weapons for defense. (*Laughing.*) And the joke is we're all afraid of the bomb! We blame everything on "They." The Pentagon—"They"! The CIA—"They." But we all have to take responsibility for the society in which we live. All America wants to do is go to the movies! Is that getting us there? Where's the leadership? Where's the dialogue? We're not talking. We're not listening. We're missing the whole point. It's not the sixties. People are just burying their heads in the sand. People will do *anything* rather than be here now. (*Pause.*) Are we getting there? No. People are just going to the office and making money . . . People suck.

Brian: (*Impressed.*) Wow. You know, you're a very passionate woman.

Fran: Well, what did you expect? Someone dumb?

Brian: No, it's just that women—

Fran: Oh brother, here we go. It's just that women what?

Brian: Just that women that you meet in bars—

Fran: Hey! You didn't meet *me* in a bar! Right? Get it?

Brian: But you said you *go* to bars.

Fran: I go to bars. I wasn't born in a bar. Right?

Brian: It's just that I think you're very smart and very passionate and very attractive. And I don't meet women like that.

Fran: Where do you meet your "woman," Brian?

Brian: Bars. I meet my women in bars.

Fran: Well, then maybe that's *your* problem, Brian. Maybe you're meeting those kind of women—the passionate, attractive, intelligent kind of women but since you're just living for the night, maybe you don't see them for what they are.

Brian: Hey. Who're you kidding? You go to bars. You have drinks. You meet guys.

Fran: That's right, Brian. And I'm the passionate, attractive, intelligent kind. (*He touches her arm.*)

Brian: Look babe, I didn't mean to—

Fran: Don't touch me.

Brian: O.k. I won't touch you.

Fran: Boy I hate your kind.

Brian: My *kind*? My *kind*? Boy if that isn't sexual stereotyping I don't know what is.

Fran: Granted. Sexual stereotyping. But in your case, it works.

Brian: Oh yeah? And what is my type?

Fran: You're—the button-down-collar-junior-executive-climbing - the - ladder - of - success - but - I'm - really - the - sensitive-young-man type. That's your type. I'll bet you haven't been to a museum in a million years.

Brian: For your information just last week I went to the Museum of Modern Art.

Fran: Oh yeah. What did you see?

Brian: Paintings.

Fran: What kind of paintings?

Brian: Modern paintings.

Fran: Oh Jesus. What a fake. What a liar. I bet you weren't even at Woodstock.

Brian: I was too!

Fran: Everybody has their little scheme don't they? Tell me, does this line work a lot? This I-like-art line? Does that work on everybody?

Brian: No. Just you.

Fran: Well, it wasn't working on me. I can assure you of that.

Brian: Yeah, come to think of it, now, I've seen you before. Sure yeah. I see you all the time in the bars.

Fran: You don't see me at bars.

Brian: Sure I do.

Fran: You do not.

Brian: The Adams Apple, Michaels, Maxwells, The Meat Place, Martys, The Satyre, Pegasus, sure you're there all the time. You're not special. I thought you were but you're not. You're like all the rest.

Fran: Fuck you.

Brian: My pleasure.

Fran: One thing though.

Brian: Huh.

Fran: If I'm like all the rest . . . so are you. (*Pause.*)

Brian: Look, I'm sorry . . . I don't know what we got so excited about . . . I mean . . . You're a nice girl.

Fran: Woman.

Brian: Woman! Woman! Woman! (*Pause.*) Look . . . you wanna smoke . . . I've got some gum . . . spearmint . . . Look I'm not like this . . . maybe I am. I didn't used to be. I don't meet women like you. I felt alive in the sixties. That's why I came here. I wanted . . . I wanted . . . then I met you. I mean. Something. In common. I don't know. Maybe not. I didn't want to go to work. I wanted to talk. (*She accepts cigarette. He lights it.*) I mean. Life goes on.

BREAKFAST WITH LES AND BESS
by Lee Kalcheim

ACT I, SCENE 2

At 8:05 A.M. every morning Les and Bess have breakfast—on the radio. It is 1961, and Les and Bess are hosts of a popular morning radio show. For the ten years they've been on the air, their audience could count on them for amusing chatter and interesting anecdotes about the many celebrities they know. Bess loves her life as a famous personality (and celebrity columnist for the *Daily News*). Les has come to find his life tiresome and wants to move to Texas and take a job as a sports announcer for a new major league team in Houston (earlier in his career Les was a sports columnist and announcer). He wants a simpler life (no more parties and no more celebrities) and he wants them to try to find a way to care about each other again.

One after another, radio talk shows are being cancelled—replaced by disc jockeys and rock and roll music. And now the ax has apparently fallen on *Breakfast With Les and Bess*. Yesterday they were cut off the air mid-show as Les, angered by Bess's disinterest in changing their lives and rebuilding their careers and relationship in Texas, blurted out on the air that their marriage was in trouble (he had been out drinking all night to celebrate his job offer and was still drunk at show time). The following scene takes place the next morning. Their children, who have been visiting and found themselves getting involved in their parents' conflict, have just left.

Les: What are you doing?
Bess: I'm going to call the station. They can't do this to us.
Les: (*He moves to her as she dials and stops her.*) Bess, don't.

(*Takes phone from her, hangs it up and crosses back to table.*)

Bess: What are we going to do? Are you going to go?

Les: You know what I'd like to do?

Bess: What?

Les: Make a deal. I'll give up Texas—if you'll give up the show.

Bess: Give it up? It's over. It gave us up!!

Les: Bess, I know you. You'll be on the phone to CBS, NBC and ABC and have us on again tomorrow!

Bess: (*With finality.*) Talk shows have had it.

Les: You'll have us playing records. You'll have us on! You get what you want.

Bess: What do you want?

Les: (*He looks at her.*) I want you.

Bess: Les . . . I can't take it when you're like that.

Les: What?

Bess: (*Starts to cry.*) Romantic.

Les: I'm not being romantic. I'm being honest.

Bess: That's worse. (*Crosses D.R. to sofa, lies down.*)

Les: Look . . . we've tried *everything*. And you know damn well, we've never really been happy since we stopped paying attention to each other. I'll make you a deal. I'll give up Texas. You give up New York.

Bess: And where would we go?

Les: I don't know. Connecticut! Yes, Connecticut. We own a home there! We've never lived in it!

Bess: And what do we *do* there?? (*Sits up slowly.*)

Les: I could *write* my book. And you could *write* yours. We could kick the sublets out of the house in Connecticut. We've never lived there. How about that? (*Crosses to sofa, sits next to her.*) We could actually live in our house. We could live there. Together. Work there together. We could even come into New York now and then.

Bess: What about my column?

Les: Give it up! You don't really like writing that crap. You're just used to the income!

Bess: No . . . it's fun . . . seeing all those people . . . going to all those . . .

Les: You don't get a Pulitzer Prize writing about who's with whom at 21!

Bess: I don't know . . . if I can write something good. I was 24. I haven't written anything of substance in years.

Les: How are you going to find out if you don't start? Starting is the hardest part. Take it from me.

Bess: What are you talking about? Starting's easy for you . . . you start hundreds of things. You never *finish* anything.

Les: OK. I'll help you start and you'll help me finish! And we'll write those damn books. And we'll have breakfasts together where we don't *have* to talk. Or we'll sleep thru breakfast. Free people can do that!

Bess: Well . . . how about the game show? Once a week? I could come in once a week and do that.

Les: Why?

Bess: (*Pouting.*) It's fun. I'm the smartest one on the panel. I like to show off!

Les: (*Laughs.*) Good. You can still do that. Once a week to New York. That sounds good. And I'll come in and drink with the boys at Toots Shors . . . and see a ball game or a fight. And then Monday . . . back to the sticks!

Bess: Would we keep this apartment?

Les: Is that really important to know now? We'll sublet it to the Dalcimers!

Bess: Oh Les . . . (*Teary.*)

Les: What???

Bess: I don't know.

Les: What??

Bess: *Yesterday* we were on the verge of divorce. How can we seriously decide to drop everything *today* and run off and live together. That's crazy!

Les: (*He puts his arm around her.*) I don't know. I think it's a hell of a lot less crazy than indoor baseball. (*She looks at him for a moment, then totally capitulates, putting her arms around him. They hug.*)

(*Phone rings. They look at each other, decide to ignore it, snuggle again. It rings again. They ignore it. It rings again.* LES *covers* BESS's *ears with his hands. It rings again. He looks at her, picks up the phone and hands it to her.*)

Bess: (*Into phone.*) Yes. What? . . . Oh . . . But . . . I . . . Yes . . . OK . . . Sure . . . OK. (*Hangs up.*)

Les: What?

Bess: (*She runs to the cabinet.*) We're on!! We're on in TWO!!!

Les: Wait a minute. We're cancelled!

Bess: (*Starts setting up the equipment.*) We have two more weeks. They have to give you two weeks notice.

Les: The hell with 'em. The way they told us. In the paper. Forget it!!!

Bess: OH Les, we owe it to our listeners. Let's go gracefully. (*No response from* LES.) Two weeks. What's two weeks?

Les: It's going to seem like two milleniums.

Bess: Nooo. Look . . . we'll do things we've never done before. We'll have fun!

Les: Yeah, sure.

Bess: (*She sets up mike, picks up studio phone. Into phone.*) Yes. All set . . . (*Into mike.*) Good morning. One two three four. (*Into studio phone.*) OK . . . thanks. (*She turns to* LES.) What do *you* want to talk about? We'll talk baseball. Every day. For two weeks. Baseball. OK?

Les: (*Rises and crosses R.*) I don't wanna talk baseball. I wanna call it quits NOW.

Bess: We owe our listeners something.

(*Yellow warning light flashes.*)

Bess: (*Cajoling him.*) Two weeks, Les. (*She flicks the monitor switch on and sits on C. chair at table.*)

YENTL
by Leah Napolin and Isaac Bashevis Singer

ACT II, SCENE 6

Yentl's father was a rabbi in Yanev, Poland, and when he taught his students the Torah, Yentl hid and listened. Yentl asked her father to teach her also. He did, but only in secret, because in the Orthodox Jewish tradition it was forbidden for girls to be educated in the Torah.

After her father dies, Yentl is determined to continue her studies and avoid the dull life of a traditional Jewish wife. She takes on the guise of a man, calls herself Anshel, and moves to the city of Bechev. She is befriended by a young man named Avigdor who arranges for Anshel to study at the yeshiva he attends. The two become close friends, though Avigdor pokes fun at Anshel for "his" shyness about disrobing and his lack of a beard.

Avigdor loves the town beauty, Hadass, and she loves him, but her mother refuses to let them marry. So Avigdor, who "need(s) a woman" marries Pesha, the town shrew. When Yentl learns that Hadass is being courted by other men, she asks Hadass to marry her. Her plan is to save Hadass for her friend Avigdor—to pass Hadass on to him whenever his marriage to Pesha ends. Hadass says yes to Yentl and soon falls in love with her. Yentl finds a way to consummate their marriage and keeps Hadass from learning that she is really a woman. But Hadass's parents and the whole town wonder why no child is forthcoming from their marriage.

Avigdor quickly discovers that he cannot remain with Pesha, but she refuses to give him a divorce. Yentl arranges for the two of them (Anshel and Avigdor) to travel together to Lublin to buy some books and see the sights. It is a joyous time for them. Then Yentl tells Avigdor that she has a secret to tell him. They enter their hotel room.

Avigdor: (*He runs into the hotel room,* YENTL *following. She closes the door behind them.*) All right, you big joker! Tell me this secret of yours! (YENTL *continues to stare at him, but doesn't reply.*) No wait. Wait. Let me guess. You've discovered a treasure buried beneath the outhouse! No? Oh, well then—you've written a commentary that revises the entire legal code of the Jewish faith! That's not it either, eh? The Cabala! You've been studying the Cabala, and you've finally learned to create doves and flowers out of thin air . . .

Yentl: (*Interrupting.*) Avigdor, I'm not going back to the Yeshiva.

Avigdor: What?

Yentl: I said I'm not going back to the Yeshiva.

Avigdor: (*Humoring her.*) So where are you going, to the Holy Land?

Yentl: I can't go back to Bechev, ever.

Avigdor: Why not?

Yentl: Hadass's love . . . Her love puts me to shame.

Avigdor: Anshel, is this a joke?

Yentl: I must leave Hadass.

Avigdor: If you love her, why would you leave her?

Yentl: I'm giving her up.

Avigdor: My God, you're not joking! If you leave her, it will kill her!

Yentl: If I leave her now, she'll be free to marry you. That's what I had in mind.

Avigdor: Me? No, it's *you* she loves!

Yentl: (*Sadly.*) Not me.

Avigdor: You're angry with her. She's done something to displease you. (YENTL *shakes her head "no." Angrily.*) Anshel, if you abandon Hadass, she'll be declared an *agunah*! Never allowed to remarry!

Yentl: A woman who's not married cannot be abandoned.

Avigdor: What are you talking about?

Yentl: By the strict letter of the law, Hadass and I were never even married.

Avigdor: How could that be? The rabbis witnessed it. It's legal.

Yentl: Witnessed what? Witnessed Hadass's marriage to a *man*!

Avigdor: So? (*Pause.*)

Yentl: So, I'm not a man.

Avigdor: What do you mean?

Yentl: I'm not a man, I'm a woman.

Avigdor: Anshel, stop it!

Yentl: Technically she's still considered a virgin, and the whole thing is null and void.

Avigdor: Don't joke about such things!

Yentl: I'm a woman!

Avigdor: (*Stares as* YENTL *starts to open her caftan.*) What are you doing . . . Anshel . . . (*Anguished,* YENTL *raises her ritual garment.*) Oh my God . . . (*He covers his eyes.*)

Yentl: I've done this only so that you can testify at the rabbi's.

Avigdor: (*In a daze.*) I don't believe it.

Yentl: (*To herself, with wonder and affirmation.*) I'm a woman . . .

Avigdor: What do you mean—testify at the rabbi's?

Yentl: Let me explain . . .

Avigdor: (*It dawns on him.*) Oh, my God—you *are* a woman! You made me commit countless sins! How could you do that to me? Why did you do that to me?

Yentl: I didn't want to waste my life! I did it out of love for learning, out of love for the Torah.

Avigdor: Love for the Torah? You broke the commandments of the Torah day and night.

Yentl: I had no choice.

Avigdor: I feel sick. (*He staggers to the bench.* YENTL *goes to comfort him. He shrinks away.*) Anshel?

Yentl: Yentl.

Avigdor: Yentl . . . Who are you, really?

Yentl: I'm Yentl, a woman. My father was a teacher, a learned man. When his pupils recited their lessons, I would hide, and I would listen! I begged my father— "Teach me too!" (*She shrugs.*) I was born with this terrible desire to learn . . .

Avigdor: He who teaches his daughter Torah is corrupting her—a learned woman is a monstrosity! (YENTL *has spoken the last words of the quote together with him.*) What you have done is what the Gemara calls iniquity for spite!

Yentl: No, Avigdor. Now it is iniquity for pleasure! Do you remember before my wedding when I was called up before the congregation to read from the Haftorah of Vayeshev? Do you remember how the whole town talked about it for days? How the women leaned out from the balcony and pelted me with raisins and almonds? Avigdor, I had waited for that moment all my life!

Avigdor: (*After a pause.*) What about Hadass? Explain that. How?

Yentl: There are ways. (*Pause.*)

Avigdor: Why?

Yentl: To save her from marrying another man. So she'd be yours someday. I was alone. You had married Pesha, Hadass loved me, and . . . (YENTL *turns away, overcome by conflicting feelings, which she masters. She turns back to him, strengthened.*) Avigdor, you and Hadass were destined for each other. You said so yourself, remember? You said, "Hadass was my destined one."

Avigdor: (*Stares at* YENTL.) Did I say that? (*Long pause. He comes back to reality.*) Her mother hates me.

Yentl: Hadass won't listen to her mother. She's not a child anymore!

Avigdor: Your beard! Oy. I don't suppose it'll ever grow in now! How could I have been so blind?

Yentl: It wasn't what your eyes saw that fooled you.

Avigdor: What was it then?

Yentl: We were— (*At a loss for words.*) we were friends.

Avigdor: Friends forever.

(*They sit on the bench laughing, comrades again. It dawns on them that things are changed. Locked into gender, they can never be the same.* AVIGDOR *becomes self-conscious.* YENTL *sits more demurely.*)

Avigdor: How old are you, really?

Yentl: Nineteen years, five months.

Avigdor: Maybe it's not too late for the two of us.

Yentl: What do you mean?

Avigdor: I mean you and I.

Yentl: It wouldn't have been any good.

Avigdor: Why not? You didn't have to marry Hadass to be close to me. You could have married *me*. . . .

Yentl: Yes, and spent my life sewing on your buttons? Oh, Avigdor, don't you understand? Without Torah I cannot breathe.

Avigdor: (*Slowly, with difficulty, he accepts this astonishing fact. Then his mind turns to more practical matters.*) Oy, what a scandal! Perhaps we can find a way to hush the whole thing up. Now what am I going to do?

Yentl: You're going to divorce Pesha and marry Hadass.

Avigdor: Pesha will never accept a divorce . . .

Yentl: If Pesha won't give you a divorce, all you have to do is collect the signatures of a hundred rabbis! Then you're free of her!

Avigdor: A hundred rabbis?

Yentl: You can do it. Look—I'll write a statement and you can testify . . . (*She grabs paper and pen.*)

Avigdor: Wait. If I testify as a witness, I might be considered an accomplice! I think it says somewhere that the witness who testifies for a deserted woman may not marry her . . . (YENTL *stops writing.*) That's right! The law calls him a "party to the affair!" What a mess! (YENTL *has spoken the last few words of the quote with him.*)

Yentl: I didn't think of that.

Avigdor: You'll have to get another witness!

Yentl: No! Let me think . . . Ah! Of course. Here's your answer! I send her a bill of divorce!

Avigdor: But since the marriage wasn't valid, the divorce papers will be meaningless . . .

Yentl: But, in the eyes of the world Hadass will be a divorced woman—therefore, no witnesses needed! Correct?

Avigdor: Correct! . . . I can't believe this is happening. I'm arguing Talmudic law with a woman.

THE HOTHOUSE
by Harold Pinter

ACT II

Gibbs and Cutts work in a government institution—a medical facility, perhaps, or a psychiatric facility. We never learn the details. But we do know there are patients who are locked in (and referred to as inmates). We also learn that all of a sudden the inmates are not behaving themselves. One died unexpectedly. Another is having a baby. And someone is making strange sounds over the public address system. The head of the institution, Roote, demands that order be restored. He wants the baby's father ("the culprit") found. But this proves to be difficult because most of the male staff, including Roote himself, commonly have sex with the female patients ("If a member of the staff decides that for the good of a female patient some degree of copulation is necessary then two birds are killed with one stone!" says Roote).

Many on the staff have also had sex with Cutts, including Roote and Gibbs. Gibbs is Roote's assistant, and Roote holds him responsible whenever anything goes wrong—so now that a great deal is going wrong Gibbs has been the constant object of Roote's rancor.

It is Christmas morning and Roote is on the verge of making his annual Christmas address to the staff. As the scene opens, Cutts enters the sitting room playing with a table tennis ball. As Gibbs walks towards the room, they both hear a series of odd sounds coming over the PA system (sighs, wails, and laughs). After the sounds fade away, Gibbs enters.

(MISS CUTTS *throws the ball at him. It falls at his feet.*)

Cutts: Catch!

(GIBBS *looks down at the ball and stamps on it.*)

Gibbs: Don't do that.

(*He takes out a packet of pills and swallows one.*)

Cutts: What's the matter, Charlie?
Gibbs: Headache.

(*He sits, closes his eyes.*)

(MISS CUTTS *goes to him.*)

Cutts: Have you got a headache, darling? Come to room 1A. (*She kisses him.*) I'll make it better for you. Are you coming?
Gibbs: I've got to go back.
Cutts: What! Why?
Gibbs: To hear his Christmas address.
Cutts: Another one? Oh, God, I thought he'd forgotten all about it.
Gibbs: He hadn't forgotten.
Cutts: Every year. Sometimes I could scream.
Gibbs: I can't stand screaming.
Cutts: Charlie, what is it? Don't I please you any more? Tell me. Be honest. Am I no longer the pleasure I was? Be frank with me. Am I failing you?
Gibbs: Stop it. I'm not in the mood.
Cutts: Let me massage your neck.

(*She touches his neck.*)

Gibbs: (*Throwing her off.*) You and your necks! You love to get your hands round someone's neck!

Cutts: So do you.

Gibbs: I'm not in the habit of touching people's necks.

Cutts: It was such fun working with you this morning.

(*She sits.*)

You're so clever. I think you're the cleverest man I've ever had anything to do with. We don't work together nearly enough. It's such fun in room 1A. I think that's my favourite room in the whole place. It's such an intimate room. You can ask the questions and be so intimate. I love your questions. They're so intimate themselves. That's what makes it so exciting. The intimacy becomes unbearable. You keep waiting for the questions to stop, to pass from one intimacy into another, beautifully, and just when you know you can't ask another one, that they must stop, that you must stop, that it must stop—they stop!— and we're alone, and we can start, we can continue, in room 1A, because you know, you always know, your sense of timing is perfect, you know when the questions must stop, *those* questions, and you must start asking me questions, other questions, and I must start asking you questions, and it's question time, question time, question time, forever and forever and forever.

Gibbs: (*Standing.*) I tell you I'm not in the mood.

Cutts: Come to 1A, Charlie.

(GIBBS *stands, looking at the door.*)

Gibbs: Did you hear anything, just now?

Cutts: What?

Gibbs: Something. Sounds. Sounds. Just now. Just before.

Cutts: Nothing. Not a thing. Nothing.

(*She looks at him.*)

What was it?

Gibbs: I don't know.

Cutts: (*A nervous chuckle.*) Don't tell me something's going to happen?

Gibbs: Something's *happening*. But I don't know what. I can't . . . define it.

Cutts: How absurd.

Gibbs: It is absurd. Something's happening, I feel it, I know it, and I can't define it. It's . . . it's ridiculous.

Cutts: I know what's going to happen.

Gibbs: That old fool in there, he sees nothing, getting drunk with that . . . bitch.

Cutts: I know what's going to happen. You're going to kill him.

Gibbs: What?

Cutts: Aren't you? You promised. You promised you would. Didn't you? Do it now. Now. Before he makes his Christmas speech.

Gibbs: Oh, stow it, for God's sake!

Cutts: But you said you would!

Gibbs: Did I?

Cutts: You said you'd stab him and pretend it was someone else.

Gibbs: Really? Who?

Cutts: Lush.

Gibbs: Lush? Lush could never be taken for a murderer. He's scum but he's not a murderer.

Cutts: No, but you are.

(GIBBS *stares at her.*)

Gibbs: (*Quietly.*) What did you say?

(*Pause.*)

What did you call me?

Cutts: Nothing.

Gibbs: You called me a murderer.

Cutts: No, I didn't call you anything—

Gibbs: (*Ice.*) How dare you call me a murderer?

Cutts: But I didn't!

Gibbs: Who do you know that I've murdered?

Cutts: No-one!

Gibbs: Then how dare you call me a murderer?

Cutts: You're not a murderer!

Gibbs: (*Hissing.*) I'm not a murderer, he's a murderer, Roote is a murderer!

(*Pause.*)

You dare to call me a murderer?

Cutts: (*Moaning.*) No, Charlie.

Gibbs: You know what that is, don't you? Slander. Defamation of character.

(*Pause.*)

And on top of that, you try to incite me to kill my chief, Mr. Roote. The man in charge. You, his own mistress. Just to satisfy your own personal whim.

(*Pause.*)

Cutts: Charlie . . .
Gibbs: Shut up!

(MISS CUTTS *falls out of her chair onto the floor.*)

Cutts: (*Whispering.*) Oh, I wish I was in room 1A. I shall never get to room 1A again. I know I won't. Ever.

(*Blackout.*)

REQUIEM FOR A HEAVYWEIGHT
by Rod Serling

SCENE 6

The "heavyweight" of the title is Harlan "Mountain" McClintock, a prizefighter at the end of his career. Mountain was once a top ranked boxer, but that was a number of years ago. All he has left now are his memories, his dignity ("one hundred and eleven fights and I never took a dive"), and a battered face and body. His manager, Maish, desperate for money, wants him to become a wrestler in an Indian costume. But Mountain cannot bear the humiliation and runs away from the sports arena to the apartment of Grace Miller. Grace works for the state employment office. She met Mountain when he came in looking for a job. She was touched by this lost, gentle soul that she found shackled in a mammoth, gnarled body.

Grace went far beyond the bounds of official operating procedures to help Mountain. She sought him out in a local fighters' bar to tell him about a possible position on the athletic staff of a summer camp. Then she confronted Maish after she learned that the reason Mountain missed his appointment with the camp director was because Maish never passed on the telephone message she left with him about the time and place of Mountain's interview. But Maish defends his action and forces Grace to face the implications of her kindness to Mountain:

> You sit across from him and you tout him, don't you? You build him up. You stick him in front of the mirror and you translate what he's supposed to see. And when you get to the end of the line with him, Miss Miller—like right now, and you've got him buying it all—that's when he's going to hold out his arms to you like any man to any woman! And unless you're blind or out of your mother grabbing head, you're going to have to turn him away. And when that happens, Miss Miller, you're going to think that it might have been kinder if you had just stripped him naked and whipped him to death.

As the scene opens Grace is in her apartment preparing for bed. There is a knock at her door. She enters, "wearing a housecoat" and "brushing her hair."

Grace: Who is it?

McClintock: It's me, Grace. It's Mountain.

Grace: (*She unlocks the door and opens it.* MOUNTAIN *enters. He enters the room almost in relief as if this were the port in the storm, as if this were heaven—but once in the room, he cannot understand why he's there. He just stands there with his big hands out in front of him while* GRACE *looks at him expectantly. Finally, after a long silence—*) Are you all right, Mountain?

McClintock: Oh, yeah. I'm all right. (*He looks at her.*) I walked out on the match tonight. I couldn't go through with it. I couldn't get laughed at, Grace.

Grace: (*In a whisper.*) Of course you couldn't.

McClintock: I tried. I wanted to do it for Maish. (*Then he* *remembers the rest of the story. His face twists.*) Maish sold me out. He bet against me my last fight. (*He turns to her, shaking his head again.*) He sold me out, Grace. Bet me to lose. *Wanted* me to lose. Maish! Maish did this to me. (*He turns away again.*) I was supposed to wrestle. I was supposed to wear this funny costume. I felt . . . I felt sick. I had to get out of there. I ran out. I ran down the street and I didn't know where to go, but I had to go someplace. I had to talk to somebody. (*He turns to her.*) And then I came here. I had to come here.

Grace: I'm glad you did. Sit down, Mountain, and rest. Sit down, Mountain.

McClintock: (*Goes over to a chair and sits. He takes a deep breath as for the first time he lets his body relax. He stares at her across the room. He wets his lips, fiddles with his hands.*) I won't stay but a minute. I didn't mean to . . . get you up.

Grace: That's all right. I wasn't in bed. (*She keeps staring at him. There's something child-like about the way he sits there, hungry to speak or just to feel another presence and there's a gripping, almost unbearable poignancy that shows in his face, his indirection, his desperate anxiety.*) Put your head back and rest, Mountain. You look very tired.

McClintock: (*Slowly lets his big frame sink back against the chair. He takes another deep breath, closes his eyes. He remains motionless for a moment. Then he opens his eyes again, staring at the ceiling. The words come out a little easier now. He speaks low, almost sonorously, because what follows are word pictures that in a sense he's speaking to himself. He can reflect where he can't project.*) It's funny. Tonight . . . tonight's the wind up. And none of us ever thought it would be this way. (GRACE *moves quietly over to sit near him. He turns to look at her.*) You know where I went first? When I went out of there? I went to the bar. I walked inside and there were all these guys talking about this fight and that fight and I just stood around with them and listened and then one of them mentioned Jerry Ueckar. He was a light-heavy. Then he turns to me and he says, "You fought him, didn't you, Mountain?"

Grace: (*A pause. In a whisper.*) Go on, Mountain.

McClintock: And I said, "Yeah, I fought him." And then I . . . and then I didn't want to say any more, Grace. Because I remember the fight. I remember every round of it. And I could have told it to them blow by blow, but if I had . . . I'd never have left there. It would have gone into another fight and then another fight and then I'd be in the graveyard. Every night. That's where you could have found me. I didn't want that. I didn't want to be one of them punchies. I wanted to say to them right there . . . I wanted to tell them, "I feel sorry for you guys. I feel sorry your heads are all scrambled. I wish it wasn't that way. I really do. But I'll come in here and I'll have a beer and listen to you. But I can't do any talking with you because I'm not a punchy. I was almost Heavyweight Champion of the World. I fought one hundred and eleven fights. I'm somebody." (*Then he whirls around and looks at her, his face twisting and contorting and his voice cracking wide open in a sob—a wracking, body-twisting, ugly, almost unbearable sob.*) Oh, Christ, Grace. I'm kidding myself. I'm nobody. I'm nobody at all. Nobody. (*He cries.*)

Grace: (*Moves to him swiftly, and takes his face in her hands, feeling the acme of pity and compassion that only a woman can feel and her voice is almost a croon.*) That's not true, Mountain. You're somebody. You're somebody, Mountain. (*Then she puts her hands down and looks at him.*)

McClintock: (*Stops crying, turns away, embarrassed, almost sick with embarrassment.*) I haven't cried . . . I haven't cried since I was a little kid. I don't know why I cried then.

Grace: You cried because you had to, Mountain. Everybody has to cry. (*He nods, not understanding, but anxious that she speaks now.* GRACE *turns away, obviously a decision is being born now and there's a different tone to her voice. A strange tone, an unsureness not unlike* MOUNTAIN's.) Mountain, do you want a drink?

McClintock: What?

Grace: A drink?

McClintock: No, thank you.

Grace: You sure? (*He nods. Then there is a moment as they stare at one another.*)

McClintock: I better go, Grace.

Grace: (*Her voice low, but imperative.*) No, you mustn't go. Not yet. Not . . . now. (*They continue to look at one another and then* MOUNTAIN *turns away.*)

McClintock: You know what I wish? I wish . . . you were blind. (*He whirls around to her.*) I didn't mean . . .

Grace: I know, Mountain. I know what you meant, but I'm glad I'm not.

McClintock: (*Looks from one corner of the room to another, moving his hands and touching his face with nervous gestures.*) Maybe I would like that drink.

Grace: (*Moves to a cupboard and takes out an unopened bottle.*) You'll have to open it.

McClintock: (*Reaches for the bottle and drops it. He bends down and picks it up.*) I'm sorry. I'm so clumsy. All . . . all knuckles. (*Then he grabs at his face.*) All knuckles and a big, freak face. So ugly. So Goddamned ugly! (*He begins to sob uncontrollably. He hits at his face.* GRACE *goes to him to try to comfort him. He at first pushes her away, but she succeeds and takes hold of him. She comforts him. Gradually, from just comforting him, they begin to make love.* GRACE's *robe is pulled off.*)

Grace: (*Whispers.*) Turn off the light, Mountain.

McClintock: I want to look at you. I want to see you.

Grace: Later, maybe. But not now. Now, I want the lights out.

McClintock: I have to see you, Grace. I have to look at you. This is . . . In my whole life this is the sweetest moment. This is the sweetest moment I've ever had.

Grace: Mountain, please turn off the light. (MOUNTAIN *lets go of* GRACE *and walks over to the lamp, picks it up, pauses a moment, then removes the shade so that the light is bright in his face. Then he grabs the bare bulb and turns it putting the room into darkness.*)

Grace: No, Mountain. It's not that.

McClintock: I have to go now, Grace. It's late and I have to go. (GRACE *has begun to sob quietly.*) Are you crying, Grace? (*Pause.*) Grace, why are you crying?

Grace: (*Still crying.*) Oh, Mountain, I'm so sorry, Mountain. I'm so sorry. Don't you understand. It's not you, Mountain. It's me. It's not you, Mountain.

McClintock: (*Going to* GRACE.) You shouldn't cry, Grace. You really shouldn't. You think you let me down, but you didn't. It's still the . . . the sweetest moment. Because you didn't run away. And I won't ever forget this, Grace. As long as I live, I'll never forget this. Thank you for not running away.

Grace: Oh, Mountain. (*They kiss and embrace.* MOUNTAIN *goes to the door and opens it.* GRACE *follows him to the door and reaches out to him. He turns and they caress each other's faces.* GRACE *takes his hand and kisses it tenderly. He exits as:*)

(*The lights fade to black.*)

Grace: Stay.
McClintock: No, Grace. There's something I gotta do.

JITTERS
by David French

Act II

Jessica and Patrick are co-stars of a new play about to open in Toronto. Indeed, the play will open in just a few minutes. Yet even now they can't end the bickering that has gone on between them ever since they started rehearsals. Patrick resents Jessica's "star" status, bestowed upon her by the Canadian theater community after she starred in two Broadway shows in New York. He also resents her top billing and thinks she is purposely trying to undermine his performance (she keeps throwing an apron in his face rather than at his chest where she has been directed). For revenge he has been calling her at three in the morning. When she finally left the phone off the hook, he ordered a pizza delivered to her at that hour.

The rehearsal process has been tense for all concerned. But the pressure on everyone is even greater now that Jessica has invited a New York producer (Bernie Feldman) to come to the opening and has interested him in moving the show to New York.

Both actors are very nervous about their performances and about their futures in the theater. This is Jessica's first play in Canada since her New York successes and her first show in two years. Patrick has had a solid and steady career in Canadian theater, but that has not brought him the kind of fame and fortune that a success in New York would bring.

The scene takes place in the dressing room. Both actors are getting into costume.

Jessica: It must be late. . . .

Patrick: Quarter to eight.

(*He takes his shirt off the hanger, examines it, then takes a needle and thread from his shoebox. He sits and sews his shirt, singing a few lines from an Irish folk song.*)

Patrick: Must be an easier way to make a living.

(JESSICA *ignores him. She is flattening out her hair with bobby pins in preparation for the wig.*)

Patrick: You know, the day I left Ireland was the day after I got married. The old man called me a lazy, shiftless sonofabitch and said I'd never do an honest day's work in my life. Imagine that.

Jessica: How prophetic.

Patrick: I know, and I wasn't even an actor yet. I think I became an actor just to spite him. To live out his prediction.

(JESSICA *turns and looks at him.*)

Jessica: How do you feel?

Patrick: Why do you ask?

Jessica: In case you haven't noticed, you only shaved on one side of your face.

Patrick: Did I? (*He looks in the mirror.*) So I did.

Jessica: Your good side, naturally.

Patrick: Instinct. (*He leans closer to the mirror.*) Jesus H. Christ . . . .

Jessica: What is it?

Patrick: The lines around the eyes. (*Beat.*) Laugh lines. No, they are. And speaking of laugh lines, I wish I had a few more in this friggin' play. (*He shaves.*)

Jessica: Tell me, Flanagan. Will you go to New York if Bernie wants you? I think you'd be a fool not to.

Patrick: (*Clicks off the razor.*) Why wouldn't he want me?

Jessica: Oh, I'm sure he will. . . . The cast works so well together. Not a single weak link. Don't you agree?

(PATRICK *clicks on his razor and goes back to shaving.*)

Jessica: Why? Who do you think's the weak one? (*Beat.*) Phil? (*Beat.*) Tommy? (*Beat.*) Well, that just leaves the two of us, doesn't it?

(*She turns and goes back to her hair.*)

Patrick: (*Finished shaving.*) Look, don't you think you're being a bit premature? Has Feldman read the play?

Jessica: And adored it. Oh, he might fault the production, but I doubt that, it's first-rate. . . . Don't you want to go?

Patrick: Between you and me, I think the New York audience is too sophisticated for this play. I think we should leave well enough alone.

Jessica: I never try to second guess. I only know what I like. You thought it was good enough to do here, didn't you?

Patrick: New York's tougher.

Jessica: You think so?

Patrick: Don't you?

Jessica: We take risks all the time, don't we? New York's just a larger arena. Higher stakes.

Patrick: Well, I'm a Catholic and Catholics are against suicide. Besides, I don't think we should judge success by New York. No, really. I've never felt that or I'd be there, wouldn't I?

Jessica: Flanagan, haven't you ever imagined yourself on Broadway? Let me tell you, it's the most exciting feeling in the world, bar none. And you know what's the nicest part? You feel you deserve it.

Patrick: Yes, but how does it feel to get clobbered?

Jessica: I wouldn't know.

Patrick: You were in two flops.

Jessica: The plays were; *I* wasn't.

Patrick: Well, I'd feel I deserved it.

Jessica: (*Into the mirror.*) Our sense of ourselves is so tentative, isn't it? I suppose that's the real risk we take.

Patrick: What's that?

Jessica: Facing our own failure.

Patrick: Look, I make a damn good living here. I have my pick of roles. I might not be a star, but who is in this country? And not everyone feels that compulsion to outshine.

Jessica: You don't need to get defensive. If you don't want to go, that's your problem. No one's twisting your arm.

Patrick: Oh, it's a problem, is it? Christ, you sound like my ex-wife. All she ever wanted was success with a capital S. The old bitch-goddess, to quote Henry James. As if there's something wrong not wanting to work your butt off for agents and accountants and Internal Revenue.

Jessica: Maybe she thought you were settling for too little.

Patrick: Well, I've seen the bitch-goddess up close. I've had a sniff or two up her skirt, I know what she's like, she's insatiable, a parasite, a cancer. She gets on your back like the Old Man of the Sea and won't get off.

Jessica: The trick is to ride success and not let it ride you.

Patrick: Well, I'm the one who has to go out there and be good. She never understood that, my wife. She. . . . (*Then, as if he has said too much already.*) Look, let's drop it, shall we? And before I forget: I don't appreciate being upstaged. You did it again last night.

(*He enters the Green Room and pours himself a coffee.*)

Jessica: When?

Patrick: You know when.

Jessica: I haven't the foggiest.

Patrick: The supper scene.

Jessica: Oh, is that why you looked so upset? I thought you had gas.

Patrick: And while we're at it, cross your legs onstage. Last night you sat on the sofa working your legs like a pair of scissors. Freud would have a field day with that gesture.

Jessica: I was simply working up a breeze. Didn't you find it stifling out there?

Patrick: The first three rows don't have to know you're wearing black lace panties.

Jessica: I bet you were the only one who noticed. Did you also notice the mark on the inside of my left thigh?

Patrick: No, I didn't. And it was your right thigh. God knows how you got *that*. I dread to think.

Jessica: From Mario, darling.
Patrick: Who's Mario?
Jessica: The little pizza boy. Don't you remember?
Patrick: Why? Is that how you paid him?
Jessica: No, tipped him.

PAINTING CHURCHES
by Tina Howe

ACT I, SCENE 1

Beacon Hill in Boston, Massachusetts: it is a bright spring morning, and the sunlight pouring through "three soaring arched windows" reveals Fanny Church (in her sixties) in the living room of her townhouse. She is packing up the contents of her home and awaiting the arrival of her daughter, Mags, a painter living in New York. She and her husband, Gardner (in his seventies)—both from "fine old" families—are selling their house and moving to their cottage on Cape Cod.

Gardner, "an eminent New England poet," is getting senile. He is unable to give readings anymore and is in a "dry spell with his poetry." Fanny is sitting on the sofa, "wearing a worn bathrobe and fashionable hat." She has been wrapping some of her family heirlooms (Mama's silver coffee service, Grandma's Paul Revere teaspoons), wondering which might have to be sold for money. Money has become a serious concern for them recently. Fanny has been calling loudly to Gardner, who has been typing a book of criticism in the next room. She wants to show him her new hat. He enters singing "Nothing Could Be Finer" and holding a stack of papers "which keep drifting to the floor."

Gardner: Oh, don't you look nice! Very attractive, very attractive!
Fanny: But I'm still in my bathrobe.

Gardner: (*Looking around the room, leaking more papers.*) Well, where's Mags?

Fanny: Darling, you're dropping your papers all over the floor.

Gardner: (*Spies the silver tray.*) I remember this! Aunt Alice gave it to us, didn't she? (*He picks it up.*) Good Lord, it's heavy. What's it made of? Lead?!

Fanny: No, Aunt Alice did *not* give it to us. It was Mama's.

Gardner: Oh yes . . . (*He starts to exit with it.*)

Fanny: Could I have it back, please?

Gardner: (*Hands it to her, dropping more papers.*) Oh, sure thing . . . Where's Mags? I thought you said she was here.

Fanny: I didn't say Mags was here, I asked *you* to come here.

Gardner: (*Papers spilling.*) Damned papers keep falling . . .

Fanny: I wanted to show you my new hat. I bought it in honor of Mags' visit. Isn't it marvelous?

Gardner: (*Picking up the papers as more drop.*) Yes, yes, very nice . . .

Fanny: Gardner, you're not even looking at it!

Gardner: Very becoming . . .

Fanny: You don't think it's too bright, do you? I don't want to look like a traffic light. Guess how much it cost?

Gardner: (*A whole sheaf of papers slides to the floor, he dives for them.*) OH SHIT!

Fanny: (*Gets to them first.*) It's alright, I've got them, I've got them. (*She hands them to him.*)

Gardner: You'd think they had wings on them . . .

Fanny: Here you go . . .

Gardner: . . . damned things won't hold still!

Fanny: Gar . . . ?

Gardner: (*Has become engrossed in one of the pages and is lost reading it.*) Mmmmm?

Fanny: HELLO?

Gardner: (*Startled.*) What's that?

Fanny: (*In a whisper.*) My hat. Guess how much it cost.

Gardner: Oh yes. Let's see . . . $10?

Fanny: $10? . . . IS THAT ALL . . . ?

Gardner: 20?

Fanny: GARDNER, THIS HAPPENS TO BE A DE-SIGNER HAT! DESIGNER HATS START AT $50 . . . 75!

Gardner: (*Jumps.*) Was that the door bell?

Fanny: No, it wasn't the door bell. Though it's high time Mags were here. She was probably in a train wreck!

Gardner: (*Looking through his papers.*) I'm beginning to get fond of Wallace Stevens again.

Fanny: This damned move is going to kill me! Send me straight to my grave!

Gardner: (*Reading from a page.*)
"The mules that angels ride come slowly down
The blazing passes, from beyond the sun.
Descensions of their tinkling bells arrive.
These muleteers are dainty of their way . . ."
(*Pause.*) Don't you love that! "These muleteers are *dainty* of their way . . . !?"

Fanny: Gar, the hat. How much? (GARDNER *sighs.*)

Fanny: Darling . . . ?

Gardner: Oh yes. Let's see . . . $50? 75?

Fanny: It's French.

Gardner: $300!

Fanny: (*Triumphant.*) No, 85¢.

Gardner: 85¢! . . . I thought you said . . .

Fanny: That's right . . . eighty . . . five . . . *cents*!

Gardner: Well, you sure had me fooled!

Fanny: I found it at the Thrift Shop.

Gardner: I thought it cost at least $50 or 75. You know, designer hats are very expensive!

Fanny: It was on the mark-down table. (*She takes it off and shows him the label.*) See that? Lily Daché! When I saw that label, I nearly keeled over right into the fur coats!

Gardner: (*Handling it.*) Well, what do you know, that's the same label that's in my bathrobe.

Fanny: Darling, Lily Daché designed hats, not men's bathrobes!

Gardner: Yup . . . "Lily Daché" . . . same name . . .

Fanny: If you look again, I'm sure you'll see . . .

Gardner: . . . same script, same color, same size. I'll show you. (*He exits.*)

Fanny: Poor lamb can't keep anything straight anymore. (*Looks at herself in the tray again.*) God, this is a good looking hat!

Gardner: (*Returns with a nondescript plaid bathrobe; he points to the label.*) See that . . . ? What does it say?

Fanny: (*Refusing to look at it.*) Lily Daché was a *hat* designer! She designed ladies' *hats*!

Gardner: What . . . does . . . it . . . say?

Fanny: Gardner, you're being ridiculous.

Gardner: (*Forcing it on her.*) Read . . . the label!

Fanny: Lily Daché did *not* design this bathrobe, I don't care what the label says!

Gardner: READ! (FANNY *reads it.*) ALL RIGHT, NOW WHAT DOES IT SAY . . . ?

Fanny: (*Chagrined.*) Lily Daché.

Gardner: I told you!

Fanny: Wait a minute, let me look at that again. (*She does, then throws the robe at him in disgust.*) Gar, Lily Daché never designed a bathrobe in her life! Someone obviously ripped the label off one of her hats and then sewed it into the robe.

Gardner: (*Puts it on over his jacket.*) It's damned good looking. I've always loved this robe. I think you gave it to me . . . Well, I've got to get back to work. (*He abruptly exits.*)

STANDING ON MY KNEES
by John Olive

ACT II

Catherine is a promising young poet with a passion for modern music and red wine. She is also a schizophrenic. Her disease can be controlled with Thorazine, but when she takes the drug her writing suffers. Robert is a stock broker. He feels trapped in his job, yet nervous about losing it. He has been fascinated by Catherine since they met. But lately, as she has cut down on the Thorazine, he has found her difficult to handle. He has not seen her for over a week. Catherine calls him in the middle of a workday and asks him to meet her in the park. He agrees.

Catherine: Robert.

Robert: (*Startled, turns.*) Oh.

Catherine: Scare you?

Robert: No, no. I'm just cold. It didn't occur to me to bring my thermals when I—

Catherine: I like the park.

Robert: I've only got time for coffee. Let's go over to—

Catherine: Let's stay here, it's nice.

Robert: Nice?

Catherine: The wind is clean.

Robert: The wind is cold.

Catherine: That's what I mean.

Robert: (*Looks at her, a beat.*) I know you detest the question, but what the hell: are you okay?

Catherine: C'mere.

Robert: What?

Catherine: Come here. (*Pause. Robert goes to her, reluctantly. Catherine takes his head in her hands, looks intently into his eyes.*)

Robert: Your hands're cold.

Catherine: I wanted to see the soft blue suns behind your eyes.

Robert: You said it was important.

Catherine: It is.

Robert: (*Slight pause.*) You've been drinking.

Catherine: Rich warm red wine. (*Catherine kisses him gently.*)

Robert: You shouldn't be drinking on top of your medication. God, I'm sorry I bought you that wine.

Catherine: San Francisco?

Robert: What?

Catherine: Going to San Francisco?

Robert: I wouldn't think so. I'll be sending my resume around, as soon as it comes back from the printer's. Cath—

Catherine: Gonna take up watercolors?

Robert: Catherine. What was so important?

Catherine: I wanted to . . . see you.

Robert: You called me away from the office just because you wanted to—

Catherine: It's been a week and a half.

Robert: (*Sharply.*) It hasn't been— (*Stops himself, looks around self-consciously.*) Well, it hasn't been a week and a half.

Catherine: I've been writing.

Robert: Good.

Catherine: And I wanted to find out what you thought of my new poems. I mean, I think . . . it's pretty important. (*Pause. Then Robert takes the envelope of poems out of his coat pocket.*)

Robert: I haven't read them yet. I've been pretty— (*Catherine suddenly giggles.*) What?

Catherine: You look good in gooseflesh.

Robert: (*Slight pause.*) Well, I've been, as you can imagine, pretty preoccupied. I'll give them back. Here. (*Holds out the envelope.*)

Catherine: This is incredible!

Robert: What?

Catherine: (*Laughing.*) I feel like I'm in the middle of some crazy magnetic field, everybody's bouncing off, I'm fucking impregnable!

Robert: It's just that this is a bad time for me.

Catherine: There's something going around.

Robert: (*Laughs nervously.*) Yeah. Look, I gotta find another job. I just don't know any other way to live, it's all I can think about. And I think it would be better if we didn't see each other, not for a—

Catherine: (*Takes a step backward.*) Yeah.

Robert: Not for a while. I'm worried about you, Catherine, and . . .

Catherine: Yeah?

Robert: And I think it might be better if I . . . stayed away from you. (*Catherine is laughing.*) Fuck. Catherine? Do you understand what I'm . . . trying to say?

Catherine: I opened the last bottle.

Robert: Jesus, I wish you wouldn't—

Catherine: It's breathing now, it's waiting for us, it's very important.

Robert: What're you suggesting, that we go drink wine? That's—

Catherine: (*Shouts.*) I love you!!!

Robert: Dammit, there are people looking at us, how dare you embarrass me like— (*Takes a beat, looks around self-consciously.*) You have a real skill, you know that? You can provoke me. I thought I divorced the only person who could do that. You're not taking your medication, are you?

Catherine: I'm writing.

Robert: Shit.

Catherine: God, how I want it, the power, the thunderstorms, screaming purple skies, clouds squealing crazy wonderful music, can you hear it? The sun, the stars, the seaside bars, and all the cars, going to Mars. (*Laughs.*) I'm working with rhyme now. Are you cold, Robert? Are you cold? C'mere. (*Embraces him hungrily.*) God, I wanna taste you, taste something rich and buttery like your wine, red wine that spurts out—

Robert: Catherine. (*Holds her hands, tightly.*) Catherine, Jesus, stop it. Stop it. Don't you know where we are? (*Beat: he looks around again.*) What's happening to you?

Catherine: I'm writing. Writers write. I love you. That's a quote. Do you love me? Listen. The sun the moon, and the darkness at noon, you'll leave again soon, I cry and I croon.

Robert: Catherine.

Catherine: Listen to the music. You'll like the music, the music is beautiful. Do you hear it? Can you hear it?

Robert: (*After a pause.*) Yes. (*Catherine looks at him for a moment, then laughs, then moves away.*)

Catherine: Yeah?

Robert: (*Goes to her, gently, carefully.*) C'mon, let's go . . . home. I'll take you home, okay? We'll make a quick phone call, then get a cab. We'll call Alice.

Catherine: I'm okay.

Robert: C'mon. (*Pulls gently.*)

Catherine: (*Firmly.*) No. I wanna stay here.

Robert: Please.

Catherine: No, I'm fine. (*Robert hesitates, then takes off his coat, wraps it around Catherine's shoulders.*)

Robert: Here. I'm gonna make a quick call, then I just wanna . . . let the office know where I am, then I'll be right back. Okay? Catherine?

Catherine: Yeah.
Robert: You'll be okay?
Catherine: Yeah, sure. (*Robert hesitates, then exits.*)

THE RISE AND RISE OF DANIEL ROCKET
by Peter Parnell

ACT I, SCENE 8

Daniel Rocket, aged twelve, can fly. He's always known he could, and tonight for the first time he demonstrated it to others—to Richard, his one friend; to Alice, the girl he has always loved (she loves Richard); and to his classmates who have always thought of him as weird and a "dork." Daniel (also called Snood) made some wings, and earlier in the evening ran off the edge of a cliff and flew into the night. No one has seen him since. His wings were an improvement on Da Vinci's design, but in fact he could fly without them— they merely increased his control.

The following scene takes place later the same night. Richard has just dropped Alice off. She enters her bedroom. The window is wide open and Daniel is there.

(*Alice enters bedroom. Stands in darkness. Goes to close window.*)

Daniel: Don't close it, Alice. I won't be able to get out. (*Alice cries out.*)
Alice: Who's there?
Daniel: It's me, Alice.
Alice: How did you get in?
Daniel: How do you think?
Alice: I don't know.
Daniel: Oh, Alice. You do. I flew straight through your window, into your bedroom. As if it was something I've

always dreamed of. (*Pause.*) Which, of course, it is, Alice. You know that.

Alice: Yes. I do. (*Pause.*)

Daniel: I won't accept less than what I want, Alice.

Alice: That's good, Daniel.

Daniel: I've decided that.

Alice: That's good if it's good for you. (*Pause.*) They were looking all over for you. The boys.

Daniel: Yes.

Alice: They've given up now, I think.

Daniel: Then I can go home.

Alice: You can.

Daniel: Yes.

Alice: But I'd stop off at Richard's and tell him you're alright. He was very worried about you.

Daniel: Was he?

Alice: Yes.

Daniel: Poor Richard. He worries about me alot. Too much, I think. Because I . . . I can pretty well take care of myself, Alice.

Alice: I know that.

Daniel: I think you're beginning to. (*Pause.*)

Alice: So, you can fly.

Daniel: Yes.

Alice: You can actually fly.

Daniel: Mmn.

Alice: You built wings and with them you've flown. (*Pause.*) Where . . . where are your wings, Daniel?

Daniel: I left them down by the rushes.

Alice: The rushes?

Daniel: Yes.

Alice: But, then—how . . .

Daniel: A secret, Alice. There's something else nobody knows. And I'm going to tell *you*. (*Pause.*) The truth is, I can fly without the wings, Alice. I can fly all by myself. It's something I've . . . always been able to do . . . (*Pause.*)

Alice: I thought so.

Daniel: Yes.

Alice: I just thought so.

Daniel: Mmn.

Alice: I remember that time I walked in on you, standing on top of Mrs. Rice's desk . . .

Daniel: Waving my arms.

Alice: Waving your arms.

Daniel: Up and down.

Alice: Up and down, yes. I saw this look, in your eyes, when you turned towards me. It was then, I guess, that I knew. (*Pause.*) When did *you* first realize . . .

Daniel: A long time ago.

Alice: When you were very little?

Daniel: First grade, Alice.

Alice: First grade?!

Daniel: It's true.

Alice: You were lying in bed . . .

Daniel: I was in my pajamas.

Alice: And you just floated?

Daniel: Well, I felt like I wanted to fly.

Alice: You just felt like it?

Daniel: I *wanted* to. Alot.

Alice: So, you stood on the bedpost.

Daniel: And I lifted up my arms.

Alice: And then what happened?

Daniel: I flew. (*Pause.*) It's been even scarier these times.

Alice: These times?

Daniel: Scarier than the first time, I mean.

Alice: The first time?

Daniel: The *very* first time. When we were in kindergarten. I floated once, around the sandbox. I was glad I didn't go very high. Besides, Mrs. Klinger saw me.

Alice: Mrs. Klinger?

Daniel: She had her heart attack the very next day.

Alice: You're kidding, Snood.

Daniel: No.

Alice: That's terrible.

Daniel: Yes.

Alice: And you blamed yourself.

Daniel: All these years.

Alice: That's *terrible*, Snood.

Daniel: For a long time I didn't want to fly. But I want to fly now. (*Pause.*) It's just something I've had locked inside me, Alice. And now that I've let it out, there's no telling what wonderful things I can do . . .

Alice: Besides, with wings you can control wherever you're going.

Daniel: Yes. With wings I can go wherever I want to. (*Pause.*) It's a nice night out, isn't it?

Alice: Yes.

Daniel: With the stars. And the moon. A nice time for a little flight, don't you think?

Alice: I suppose.

Daniel: Would you care to join me?

Alice: Are you serious?

Daniel: I could lift you up. On my back. I'm strong enough now. I've been practicing.

Alice: Have you?

Daniel: So I could take you with me.

Alice: Where are you going?

Daniel: I don't know. Away. Far away.

Alice: When?

Daniel: Soon. Very soon. (*Pause.*)

Alice: We can't do that, Snood.

Daniel: Why not?

Alice: Because. We're only twelve years old.

Daniel: Yes.

Alice: We've got another twenty years in us at least.

Daniel: At *least* another twenty years.

Alice: Yes.

Daniel: Well, yes. I guess. That's true. (*Pause. Daniel lowers his head. Sobs. Alice is surprised. Moves to him. Touches his head.*) It's going to be horrible. Being with the other kids.

Alice: Yes.

Daniel: They already hate me.

Alice: They don't hate you.

Daniel: They do! And now that they've seen me fly . . . I can't stay here, Alice. I've got to go, I think. Don't you? (*Pause. Alice embraces Daniel.*)

Alice: It will be alright, Daniel. Everything will be alright.

Daniel: You sure you wouldn't like a ride?

Alice: Not tonight, Snood.

Daniel: But soon?

Alice: Soon.

Daniel: Soon! Alice! Soon! We'll both be flying, Alice! You and me! We'll both live in the sky! (*Pause.*) If I *do* decide to go away, Alice, I'll come back for you someday.

Alice: You will?

Daniel: Yes. Will you come with me?

Alice: I . . . Yes, Daniel.

Daniel: Do you promise?

Alice: I . . . I'll think about it.

Daniel: Good.

Alice: We . . . we have a whole lifetime ahead of us, Daniel.

Daniel: Yes. I guess. We do. And now, I'm going to show you what I've wanted to show you. All these years. The special secret between you and me, Alice. The secret of what I can *really* do . . . (*Pause. Daniel closes his eyes. Lifts up his arms. Utters low sound. Almost a hum. He floats to the ceiling. He flies around the room. Alice watches, spellbound. Daniel flies out bedroom window. Alice rushes after him. Looks out window. Waves. Dog heard barking, off.*)

ACCOMMODATIONS
by Nick Hall

ACT II, SCENE 1

Tracy Varetta is a serious student majoring in research psychology at New York University and studying "the effects of pollution and poor air quality on the lives of overcrowded rats." He is *very* serious . . . and *very* attractive. Through a mix-up at the roommate agency he finds himself living in a tiny apartment in Greenwich Village with two women, Lee (thirtyish), and Pat (early twenties). Pat is an actress who loves men and loves to wear elaborate costumes in her everyday life, costumes that she borrows from her gay landlord, Simon (at the opening of the play she is dressed as Shirley Temple, including hair and make-up). Her attitude toward life is: "Look on the bright side. The worse the situation, the funnier it is." Her attitude toward Tracy is lust at first sight.

In the scene that follows, the trio has been living together for a week. Tracy is reading diligently and making notes. Pat enters from the bedroom. Today she looks like "a very Middle European cross between Garbo and Dietrich. She wears spiked heels, a belted trench coat with the collar turned up, possibly dark glasses, and definitely, a huge slouch hat. Occasionally she remembers to speak with an ersatz Hungarian accent. She is smoking ostentatiously. She strikes the classic, cliché pose: one leg up on the seat of a chair."

Tracy ignores her. She crosses to the tape deck and turns off the classical music that has been playing.

Pat: Did you know I vas madly in love with you?

Tracy: (*Deep in the book.*) Yes, you told me yesterday.

Pat: Und I vill probably tell you again tomorrow. A good book? (*No reply.*) Lots of pictures of rats in it? (*No reply.*) What are you reading? (*No reply. Sharply.*) Hein!

Tracy: What?

Pat: We're gonna have to work out a system, Tracy, like secret agents. I'll carry ninety percent of the conversation, talking for both of us, and you can consider most questions rhetorical, but if you hear a twelve second pause at the end of a question and I don't answer myself, that means it's your turn. Okay? Don't answer that. Throw in an occasional grunt when the mood strikes you. It'll help me carry your end of the conversation. I think I wanted to know what you're reading, but it was so long ago, I don't care anymore. You know, it would be easier talking for you if I knew what you were like. I mean, I know you're Tracy Varetta, twenty-five years old, medium height, gray eyes (*Adjust to fit actor.*), currently doing graduate work in psychology at N.Y.U. But what does it all add up to? Not that I think you're hiding things, you understand. It's very hard to have secrets when the bathtub's in the kitchen. It's just that I want to know who you are. So prepare yourself, 'cos I'm going to ask you a question and pause for twelve seconds. Ready? (*Back into mystery woman part.*) Then I begin. Who are you? (*Very long pause.*) Now for those of you who may not have heard that, I repeat it. Pay attention. There's someone under my skin and I vant to know who it is. (*Long pause,* TRACY *studying.* PAT *shouts.*) Tracy, I want an answer!

Tracy: (*Looking up, startled.*) Clinical Studies of Reaction to Aversive Stimuli in a Deprived Environment.

Pat: What?

Tracy: (*Holding out the book for her to look at.*) That's what I'm reading.

Pat: I'll wait for the movie. (TRACY *goes back to the book.*) You know, I think if we're going to live here in close quarters, we ought to get to know each other better. We should understand each other's moods and feelings. First off, let's consider your feelings. Okay, that's done. Now let's consider mine. You know I'm in love with you. I actually knew it the first day but I didn't tell you then because I was hoping it was just a twenty-four hour virus. Sure enough, it was love. It wasn't even for the right reasons like you were easy to talk to or a producer. I think it was the way the hair grew down the back of your neck and how you brushed your teeth without spattering toothpaste anywhere. (*Mystery woman again.*) Vy don't we do something mad like make hungry sveating love? Doktor, with your mind and my body we can rule the world. Or as we used to say in Lithuania, "Si el tren se para entre la estaciones quedesa adentro." Which translates as . . . (*She pushes his book up against his chest so that he cannot read and has to focus on her.*) . . . Do you love me?

Tracy: No.

Pat: Will you marry me anyway?

Tracy: No.

Pat: (*Brightly.*) Well, I'll try again tomorrow.

Tracy: I like you.

Pat: Thanks a lot. How are the rats?

Tracy: Pretty good. I think my theory is going to hold up. The general apathy has worn off and in the last few days there's been a marked increase in the incidence of cannibalism and incest.

Pat: See, I just knew, once you'd put that book down, we'd have a great conversation. Tell me about your love life.

Tracy: I don't think I have one.

Pat: Of course you do. Everyone has one. They may not be sleeping with anybody, but they do have a love life.

Tracy: I never thought about it.

Pat: You're twenty-five. Start thinking. What type of girl do you like?

Tracy: I don't like types. I like individuals.

Pat: Do you like these individuals to be blonde or brunette?

Tracy: Why?

Pat: Because Simon has dozens of wigs I can borrow. I mean are you looking for a mother, a sex object, or a pal? I do pal very well, but I'll work on mother or sex object if that's what you want. Here I am. What would you like me to be?

Tracy: Quiet.

Pat: What do you think of Lee?

Tracy: She's nice.

Pat: Do you think she's attractive?

Tracy: Yes.

Pat: Very attractive?

Tracy: What do you mean by very?

Pat: Does she turn you on?

Tracy: I'm not a light bulb.

Pat: What are you going to do when you graduate? Open an office?

Tracy: No, I'm going to be a research psychologist.

Pat: No plush office with a leather couch and rich, bored ladies lying on it?

Tracy: No.

Pat: What a shame, I was hoping for a free consultation. If I don't get professional help soon, I don't think I'll make it.

Tracy: You're as healthy as a horse.

Pat: No, I'm not, I know I seem normal, but underneath I'm sick, really sick. (*Who by this time is lying on the couch.*) Tell me, doctor, is it too late for help?

Tracy: I'm not a doctor.

Pat: Would you like to hear about my childhood?

Tracy: Not particularly.

Pat: I have an older sister and a younger brother and my parents loved us all very much. They loved my sister because she was the oldest, and they loved my brother because he was the youngest, and they loved me because there I was in the middle and there wasn't much else they could do with me. (*Beat.*) There, now you can see how it all began.

Tracy: How all what began?

Pat: This craving, this desperate need to be oldest or youngest or something.

Tracy: What do you want anyway?

Pat: What do you mean, what do I want? I wanta know who I am. I wanta find someone else who knows who I am. (*Sincere.*) What does anyone want, love and happiness.

Tracy: (*Quietly.*) Oh.

Pat: (*Brightly.*) That's the first time you've ever really talked to me.

Tracy: I . . . er . . . got carried away.

Pat: It's okay.

Tracy: Maybe you try too hard.

Pat: Maybe. I was just trying to be what you wanted.

Tracy: What's that?

Pat: An in-depth study. Maybe I do try too hard, but you think too much and don't try at all. Anyway, I have no objection to being treated as a sexual object. I think I'd like it.

RICH AND FAMOUS
by John Guare

SCENE 1

Bing Ringling is finally having a play produced—after 843 tries—and he hopes to become rich and famous. John Guare's fanciful comedy opens with the young playwright standing on a street corner in Manhattan "in a rented tux," clutching his script "to his heart." His girlfriend Leanara is with him. She carries two shopping bags.

Leanara: To walk to the theater with the playwright on opening night!

Bing: Oh, Leanara, we're going to have the best life. A life you'll want to read about. A life they'll write musicals about in twenty years. John and Yoko. Scott and Zelda. Dante and Beatrice. Bing and Leanara.

Leanara: Oh, Bing, I'm so honored to be in your play. All those years wasted on Shakespearean comedy. Lovers in the woods. All that Chekhov crap. Chopped down cherry trees.

Bing: Wait. Don't say that about Chekhov.

Leanara: I hate people like Chekhov.

Bing: He tried.

Leanara: But people like that are so good they don't leave room for the new people. For the Bing Ringlings. I want to do Ringling for the rest of my life. (*The music swells into this terrific Bossa Nova. Bing embraces Leanara.*)

Bing: (*Sings*)

> I. I. I will always love you
> Don't Be Sure
> I. I. I will never leave you
> Don't Be Sure
> I promised I could be relied on
> Remember the shoulder you cried on
> Well, here is the Bible I lied on
> When I swore
> Forevermore
> I. I. I will drive you crazy
> Don't Be sure
> I. I. I cannot be trusted
> Don't Be sure
> Darling, if you're into trust
> Possibly I might just
> Surprise you
> If you want surprises
> Like a love that's pure
> Can I deliver?
> Will I deliver?
> I will deliver!
> Don't Be Sure.

I went into that little all-night bookstore over there on the corner to see where I'll fit in and I'll be between Rimbaud and Rin Tin Tin. Beloved Hollywood dog reveals all in touching memoir.

Leanara: Do you like me in your play? Honest. I mean, really honest.

Bing: As simple as this. If you were not in it, it would not be worth doing. As if you stepped out of my brain right onto the page.

Leanara: Recite my favorite part. Right from the playwright's mouth.

Bing: "I ran down into the subway. In a panic. I'll go anywhere. Trains rush past me. E trains. F trains. A's. GG's. RR's. C's. Pursued by the entire alphabet."

Leanara: I love it. I love you. Are you in as much pain as the play says?

Bing: Oh, yes. More.

Leanara: How do you stand it? How do you live?

Bing: Well, no, not really. You see I make up bad things about myself so I'll be more interesting. I read about O'Neill and I think Christ, I could have been a great playwright too if my Mother was a junkie and my father was a miser who ran around playing the Count of Monte Cristo all the time. So I write my autobiographical play, based on Dante's *Inferno,* and it's close enough to the way I'd like my life to be. With a few songs thrown in. Oh, God!

Leanara: What is it?

Bing: (*Pulls a small box out of his shopping bag.*) I bought these cufflinks at a little magic store on Fourteenth Street. One set has the initial R and the other set has the initial F. I mix them up and wear them R and F. For rich and famous. Sometimes I wear them the other way around. F and R. For famous and rich. I don't care which one comes first. But if my play stinks. If my play flops. I'm going to be wearing them D & B. For dead and buried. O & O. For over and out. I'm not going to be the World's Oldest Living Promising Young Playwright.

Leanara: Your first produced play. After 843 plays. My God, the typing alone. What those fingers have been through. (*Bing gets his cufflinks set in his cuffs.*)

Bing: Sorry, Aeschylus. Sorry, Brecht. Sorry, Chekhov. Sorry, Molière. Feydeau. Racine. Sorry, guys, but I got a machine gun attached to my typewriter and you haven't seen the plays I've got in my head.

Leanara: (*A gun moll.*) Ratatatatatatatatatatatatatata!!!!!!!!!!!!

(*An ominous chord plays. Overhead an enormous billboard appears in the process of being painted. It is a bill-*

board dominating all of Times Square. It announces a new film: GANGLAND, *and the music plays again and a face appears on the billboard and it's the face of that hot young actor, none other than Tybalt Dunleavy. The music plays again. Tybalt smiles malevolently down at us. Bing looks up at the billboard. Leanara takes his arm.)*

Bing: There he is again. My old friend, Tybalt Dunleavy, on a billboard at the crossroads of the world. Here I am, my play opening in a toilet on Lower Death Street and my boyhood chum up there like a plague—

Leanara: Bing, calm down. Will you stop it with Tybalt Dunleavy already? I hate to say it, but sometimes people become stars because they're very good and Tybalt Dunleavy happens to be very good.

DANCING IN THE END ZONE
by Bill C. Davis

ACT I

James is the star quarterback for a major university football team. All seemed to be going well: the team was undefeated, he was befriended by the coach who became a much-needed father figure for him, and he was on the dean's list. Then a newspaper story revealed that the teachers were giving the football players "gift grades"—something James had not known. So Coach Biehn arranged for a tutor for him. The tutor, Jan, a graduate student in journalism, was the one who anonymously wrote the "gift grades" story. She is now working on another story and wants to get James on her side. She suspects that the coach is giving James Novocain to kill the pain in his injured knee. She has letters from former football players who claim to have had permanent injuries because they too were given painkillers by Coach Biehn. Jan wants to expose the coach. She gave copies of the letters to James at their last meeting.

Jan (who is married but separated from her husband) has been educating James in areas other than his school courses. She has been trying to get him to see football as a brutal sport that glorifies human aggression. She has been making headway with him, perhaps because he has been falling in love with her. In his last game James didn't use Novocain, and the team lost. As he reveals in the scene, he also didn't "throw up" before the game. A teammate, Pagones, had the habit of forcing himself to throw up before a game. James, in a kind of sympathetic reaction, would always throw up with him.

The scene that follows takes place in Jan's apartment where James goes for his tutorials.

Jan: You're ten minutes early. (*Pause.*) I wasn't even sure you were coming.

James: Listen—I want to keep those letters you gave me. I read them all—twelve times. I can't talk about it yet.

Jan: All right.

James: Please don't print them. Please.

Jan: (*Pause.*) How's the knee?

James: It's fine.

Jan: Really?

James: No—it hurts.

Jan: Did it hurt during the game?

James: Hm—Hmm.

Jan: You played without it?

James: Hm—Hmm.

Jan: You think that's why you lost?

James: I don't know. The team is certain we lost because I didn't throw up.

Jan: You didn't?

James: First game this season I didn't. I think Pagones was kind of hurt too. (*Pause.*) So what are we learning today?

Jan: German Philosophers. They're the toughest. You should have brought your helmet.

James: What's your husband's name?

Jan: (*Pause.*) Rich.

James: As in Richard?

Jan: Yes.

James: That's Coach Biehn's name, except his friends call him "Dick."

Jan: I'm sure.

James: You shouldn't be so hard on him.

Jan: Sorry.

James: He is my best friend.

Jan: But why do you always call him "Coach Biehn"? You never call him Dick.

James: He wants it that way. I understand that. I have to be the same as every other player.

Jan: Are you?

James: (*Pause*—JAMES *doesn't answer.*) He's a good man. You know, once a month he volunteers a free day to drive kids with cancer to the Marion clinic.

Jan: That's very nice of him. He could be a saint for all he knows. But, Jimmy, please understand, I can't forget the letters.

James: Couldn't you just show the letters to the board of directors? They'll give him a warning. But don't print them. It'll kill him—I know it.

Jan: (*Pause.*) Let's get down to business.

James: What does Rich do?

Jan: That's not business.

James: But I want to know about you.

Jan: He's a lawyer. A public defender. The first German philosopher we're going to . . .

James: Where is Rich now?

Jan: We don't have time for this. We have to tackle Hegel today. Sorry—I didn't mean to say "tackle." (JAMES *laughs—she joins him—silence.*)

James: Where is Rich?

Jan: He's in prison.

James: Are you kidding me? Your husband's in jail? Oh my God. What's he in for? I've always wanted to say that. "What's he in for?"

Jan: (*Laughing.*) This isn't Dodge City, Jimmy. He's not in "jail." He's in prison.

James: But what for?

Jan: Tax evasion.

James: He made a mistake?

Jan: No. He did it on purpose. He figured out the percentage of his taxes that went to nuclear arms, and he refused to pay that amount.

James: That's gutsy. You married a gutsy guy.

Jan: Yeah—but I told him, I don't think it's going to help. Bombs exist. Plans for bombs exist. You could defuse all of them tomorrow, but sooner or later they'll come back. *We* have to be defused. If all the guys on your team quit, and grew zucchini, and broccoli on the football field, I think that would do more for world peace than everyone going to prison for unpaid taxes. (JAMES *laughs*.) I mean it.

James: I know.

Jan: You think I'm crazy—don't you?

James: No, I just never knew anyone who thinks like you. Was that why you and he separated? Because he got arrested?

Jan: No—we separated a month before that.

James: Why?

Jan: (*Pause*.) He wanted children. I didn't. Simple.

James: Why not? Why don't you want children?

Jan: As I told him—if we have a boy, he'll get his legs blown off in a war. Or, if it's a girl, she'll have deformed babies from nuclear waste. And he'd say to me—"Jan—you don't need to take the pill—You can *talk* yourself out of ovulating."

James: What are you going to do about him? Are you going to divorce him?

Jan: I don't know. I have a lot to figure out.

James: Could he divorce you in the meantime?

Jan: He could.

James: Would that upset you?

Jan: I haven't thought about it.

James: Do you still like him?

Jan: Of course.

James: What do you like about him?

Jan: A lot.

James: Like what?

Jan: Well—He can be funny—in a sick sort of way. He wrote a country Western song for me, as an anniversary present. The title of the song is, "There's Only You and Me and World War Three." He was making fun of me. I laughed when I read it, but I believe it.

James: Does he?

Jan: He's not sure. But he's willing to risk having children. I'm not. (*Pause.*) What do you think?

James: (*Pause—slowly.*) I think *you* having . . . I mean—I think *your* having children would do more good than going to prison, or quitting the team, or anything anyone could do. (JAN *touches his face.*)

Scenes for Two Women

ISN'T IT ROMANTIC
by Wendy Wasserstein

Act II, Scene 5

The scene takes place in Harriet Cornwall's apartment. Janie Blumberg, her closest friend, has just learned that Harriet is going to marry a man she has been dating for only two weeks—and Janie is puzzled and upset. Both women are in their late twenties. They were friends at Harvard and decided together to come back to New York (where they grew up) in the hopes of building successful careers and finding exciting love lives. Harriet, beautiful and poised, has been doing very well in the career category. She's rising up the ranks as an executive at Colgate-Palmolive. But her love life hasn't worked out well. She had a disappointing affair with a married man (Paul Stuart), a vice-president at her company, and she often spends her evenings with her mother, Lillian, watching *The Rockford Files* reruns.

Janie, more of an oddball than Harriet (and plumper), hasn't been very successful in either category. Earlier in the week she turned down marrying Marty, a "nice Jewish doctor" who her mother, Tasha, thought would bring her lots of *naches* (the Jewish word for happiness). She turned him down because he needed a traditional wife, that is, one who lets him make all the decisions. But Janie has been trying to feel good about herself as a capable and independent woman, and wants a relationship in which she is an equal partner.

Janie's career as a writer hasn't been working out very well either, although she just had some hopeful news: *Sesame Street* hired her part-time to work on the letter "B."

As the scene begins, Lillian, who is fond of quoting the

141

latest wisdom from the popular women's magazines, has just left.

Janie: She's in a good mood.

Harriet: She's been reading *Redbook*. So, what 'do you think?

Janie: It's wonderful. Mazel tov.

Harriet: (*Exiting to kitchen.*) I didn't mean to surprise you like this. I wanted to have you and Marty to dinner. Are things O.K. with Marty?

Janie: Yeah. Fine.

Harriet: (*From kitchen.*) You O.K.?

Janie: Harriet, have you thought maybe you should live with Joe first? Better yet, maybe you should have dinner with him first?

Harriet: I want to marry him. Janie, he's the only person who's even cared about me in a long time. He listens to me. (*Harriet re-enters with flowers in a vase.*) Tasha's right. You and I deserve a little nachos.

Janie: Naches.

Harriet: Joe makes me feel like I have a family. I never had a family. I had you and Lillian, but I never felt I could have what other women just assumed they would get.

Janie: I want to know one thing. I want to know why when I asked you about my living with Marty, you told me you didn't respect women who didn't learn to live alone and pay their own rent? And then, the first chance you have to change your life, you grasp it.

Harriet: What? Marrying Joe is just a chance that came along.

Janie: I see. You've been waiting for some man to come along and change your life. And all the things you told me about learning to live alone and women and friendship, that was so much social nonsense. I feel like an idiot! I made choices based on an idea that doesn't exist anymore.

Harriet: What choices?

Janie: Never mind.

Harriet: Janie, when I told you that, I didn't know what it would be like when Paul Stuart would leave at ten and go home to Cathy and I would have to pretend I wasn't hurt. I didn't know what it would be like to have lunch with Lillian and think I'm on my way to watching "Rockford File" reruns. Of course you should learn to live alone and pay your own rent, but I didn't realize what it would feel like for me when I became too good at it. Janie, I know how to come home, put on the news, have a glass of wine, read a book, call you. What I don't know is what to do when there's someone who loves me in the house.

(*Pause.*)

Janie: I could throw this table at you.

Harriet: Why? Janie, we're too good friends for you to be jealous.

Janie: I'm not jealous.

Harriet: Don't blame me for your doubts about Marty.

Janie: Harriet, I don't blame you for anything. I'm sorry. Right now I just don't like you very much.

Harriet: Why? Because I'm leaving you? Because I'm getting married?

Janie: Because our friendship didn't mean very much to you. You bring me the sugar, the bread, and the salt, and then you stand there and tell me you never had a family. Harriet, you never really listened to me and you never really told me about yourself. And that's sad.

Harriet: Janie, I love you. But you want us to stay girls together. I'm not a girl anymore. I'm almost thirty and I'm alone.

Janie: You lied to me.

Harriet: I never lied to you. I lied to myself. It doesn't take any strength to be alone, Janie. It's much harder to be with someone else. I want to have children and get on with my life.

Janie: What do you do? Fall in with every current the tide pulls in? Women should live alone and find out what they can do, put off marriage, establish a vertical career track, so you do that for a while. Then you almost turn thirty and *Time* magazine announces, "Guess what, girls, it's time to have it all." Jaclyn Smith is married and pregnant and playing Jacqueline Kennedy. Every other person who was analyzing stocks last year is analyzing layettes this year. So you do that. What are you doing, Harriet? Who the hell are you? Can't you conceive of some plan, some time-management scheme that you made up for yourself? Can't you take a chance?

Harriet: I am taking a chance. I hardly know this man.

Janie: You don't have to force yourself into a situation—a marriage because it's time.

Harriet: You're just frightened of being with someone, Janie. You're just frightened of making a choice and taking responsibility for it.

Janie: That sounds romantic.

Harriet: That's life.

Janie: Harriet, you're getting married to someone you've been dating for two weeks. I am much more scared of being alone than you are. But I'm not going to turn someone into the answer for me.

Harriet: Then you'll be alone.

Janie: Then I'll be alone. (*Pause.*) I better go. I have to get up early with the letter "B." If they like this, they'll hire me full time. In charge of consonants.

Harriet: Give my love to Marty.

Janie: I can't. I told him I won't move with him to Brooklyn.

Harriet: So you'll get an apartment in Manhattan.

Janie: (*She cries.*) We broke up. I decided not to see him anymore.

Harriet: Won't you miss him?

Janie: I missed him today when I saw someone who looks sweet like him walking down the street, and I'll miss him late tonight.

Harriet: Maybe you should call him.

Janie: No.

Harriet: Life is a negotiation.

Janie: I don't believe I have to believe that.

Harriet: Janie, it's too painful not to grow up.

Janie: That's not how I want to grow up. (*She kisses* HARRIET *and starts to go.*)

Harriet: You don't have to separate from me. I'm not leaving you.

Janie: (*Picking up the trash.*) Want me to throw this out for you?

Harriet: Sure.

Janie: Do you really think anyone has ever met someone throwing out the garbage?

(*They shake their heads no.* JANIE *exits.*)

COME BACK TO THE 5 AND DIME, JIMMY DEAN, JIMMY DEAN
by Ed Graczyk

Act II

It is a hot, dry September 30th in McCarthy, Texas, in the year 1975, and the H. L. Kressmont five-and-dime store is decorated for a most unusual celebration. As the sign on the wall says, it is "The 20th Anniversary Reunion of the Disciples of James Dean." Twenty years have passed since James Dean died, and the Disciples—now women in their late thirties— are gathered to reminisce about their teenage fan club and their deceased idol. Mona was and is the most devoted of the Disciples. She has always claimed that her son was fathered by James Dean during the time he was filming *Giant* in a nearby town.

Unlike the other women, Mona has never left McCarthy. She works in the five-and-dime. Her son, whose name is Jimmy Dean, is now twenty years old, and, without saying a word to his mother, has driven off in a car belonging to one of the women. His mother is beside herself with worry. She tells the women that the boy is retarded and alerts the state police about his disappearance.

This scene follows a series of revelations by the women about how their lives have evolved. Sissy, who returned to live in McCarthy a few years ago, has revealed that her enormous breasts—always her most prominent feature—are now rubber replacements for those removed in a cancer operation. As the scene below opens, Sissy has been mocking Mona's self-righteousness.

(For scene-study purposes, the reference to Joanne can be ig-nored.)

Mona: *(Goes to the phone.)* I just don't understand what is takin' them so long. Maybe the phone is out of order, along with everythin' else.

Sissy: (*Goes after her.*) There's nothin' wrong with the God-damn phone. (*Grabs it from her.*) He's gone!

Mona: (*Innocently.*) Well, I know that he's gone, Heavens, I'm not blind am I?

Sissy: Then why do you think everybody else is?

Mona: I don't understand your point.

Sissy: Stop all the crap, Mona . . . He's run away . . . Flew the coop . . . Gone!

Mona: (*Small laugh.*) He couldn't run away . . . he doesn't even know what it means . . . He doesn't know how to do anythin' without me to help him. (*Moves away.*) He's only a child . . . a poor helpless . . .

Sissy: That's what you are, for Chrissake, not him! He's all grown up, Mona . . . Open your damn eyes an' see it.

Mona: His mind isn't . . . his mind is like a . . .

Sissy: The only thing wrong with his mind is that he couldn't make it up soon enough to get the hell outta here . . . away from you an' your crazy ideas about him. He finally made it up, Mona . . . He's gone!

Mona: No, he couldn't decide somethin' like that by himself.

Sissy: I helped him!

Mona: You?!

Sissy: Yes, me, Mona . . . an' I gave him every damn red-cent I had . . . (*Gestures.*) there in my purse to get him started . . . someplace else . . . away from you!

Mona: (*Charging at her.*) You are a disgustin', deceitful . . . (*Slapping at* SISSY. *A crazed woman.*) Hypocrit . . . claiming all these years to be my friend. He was none of your Goddamn business. (JOANNE *tries to pull her off* SISSY.) . . . putting crazy ideas like that into the head of a helpless moron.

Sissy: He is not a moron, Goddammit!

Mona: (*Simply to* JOANNE.) Take your hands off me. (*To* SISSY.) You should be arrested an' locked up.

Sissy: Mona, dammit . . . there is nothin' wrong with that boy.

Mona: (*Covers her ears.*) Lies! . . . lies, nothin' but lies! All those doctors . . . those doctors said he was a . . .

Sissy: (*Prying her hands away from her ears.*) You never took him to no doctors . . . he told me so!

Mona: He's lyin' . . . He doesn't know the truth.

Sissy: And neither do you anymore, Mona. Where the hell did you get the idea anyhow? . . . Did you see it in some

movie, or did it jump out at you from the pages of some
damn novel-of-the-month?

Mona: I am his mother and I know what he is! I don't believe one word you have just said . . . This is a trick isn't
it? (*Gestures to* JOANNE.) The two of you got together,
didn't you? . . . Got together to trick me into sayin' . . .
sayin' . . .

Sissy: Sayin' what, Mona? . . . That he isn't the son of James
Dean? . . . Hell, we've all known that for years . . . everybody's known it, an' accepted it, but you.

Mona: He needs me!

Sissy: Not anymore, he doesn't. You tried to make him helpless an' dependent on you to keep him to yourself . . . to
keep James Dean alive . . . (*Pleading.*) Let him go, for
Chrissake.

Mona: (*Reaching for breath.*) I knew it would come to this
in time. I could feel it inside me . . . I had a premonition.

Sissy: You had gas.

Mona: (*A cornered child.*) I don't know why you have done
this. We were friends . . . I gave up a formal college education just to come back here . . . (*Starts to wheeze.*) so
we could . . . could be together . . . my pills, Sissy, get me
my . . .

Sissy: That asthma of yours is as phony as my rubber tits an'
you know it.

ANTON CHEKHOV'S "THE DUEL"
adapted by Michael Schulman and Eva Mekler
from the translation by Ann Dunnigan

ACT II, SCENE 2

Nadyezhda Fyordorovna left her husband in St. Petersburg and ran away with her lover, Ivan Andreich Layevsky, to
a village in the Caucasus on the Black Sea. She quickly became bored with her new life (as did Layevsky), but she was
trapped without money or family to help her return home. She
longs desperately for the excitement of city life—the balls, the
flirtations, the impassioned conversations. Now Nadyezhda

has received word that her husband has died, but at this point in time neither she nor Layevsky are thinking about marriage. They still care for each other, but Layevsky finds himself irritated at almost everything she does, and she has had an affair with a land official.

The scene below takes place in the kitchen of Nadyezhda and Layevsky's cottage. There are soiled dishes and glasses on a table. Marya, a local townswoman who is married to a village official, has come to pay a condolence call. She hands Nadyezhda a basket of fruit and flowers.

(For more information, see other scenes from this play in other sections of this book.)

Marya: My dear, I'm so distressed and shocked! This morning our dear, sweet doctor told my Nikodim Aleksandrych that he heard your husband had passed away. Tell me, my dear . . . tell me, is it true?

Nadyezhda: Yes, it's true, he's dead. Thank you for these.

Marya: That's dreadful, dreadful, my dear! But there's not evil without good. Your husband was, no doubt, a wonderful, noble, saintly man, and such men are more needed in heaven than on earth . . . Yes, and so you are free, my dear. Yes, now you can hold up your head and look people boldly in the eye. From now on God and man will bless your union with Ivan Andreich. I'm so excited for you that I'm trembling with joy. My dear, we'll give you away . . . It will give us such pleasure. Nikodim Aleksandrych and I are so fond of you. You will allow us to give our blessing to your pure lawful union? When, when do you intend to be married?

Nadyezhda: I haven't even thought about it.

Marya: That is not possible, dear. You have thought about it, you must have!

Nadyezhda: No, I really haven't. Why should we get married? It wouldn't make things any better. On the contrary, it would make them worse . . . We should lose our freedom.

Marya: My dear, my dear . . . what are you saying? Come to your senses. You must settle down!

Nadyezhda: What do you mean, "settle down"? I haven't even lived yet and you tell me to settle down. Do you realize that as soon as I completed my studies at the institute I married a man I did not love and then I ran away with Layevsky and have been living the whole time with him on this dull, desolate shore? Always in the expectation of something better. Is that life? No! It is not life when from morning to night one has no idea how to spend the useless hours. I'm wasting my youth!

Marya: (*Taking back her basket.*) Good-bye, my dear. Forgive me for having troubled you. Although it is not easy for me, I am obliged to tell you that from this day on, all is over between us, and in spite of my profound respect for Ivan Andreich, my door is closed to you! (*She begins to walk off.*)

Nadyezhda: Ivan Andreich did not even come home to me last night!

(*Marya returns and puts down basket. There are tears in her eyes. She holds out her hands to Nadyezhda. Nadyezhda rushes to her, they embrace, and both begin to weep. They sit, continue to weep, and while weeping Marya begins.*)

Marya: Oh, my dear, my dear child. I wish I could spare you, but I must tell you some hard truths. Trust me, my dear, as you would a mother or older sister. Remember, of all the ladies here, I was the only one to receive you in my home. I was scandalized by you from the first day, but I didn't have the heart to treat you with contempt, as everyone else did. I grieved for dear, good Ivan Andreich as if he were my own son—a young man in a strange place, inexperienced, weak, without a mother . . . But I was uneasy about you . . . I have a daughter, a son . . . You understand . . . the tender mind, the pure heart of a child . . . "Whoso offendeth one of these little ones . . ." I received you, but I trembled for my little ones. And everyone was surprised at my receiving you—you will forgive me—like a respectable woman.

Nadyezhda: But why? Why? What harm have I done anyone?

Marya: You are a dreadful sinner. You broke the vow you made to your husband at the altar. You seduced a fine young man. You have ruined his future. Don't speak, don't speak, my dear! I will not believe that it's the man who is to blame for our sins. It is always the woman's fault. Men are frivolous in these matters; they are guided by their hearts, not by their heads. Oh, my dear, if women were more foolish than men, or weaker, God never would have entrusted them with the upbringing of little boys and girls. Any other woman in your position would have hidden herself away, would have been seen only in church. But you flaunted yourself and lived openly, waywardly. And watching you I trembled fearing that a thunderbolt from heaven would strike our home when you visited us. Don't speak, don't speak, my dear! Listen to me . . . God marks the great sinner and you have been marked. It's not by accident that your style of dress has always been appalling.

Nadyezhda: I thought I dressed very well.

Marya: No, appalling. Anyone could judge your behavior from the showiness and gaudiness of your attire. And I grieved, grieved . . . And forgive me, my dear, but you are not clean in your person. When we meet in the bath-house, you make me shudder. Your outer clothing is pass-able, but your petticoat, your chemise . . . My dear, I blush. And your house—it's simply dreadful, dreadful. No one else in the whole town has flies, but you are plagued by them, your plates and saucers are black with them. Just look at your windows . . . and the table-tops—they are covered with dust, dead flies, soiled glasses . . . And one is embarrassed to go into your bedroom; under-clothes flung about everywhere, and your various rubber things hanging on the wall, basins standing about . . . My dear! A husband ought to know nothing of these things, and a wife ought to appear before him as immaculate as a little angel.

Nadyezhda: All this is not worth bothering about. If only I were happy, but I'm so unhappy!

Marya: Yes, yes, you're unhappy, and terrible grief awaits you in the future. A solitary old age, illness, and then you will have to answer at the Last Judgment . . . Dreadful! . . . Dreadful! Now fate itself holds out a helping hand and you foolishly thrust it aside. Get married . . . get married quickly!

Nadyezhda: But it's impossible.

Marya: Why?

Nadyezhda: I can't. I'm going away. Ivan Andreich may re-main here, but I'm going away.

Marya: Where?

Nadyezhda: To Russia.

Marya: But how will you live there? Why, you have nothing!

Nadyezhda: I'll do translations or . . . or open a bookshop . . .

Marya: These are childish fantasies, my dear. You need money for a bookshop.

Nadyezhda: I can't live this kind of life . . . I'm not worthy of him.

Layevsky: (*He calls from off-stage.*) Nadyezhda.

Marya: Well, I'll leave you now.

Nadyezhda: I must do something, what can I do?

Marya: You calm yourself and think things over and tomorrow come and see me in a gay mood. That will be lovely. Well, good-bye, my little angel. Let me kiss you.

LYDIE BREEZE
by John Guare

ACT I, SCENE 2

Lydie Hickman is fifteen years old. She lives in an old house in Nantucket with her father and their "serving girl," Beaty. The year is 1895. When Lydie was a baby her father caught her mother with a man, a friend (Dan Grady), and killed him. The father spent three years in jail and was pardoned through the aid of another friend, Amos Mason, a U.S. Senator. Shortly after her father returned home, her mother (whose name was Lydie Breeze) committed suicide by hanging herself. Beaty was a teenager at the time of the suicide and has stayed on in her position through the years. She has told Lydie all she knows about Lydie's mother, and they enact rituals together to keep her spirit alive.

Lydie's sister Gussie is twenty-two years old. She left home five years ago for Washington, D.C. There she became Amos Mason's secretary and her life has been filled with excitement ("I thank God for my shorthand and my typing"); she is also Amos's mistress. She and Amos have returned to Nantucket on William Randolph Hearst's yacht, and Amos plans to announce that he is a candidate for the presidency.

Gussie has an asthmatic wheeze, and whenever it comes upon her she lights one of her cigarettes, which she refers to as "Dr. Benson's Magic Asthma Stick."

Just before the scene below, Beaty accused Gussie of having become a whore and of dressing like a whore. As Beaty storms off, Gussie and Lydie are left alone. Gussie's opening lines are to Beaty (already off-stage) in reply to her criticism of her clothes. Lydie wears dark glasses because a firecracker exploded near her eye.

(For more information on this play, see the section of this book with "Monologues for Men.")

Gussie: You're damn right! I dress as good as any girl can! *(To Lydie.)* Feel my dress. Can you feel the silk?

Lydie: I never felt silk.

Gussie: Well, that's English silk, goddammit. And these are my beautiful English shoes. And these are beautiful English hairpins. I am doing so fine!

Lydie: You went to England?

Gussie: Those English make me so mad. Can you imagine— We tell England to frig off in 1776. Not till 1894 does England finally decide to open an embassy in Washington. But Amos says I must forgive. So Amos and I had to return the honor and go over there.

Lydie: Did you meet the Queen? Is everything gold?

Gussie: I've been in Buckingham Palace. Saw Prince Edward. The Prince of Wales. He's Queen Victoria's son. The next King. We talked.

Lydie: You talked to the next King of Wales?

Gussie: England! England! Are you an idiot? We were talking back and forth. If I ever get to England, I wouldn't mind looking him up. Buckingham Palace.

Lydie: What did you talk about?

Gussie: Most of our chat revolved around the theater. When you meet people of that royal ilk, you have to have cultural things to talk about.

Lydie: The theater?

Gussie: We saw *Frankenstein*. It was worth sailing an ocean for.

Lydie: *Frankenstein?*

Gussie: Frankenstein is this wonderful scientist who cuts up old corpses . . .

Lydie: Right on the stage?

Gussie: He makes this monster who's controlled by all the dreams of the parts he's made out of. Other people's dreams. Other people's nightmares. It scares the bejesus out of you. To hear all those tight-lipped English tiaras and white ties in the audience screaming like residents of Bedlam.

Lydie: Is he hideous? Is he ghastly?

Gussie: No . . . Dr. Frankenstein must've got hold of the best-looking parts of all the corpses because the monster is . . . truly attractive. He pulls you toward him.

Lydie: I don't want to go near him.

Gussie: In the last scene, the doctor goes up to the North Pole where he's chased the monster!

Lydie: They have the North Pole right on stage!

Gussie: And they walk across the ice! And its quiet . . . It's very still . . . (GUSSIE *spins* LYDIE *around*.) And you hear the wind swirling . . . And you know the monster is out there somewhere . . . Woooo . . . Woooo . . . ! (GUSSIE *hides*.)

Lydie: Gussie? Gussie, don't scare me! (GUSSIE *sneaks up from behind* LYDIE.)

Gussie: And the monster leaps up . . . (GUSSIE *grabs* LYDIE. LYDIE *screams with pleasure*.) And he grabs Dr. Frankenstein and pulls him down, down under the ice. (LYDIE *and* GUSSIE *fall to the floor*.)

Lydie: No!!

Gussie: And the monster looks out into the audience in the dark theater. "Come, my enemies, we have yet to wrestle for our lives. My reign is not yet over." Every evil ugly thing that ever happened woke up inside me. Ma killing herself. Pa going to prison. I got asthma worse than ever.

Lydie: (*Hugging* GUSSIE.) I hate the evil ugly things inside of me.

Gussie: You're a goddamn little saint. You never did anything bad.

Lydie: Ma killed herself. Maybe over something I did.

Gussie: You were just a baby. Ma killed herself because she was still in love with the other man.

Lydie: Dan Grady. I know the name of Dan Grady.

Gussie: Pa killed Dan Grady and Pa went to prison. And then Pa came home and then Ma died. It was all for love. All for love.

Lydie: Gussie, were you ever afraid of Pa?

Gussie: Yes, I was afraid of Pa. After he came home from jail, I could never sleep at night. If I was a bad girl, I was sure Pa would come in and kill me the same as he did to Dan Grady.

Lydie: Is that why you left home?

Gussie: (*Rise.*) I dream all the time I'm going to be killed. I'd rather be killed by a stranger than have Pa be the one.

Lydie: Don't say that about Pa. (GUSSIE *takes a comb from her purse and goes to the mirror to adjust her hairdo.*)

Gussie: Sometimes I wish they had left Pa in that Charlestown prison. What'd he ever do for any of us? Look at you. What's he doing for you? You can't read.

Lydie: I can. A bit.

Gussie: You get decent grades in school?

Lydie: I don't go to school.

Gussie: Do you know your ABC's?

Lydie: Beaty teaches me.

Gussie: Those letters you write to me.

Lydie: They're love letters.

Gussie: I can't read your letters. Zulus in Darkest Africa send out better love letters.

Lydie: It's very hot in here.

Gussie: (*Taking* LYDIE'*s arm.*) How're you going to learn shorthand if you don't even have any longhand?

Lydie: (*Pulling away.*) I don't want to learn shorthand.

Gussie: Don't you care about your life?

Lydie: I care! I'm fine!

Gussie: Don't Pa care?

Lydie: Pa cares.

Gussie: Some people even say Pa is not your real father. Amos Mason says Dan Grady is your father. If he is, I envy you.

Lydie: You never come home. You never answer my letters.

Gussie: Baby, maybe I have kind of ignored the family the past few years. But I come back—see this—I think Ma'd like you travelling with me.

Lydie: But Ma is here. I hear Ma's voice everyday.

Gussie: I only hear my own voice. And my own voice is saying that I want you to learn shorthand so bad. That's the ticket. When I went down to Washington, I just showed up at the Capitol building. Amos could've thrown me out with a gold piece. But he didn't. He took me in and he's taught me to read and recognize the good things. (*She strokes* LYDIE'*s face.*)

Lydie: Your hand feels so nice.

Gussie: Oh, baby, I'd love you to meet Amos. You'd score a bull's eye, Lydie. A pretty young girl in Washington. And you could keep me company.

Lydie: But I have to stay here with Pa . . .

Gussie: Pa!? Pa lost Ma. Pa lost me. Pa lost Amos as a friend. Pa won't even notice you're gone. Baby, electricity's been invented. I'm introducing you to power. You got a bag? I'm packing you up and taking you away.

Lydie: I don't want to be like you. I don't want to go into bed with everybody.

Gussie: What do you know about going into bed?

Lydie: Beaty tells me about going into bed.

Gussie: Beaty don't know nothing! Hills of beans have flags in them announcing what Beaty knows! (GUSSIE *wheezes. She hurries to get another Dr. Benson's Magic Asthma stick. She wheezes again.*)

A YOUNG LADY OF PROPERTY
by Horton Foote

The scene takes place in the yard of Wilma's house in Harrison, Texas, in 1925. Wilma is fifteen years old and "a young lady of property." She owns this house. Her mother bequeathed it to her just before she died in order to prevent Wilma's father, a chronic gambler, from betting it away. But Wilma doesn't live in the house now. She lives with her Aunt Gert, but she loves to visit her house (when it isn't occupied by tenants) and reminisce about her childhood and her mother.

Today Wilma is doing more than reminiscing. She has been waiting all day for a letter from Mr. Delafonte, the famous Hollywood director, who is in Houston interviewing young women for Hollywood screen tests. She has written him asking for an appointment. She dreams of being a movie star: "Hollywood or bust" is her motto. Today will be different for Wilma in another way. She will learn that her father is planning on marrying Mrs. Leighton, a woman he has been dating, and that he plans to sell the house and move away (he doesn't accept that it belongs to Wilma).

The author describes Wilma as "a handsome girl with style and spirit about her." Her friend, Arabella, who has also written to Mr. Delafonte, is described as "a gentle looking girl, so shy about growing into womanhood, that one can't really tell yet what she is to look like or become."

(*Wilma comes in from U.C. of the D.R. area. It is the yard of her house. She sits in the swing rocking back and forth, singing "Birmingham Jail" in her hillbilly style. Arabella comes running in R.C. of the yard area.*)

Wilma: Hey, Arabella. Come sit and swing.

Arabella: All right. Your letter came.

Wilma: Whoopee. Where is it?

Arabella: Here. (*She gives it to her.* WILMA *tears it open. She reads.*)

Wilma: (*Reading.*) Dear Miss Thompson: Mr. Delafonte will be glad to see you any time next week about your contemplated screen test. We suggest you call the office when you arrive in the city and we will set an exact time. Yours truly, Adele Murray. Well. . . . Did you get yours?

Arabella: Yes.

Wilma: What did it say?

Arabella: The same.

Wilma: Exactly the same?

Arabella: Yes.

Wilma: Well, let's pack our bags. Hollywood, here we come.

Arabella: Wilma . . .

Wilma: Yes?

Arabella: I have to tell you something. . . . Well . . . I . . .

Wilma: What is it?

Arabella: Well . . . promise me you won't hate me, or stop being my friend. I never had a friend, Wilma, until you began being nice to me, and I couldn't stand it if you weren't my friend any longer . . .

Wilma: Oh, my cow. Stop talking like that. I'll never stop being your friend. What do you want to tell me?

Arabella: Well . . . I don't want to go to see Mr. Delafonte, Wilma . . .

Wilma: You don't?

Arabella: No. I don't want to be a movie star. I don't want to leave Harrison or my mother or father . . . I just want to stay here the rest of my life and get married and settle down and have children.

Wilma: Arabella . . .

Arabella: I just pretended like I wanted to go to Hollywood because I knew you wanted me to, and I wanted you to like me . . .

Wilma: Oh, Arabella . . .

Arabella: Don't hate me, Wilma. You see, I'd be afraid . . . I'd die if I had to go to see Mr. Delafonte. Why, I even get faint when I have to recite before the class. I'm not like you. You're not scared of anything.

Wilma: Why do you say that?

Arabella: Because you're not. I know.

Wilma: Oh, yes, I am. I'm scared of lots of things.

Arabella: What?

Wilma: Getting lost in a city. Being bitten by dogs. Old lady Leighton taking my daddy away . . . (*A pause.*)

Arabella: Will you still be my friend?

Wilma: Sure. I'll always be your friend.

Arabella: I'm glad. Oh, I almost forgot. Your Aunt Gert said for you to come on home.

Wilma: I'll go in a little. I love to swing in my front yard. Aunt Gert has a swing in her front yard, but it's not the same. Mama and I used to come out here and swing together. Some nights when Daddy was out all night gambling, I used to wake up and hear her out here swinging away. Sometimes she'd let me come and sit beside her. We'd swing until three or four in the morning. (*A pause. She looks out into the yard.*) The pear tree looks sickly, doesn't it? The fig trees are doing nicely though. I was out in back and the weeds are near knee high, but fig trees just seem to thrive in the weeds. The freeze must have killed off the banana trees. . . . (*A pause.* WILMA *stops swinging—she walks around the yard.*) Maybe I won't leave either. Maybe I won't go to Hollywood after all.

Arabella: You won't?

Wilma: No. Maybe I shouldn't. That just comes to me now. You know sometimes my old house looks so lonesome it tears at my heart. I used to think it looks lonesome just whenever it had no tenants, but now it comes to me it has looked lonesome ever since Mama died and we moved away, and it will look lonesome until some of us move back here. Of course, Mama can't, and Daddy won't. So it's up to me.

Arabella: Are you gonna live here all by yourself?

Wilma: No. I talk big about living here by myself, but I'm too much of a coward to do that. But maybe I'll finish school and live with Aunt Gert and keep on renting the house until I meet some nice boy with good habits and steady ways, and marry him. Then we'll move here and have children and I bet this old house won't be lonely any more. I'll get Mama's old croquet set and put it out under the pecan trees and play croquet with my children, or sit in this yard and swing and wave to people as they pass by.

Arabella: Oh, I wish you would. Mama says that's a normal life for a girl, marrying and having children. She says being an actress is all right, but the other's better.

Wilma: Maybe I've come to agree with your mama. Maybe I was going to Hollywood out of pure lonesomeness. I felt so alone with Mrs. Leighton getting my daddy and my mama having left the world. Daddy could have taken away my lonesomeness, but he didn't want to or couldn't. Aunt Gert says nobody is lonesome with a house full of children, so maybe that's what I just ought to stay here and have . . .

Arabella: Have you decided on a husband yet?

Wilma: No.

Arabella: Mama says that's the bad feature of being a girl, you have to wait for the boy to ask you and just pray that the one you want wants you. Tommy Murray is nice, isn't he?

Wilma: I think so.

Arabella: Jay Godfrey told me once he wanted to ask you for a date, but he didn't dare because he was afraid you'd turn him down.

Wilma: Why did he think that?

Arabella: He said the way you talked he didn't think you would go out with anything less than a movie star.

Wilma: Maybe you'd tell him different . . .

Arabella: All right. I think Jay Godfrey is very nice. Don't you?

Wilma: Yes, I think he's very nice and Tommy is nice . . .

Arabella: Maybe we could double-date sometimes.

Wilma: That might be fun.

Arabella: Oh, Wilma. Don't go to Hollywood. Stay here in Harrison and let's be friends forever. . . .

Wilma: All right. I will.

Arabella: You will?

Wilma: Sure, why not? I'll stay here. I'll stay and marry and live in my house.

Arabella: Oh, Wilma. I'm so glad. I'm so very glad. (WILMA *gets back in the swing. They swing vigorously back and forth.*)

SALLY AND MARSHA
by Sybille Pearson
•

SCENE 3

Sally and Marsha live across the hall from each other in an apartment building in New York City. They have become friends despite the fact that they are so different from each other. Sally has recently arrived, with her husband Ted, from South Dakota. She is a homebody and loves being a mother (she has two children and one on the way); she is unsophisticated and uncomfortable in New York. Marsha is a native New Yorker who loves museums and foreign films, who hates cooking, who is not a devoted wife and mother (she has two children), and who visits her analyst, Dr. Heintz, every afternoon.

Before long Sally and Marsha are sharing intimate details of their lives with each other and helping each other overcome some of their fears and difficulties. Marsha tells Sally about her problem with her overbearing mother and with her husband, Martin, who is in residency to become an orthopedic specialist. Marsha is also determined to introduce Sally to great art and literature. Sally confesses her jealousy of people with money, particularly her resentment of a friend from back home named Joni whose husband makes over a hundred thousand dollars a year (initially, she talked about Joni only in glowing terms).

Ted is a door-to-door soap salesman for one of those pyramid companies (Sim's) in which someone sponsors you for a percentage of your sales and you try to find others to sponsor. (In this company the senior sponsor is called an "uncle" and the people you sign on are your "cousins.") Joni's husband Rusty is Ted's "uncle" and he has sent Ted to New York to open the eastern market.

In the scene that follows, the women have known each other for about five weeks. They are in Sally's apartment. Sally is making puppets out of peanuts while Marsha (with a new short hairdo) sits in the rocker "happy and restless," attempting to juggle peanuts. There is a tray on the table with yarn, beads, glue, and an open scrapbook.

Sally: Come sit next to me.

Marsha: What about a movie? Where's the *Times*? (*She jumps up.*)

Sally: Don't have it.

Marsha: I thought you were buying it.

Sally: Forgot.

Marsha: Shit. No, not shit. There's always a theater in the Village that has Bertolucci. You like him?

Sally: Don't know him.

Marsha: That's it! (*She gets* SALLY*'s coat out of the closet.*) First, we're going to Rienzi's, have a fat cappucino, then there's a hero place on . . .

Sally: It's almost noon.

Marsha: (*Tosses coat to* SALLY.) So I'll tell the cab driver you're having the baby. We'll get meat-ball heroes with five napkins, eat them in the movies, get a cab back and you'll be here by three.

Sally: I don't feel like a movie.

Marsha: Why not!

Sally: I got a headache.

Marsha: I'll buy you an aspirin hero.

Sally: Not today . . . Come. Sit quiet next to me and make a peanut puppet. (MARSHA *grabs a handful of peanuts and walks to rocker. She stops midway and freezes.*)

Marsha: I hear it. My mother's packing her little broomstick. (*She bends her ear to stomach.*) Tell me. When will mother arrive? Eight days! Mother and Thanksgiving will be here in eight days. (SALLY *gets up and goes to kitchen.*)

Sally: You're losing your marbles. (MARSHA *flops in rocker, shells peanuts on floor, and eats them.*)

Marsha: You see, the Japanese think the soul resides in the stomach, but I know that tucked under the pancreas, undetectable by x-rays, there's a clock that tells people when their mother is coming to visit. And exactly eight days before her arrival, it sends up a message of uncontrollable hunger. (SALLY *sticks a Saltine in* MARSHA'*s mouth.*)

Sally: Whistle Yankee Doodle. (SALLY *returns to couch and her scrapbook and puppet.* MARSHA *attempts whistling and inadvertently spits all over scrapbook.*) Damn you're a kletz!

Marsha: Klutz. (*She cleans off page of scrapbook.*) I'm sorry.

Sally: Didn't mean to yell.

Marsha: (*Flipping through scrapbook.*) Painting with lard! (*She takes book to rocker.*) Whose is this? How to make hats or bird feather out of bleach bottles.

Sally: Can I have it back?

Marsha: Who devoted their life to this?

Sally: It's a friend's.

Marsha: I bet you it's Joni's. Joyful Joni. The one who opened the champagne to let it breathe.

Sally: I never told you that.

Marsha: She locks herself in the bathroom and reads "Heloise's Household Tips," and I bet you her fucking pineapple upside down cake that I'm right.

Sally: What she just got is a twenty-three caret gold Oneida table setting, a twelve-hundred-dollar modular sofa, AND, any day now, Rusty's going to buy her a motel.

Marsha: A motel?

Sally: Going to give it her name. Going to be under Mt. Rushmore.

Marsha: That's obscene. (*She jumps up.*) Let's go out. Let's have lobsters!

Sally: I got tuna in the fridge.

Marsha: Is it that you're ashamed to go out with me now that I'm so beautiful?

Sally: (*Excited.*) You didn't tell me? Did Martin like your hair?

Marsha: He said I looked less Chekhovian.

Sally: That mean he liked what I did?

Marsha: You haven't read Chekhov!

Sally: No.

Marsha: (*Running to bookcase.*) Where's the list? He's got to go on the list. (*She finds list and pencil and writes.*) Did you finish "Little Dorrit"?

Sally: No.

Marsha: (*Writing.*) Finish it, and then we'll do Fielding before we hit Austen. And the entire Bronte family including Branwell. (*She tosses paper aside and goes to* SALLY.) We're going. We're going to the Strand. Twenty dollars can get you twenty, forty books. We'll take a cab down. I'll take my cab from there to Heintz. You'll take your cab . . .

Sally: I can't.

Marsha: Yes. You can.

Sally: Why can't you just sit down next to me!

Marsha: Anybody can do that.

Sally: Then make a puppet with me! I promised the kids a puppet show the first rainy afternoon.

Marsha: All children should go to boarding school, then there wouldn't be anything like afternoons.

Sally: You couldn't live without afternoons. You see your doctor every one . . . Look at this mess. (SALLY *gets up and picks peanut shells from floor.*)

Marsha: I was going to do it. (*She gets ash tray and helps pick up shells.*) I'll pay you for them.

Sally: (*Picking up shells.*) Don't ever talk about paying me. Besides, you've given me too many things already.

Marsha: I only gave you what I didn't need.

Sally: You're going to want your blender back.

Marsha: I can't stand appliances.

Sally: (*Finding peanuts under couch.*) Sure gota lot of things you can't stand.

Marsha: I didn't buy them.

Sally: Still got them.

Marsha: Men give you appliances to take away your right to complain. (MARSHA *starts to kitchen with shells.*)

Sally: I'll do it.

Marsha: I can carry them to the kitchen.

Sally: I'll do it! (SALLY *brings ash tray to kitchen.*)

Marsha: *I'll* do the living room. (*She takes tray of puppet materials and a book that's lying on the coffee table and brings them to bookcase.*) How can you have this in the house where the kids can see it?

Sally: (*Returning.*) What?

Marsha: Dale Carnegie.

Sally: (*Entering.*) That man is like a part of our family.

Marsha: Burn it! This asshole is responsible for more frozen smiles than Birdseye. (SALLY *takes book from* MARSHA, *sits on couch and reads, aloud, to herself.*) I'll race you for a bagel and lox. (SALLY *doesn't respond.*) I'm sorry . . . (MARSHA *nudges* SALLY.) Hey, I said I'm sorry.

Sally: I am reading. Can't you see I am reading.

Marsha: I see that.

Sally: You read when I talk to you. I read when you talk to me.

Marsha: What are you cracking up for?

Sally: On your way *out* take "Little Dorrit" with you. It's boring and the pages fall out when you turn it.

Marsha: Fine. (*She picks up scrapbook.*) Why don't you read this shit, too. (SALLY *pulls book out of her hands.*)

Sally: That's mine! I made it. (*The cover tears.*) Look what you did.

Marsha: I didn't do a thing. You pulled it.

Sally: (*Trying to fix cover.*) What you have to touch it for?

Marsha: Why didn't you tell me it was yours?

Sally: And have to sit through a five-hour lecture on art? You can't even knit a pot holder.

Marsha: I'm proud of that.

Sally: Cause you're a blank on imagination.

Marsha: All I have is imagination!

Sally: All you have is opinions.

Marsha: Because I don't have orgasms over blenders? (SALLY *heads for kitchen to get blender.*)

Sally: You're taking it back.

Marsha: (*Following.*) I'll put it in the incinerator. (SALLY, *with blender in hand, stops in archway and blocks* MARSHA's *entry to kitchen.*)

Sally: Don't come in my kitchen!

Marsha: Why am I never allowed . . .

Sally: And you'll never be. I'm giving your blender to the church and going to get my own when Ted gets his first Cousin.

Marsha: I was in the best mood I was ever in in my life this morning! I wanted to go out. When in my life have I ever wanted to go out and all you could relate to was putting wigs on peanuts!

Sally: (*Irrationally angry.*) Where do I live?

Marsha: Here.

Sally: How many rooms I got?

Marsha: Two and a half.

Sally: Do I sleep in a fold-up bed?

Marsha: (*Beginning to be exasperated.*) Yes.

Sally: Do I have a vacuum of my own?

Marsha: No.

Sally: Do I have a TV, dishwasher, dryer, orange juice squeezer?

Marsha: No. No. No. No.

Sally: Where do you live?

Marsha: (*Starting to shout.*) There.

Sally: How many rooms you got?

Marsha: Eight.

Sally: Why can't I go out with you?

Marsha: (*Shouting louder.*) Why the fuck can't you go out with me?

Sally: (*Shouting louder.*) Because I don't have the money.

Marsha: (*Shouting louder.*) I would have given it to you.

Sally: I don't take charity!

Marsha: I'm shouting!

Sally: YES.

Marsha: I've never shouted at another woman before.

Sally: (*Still shouting.*) Me neither.

Marsha: You didn't shout at Joni?

Sally: NO.

Marsha: (*Shouting.*) I'm the first woman you ever shouted at?

Sally: YES.

Marsha: Thank you . . . thank you.

Sally: I got to get some O.J.

Marsha: Don't move. I want to get it for you. I'm going to serve you.

Sally: (*Softly.*) I don't want you to go in there.

Marsha: Why?

Sally: (*With difficulty.*) The place is crawling with roaches.

Marsha: Everybody in New York has roaches. Even Greta Garbo and she's Nordic.

Sally: I'd like very much for you to get me an orange juice. (SALLY *sits on couch.* MARSHA *goes in kitchen.*)

Marsha: I feel like Richard Burton going into Mecca.

Sally: What picture was that?

Marsha: Different Burton. (*She gets juice out of ice box.*) Sir Richard. He was a nineteenth-century explorer . . . You too must die. (*She slams spatula on roach. She enters living room and speaks excitedly as she finishes* SALLY'*s glass of juice.*) You are going to flip over Burton. Not only was he the first white man to go to Mecca, but he discovered Lake Tanganyika, translated the Arabian Nights which is part pure erotica, spoke twenty-eight languages, AND married Isabel Arrundel who was as exciting as he . . . (*She sees* SALLY'*s expression.*) Shit, I'll never change. I'm a twentieth-century neurotic and a lecturing bore.

Sally: I agree.

Marsha: You're not supposed to agree.

Sally: No? Whose orange juice was that?

Marsha: Yours. (*She goes to kitchen quickly to get more juice.*) You're so fucking good, good, good, and I'm a shit.

Sally: H. I'm not so great. (MARSHA *re-enters with juice.*) I'm turning ugly, Mash . . . I'm a shit.

Marsha: Sally.

Sally: I'm a jealous woman.

Marsha: Who? Of me?

Sally: You, Joni, people in the subway. Anybody that's got things.

Marsha: I've got things and look at me. Money's not . . .

Sally: I know money's not happiness. I was bred on that.

Marsha: You don't need things.

Sally: I thought that. It was easy. I'd flip through magazines, look at a nice set of china. But if you only see a picture, it looks like a dream. And if it's not meant, you close the page and go on with your life. But here. God, when I took the kids to ride the escalators at Macy's, nothing seemed like a dream. I could touch everything. Watch people picking things out, carrying things out. I don't even know what's in the packages, but I sit in the subways now guessing what's in them and *wanting* it. I can't close that store out of my mind. And Ted comes home after twelve hours killing himself, bringing home nothing. And I'm wanting things. I can't tell him that. Unless I walk blind in this city, I don't know how I'm going to shake it. I want to wake up tomorrow morning and be a hundred-thousand-dollar wife. *I want it*. . . . . . You haven't heard anything uglier than that, have you?

Marsha: (*After a beat between them.*) I don't think you're ugly. (*After a moment of silence,* MARSHA *sits next to* SALLY *on the couch.*)

Sally: It's nice. Sitting quiet next to a gal. It's nice.
Marsha: You do that with Joni?
Sally: She wasn't a friend.
Marsha: You said she was your best friend.
Sally: (*Smiling.*) I know what I said. (*The two women sit quietly as the lights dim.*)

PIAF
by Pam Gems

ACT I, SCENE 1

The play tells the story of Edith Piaf, the French singer—of her rise from an impoverished street life to international stardom. Her audiences were thrilled by her voice and her honest, emotional singing style, and they were titillated by reports of her tempestuous love affairs, her bouts of drinking and drug use, her breakdowns and her comebacks.

As the play opens we see Piaf, already a star, staggering during a song and having to be helped off the stage. The scene then changes to an earlier time and we are outside a posh Paris nightclub, the Cluny Club. The young Piaf is singing in the streets for money. The owner of the club hears her, hires her on the spot, and hands her some money. Then we are in Piaf's apartment a short while later. Her friend, Toine, enters, "throws down her large Thirties' clutch bag, and sits heavily, taking off her shoes and massaging her feet, wincing." Toine is a prostitute—as is Piaf.

Piaf: Toine—here—guess what!
Toine: Fuck off.
Piaf: Wassa matter with you?
Toine: Fucking pimp's had me on that corner, I thought my bleeding toes would burst. I haven't seen more than a couple of fellers all night . . . he's gotta change my shift.
Piaf: Here, listen—
Toine: Him with his bloody favorites, think I don't know?

Piaf: Listen! You're never going—

Toine: That fat Hélène, sits in the fucking caff half the time, I'm not going to stand for it—

Piaf: This bloke . . . !

Toine: (*Irritable.*) What?

Piaf: Me big chance! —you know, like on the movies.

Toine: (*Baffled.*) Eh?

Piaf: This bloke comes up to me—hey! Remember what the fortune teller told us—!

Toine: Hang on . . .

Piaf: *You* remember! I was standing outside the Cluny Club, singing—

Toine: Singing?

Piaf: Yeah, you know . . . for a lark . . . I'm just getting going when up he comes . . . real swell . . . top hat, silk scarf, silver cane, the lot. Next thing I know he asks me inside.

Toine: Iyiy!

Piaf: Toine, you've never seen nothing like it—white tablecloths, little velvet chairs with gold tassels, anything I wanted to drink—

Toine: Hah, I get it—another fucking funny, Christ he must be hard up . . ∴ here, can you see any crabs?

Piaf: (*Looks perfunctorily.*) No, listen! He says to me, he says 'You've got a good voice, kid . . .'

Toine: Hah!

Piaf: Shut up . . . 'I want you . . .' (*She fixes* TOINE *with a magnetic stare.*) . . . 'I want you to star in my club!' Whatcha think of that!

Toine: Oh Christ, she's away.

Piaf: It's true!

Toine: Ede—

Piaf: Look, I'm not saying he's young or goodlooking or anything—

Toine: Ede, have you gone off your head or something?

Piaf: I keep trying to *tell* you! (*Her rage subsides as she concedes the unlikeliness of the tale.*) He wants me to sing . . . in his show . . . Cluny Club.

Toine: Where all the swells go? Get away.

(*But* PIAF *is counting the money.*)

Listen . . . where did you get that?

Piaf: He *gave* it me . . . honest. For nothing!

(*They both look at the money.* TOINE *shakes her head slowly.*)

Toine: Nah.

(PIAF *waits patiently for the verdict.*)

Nah . . . sounds funny to me. Look, kid, I wouldn't have nothing to do wiv it. He's got a little business going, he's short of girls— (*She laughs.*) haha, hahaha . . . he must be!

Piaf: Speak for your bloody self!

Toine: (*Threatening.*) Get off.

(PIAF *backs away prudently.*

Hiatus.

She scuffs moodily . . . picks up the dress TOINE *has taken off.*)

Toine: (*Without raising her eyes from her magazine.*) It's too big for yuh.

(PIAF *hums moodily, ruining* TOINE's *efforts to read.*

She puts down her book with a martyred sigh.)

Oh all right. You can have this. (*She proffers her long, thin, dark-purple Thirties-style scarf.*)

Piaf: Thanks! (*She arranges it around her neck.*) Here, don't laugh. He told me to have a bath . . . wash me hair.

(*They laugh, jeering.*)

Toine: Tell you what, though. (*She finds a comb in her bag . . . tidies* PIAF's *hair, arranges a spitcurl on her forehead.*) That's better—we-ell, you wanna look decent.

Piaf: Thanks. (*She makes to go . . . pauses.*)

Toine: (*Without looking up from her book.*) OK, what is it now?

Piaf: Can I have a lend of your handbag?

Toine: No.

(*But* PIAF *knows the value of fidgeting.*

TOINE *grinds her teeth, hurls the bag at her.*)

Piaf: Thanks! (*She tucks the unsuitably large poche under her arm and struts off proudly, causing* TOINE *to grin.*)

Toine: Take it easy, squirt. (*To the audience, tired*) Well, can't be for the fucking singing, can it—he can hear that for nothing in the street. Be Tangier for you, I shouldn't doubt. (*She picks up her things and goes.*)

COURTSHIP
by Horton Foote

Elizabeth Vaughn is twenty years old. Her sister Laura is seventeen. There is a dance tonight, but they can't go because their father doesn't like dancing. It is 1914 in Harrison, Texas, and Elizabeth and Laura are concerned about their futures—about whether they'll find love and what their marriages will be like. Their parents are strict, overprotective, and constantly point out all the bad examples of abandoned women and marriages gone awry. Unbeknownst to Laura and their parents, Elizabeth has become very serious about her new beau, Horace Robedaux, a young man from town who has become a traveling salesman. Her father has tried to discourage the relationship, but Elizabeth has an independent spirit and has accepted a ring from the young man.

In the scene that follows, Elizabeth and Laura are alone on the porch of their home. Their parents have just gone off to pay a condolence call on Mrs. Thomas, whose daughter Sibyl died earlier in the day giving birth to a stillborn baby conceived out of wedlock.

Laura: How old was Sibyl Thomas?
Elizabeth: Twenty-one. She was one year older than I am.
Laura: She wasn't in your crowd though.
Elizabeth: Sometimes.
Laura: Did you like her?
Elizabeth: She was always jolly and had a very sweet disposition.
Laura: I thought she was pretty. Didn't you?
Elizabeth: Yes, I did.
Laura: I think you're very pretty, Elizabeth.
Elizabeth: Thank you.

Laura: I love the way you do your hair and the way you dress.

Elizabeth: Thank you.

Laura: Do you think I'm going to be pretty?

Elizabeth: I think you're lovely now.

Laura: If it wasn't for the scar on my throat.

Elizabeth: I don't even notice it.

Laura: I do. I'm very conscious of it.

Elizabeth: You're lucky to be alive.

Laura: Yes, I am. I guess they thought I would die. Do you remember it at all when I drank the carbolic acid?

Elizabeth: Of course, I do.

Laura: I was two, wasn't I?

Elizabeth: Yes. I remember hearing Mama scream when she discovered it. I remember Mama and Papa both yelling at the nurse for being so careless and letting you near the bottle of acid and I remember Mama sitting by your bed, night and day nursing you. I remember Papa saying she would kill herself if she didn't get some rest.

Laura: I try to forget the whole thing and just when I think I have, Mrs. Jordan will say to me, "We didn't expect you to live, Honey. We thought for sure we were all going to your funeral." (*A pause.*) Do you ever think about dying?

Elizabeth: Sometimes.

Laura: I wonder why did the two little girls die and not us? Why are they out in the graveyard and we are here?

Elizabeth: I don't know.

Laura: You're not half listening to me. What are you thinking about?

Elizabeth: I don't know.

Laura: I bet I know what you're thinking about.

Elizabeth: What?

Laura: Horace Robedaux.

Elizabeth: Maybe. (*A pause.*) I'm in love with him.

Laura: How can you know that?

Elizabeth: I know.

Laura: How can you be sure of that?

Elizabeth: I'm sure.

Laura: I hope someday I can be sure of something like that.

Elizabeth: You will be.

Laura: Be careful though, Elizabeth. You were sure about Syd, but then you changed your mind. You could change your mind again. (*A pause.*) Ruth Amos said if Miss

Agnes Sweet didn't stop singing so loud in the choir she was going to quit.

Elizabeth: Ruth Amos is the most sensitive human being I've ever heard of. She's always getting her feelings hurt about something and walking out of the choir.

Laura: Mrs. Cookenboo said she only joined the Methodist Church so she could sing solos in the choir. (*A pause.*) Do you smell the honeysuckle?

Elizabeth: Yes.

Laura: I think my favorite smell is chinaberry blossoms in the Spring. (*A pause.*) It's been a dry Fall. I hope we make a good cotton crop. Papa says he needs a good cotton crop to get me to school in Virginia. I wish I weren't going quite so far away. I'm afraid I'll get lonesome. (*A pause.*) Do you think I'll get lonesome?

Elizabeth: If you do, you'll get over it.

Laura: Were you lonesome off at school?

Elizabeth: At first.

Laura: How long were you lonesome?

Elizabeth: Not long.

Laura: The dance music has stopped.

Elizabeth: It stopped quite a while ago.

Laura: I wonder why it stopped so early?

Elizabeth: Maybe they heard about Sibyl Thomas.

Laura: Maybe they did.

Elizabeth: Why did you ask Mama about Mrs. Borden?

Laura: I don't know. Wasn't I supposed to?

Elizabeth: When I tell you secrets I like to feel you won't repeat them.

Laura: I didn't know that was a secret.

Elizabeth: It was a secret, my knowing anything about it. My being in love with Horace Robedaux is a secret.

Laura: I know that. I would never tell that. (*A pause.*) Does Horace know how you feel?

Elizabeth: I don't know.

Laura: Do you think he feels that way about you?

Elizabeth: I don't know.

Laura: Are you going to tell him how you feel?

Elizabeth: Certainly not!

Laura: What if he tells you first he feels that way about you? Would you tell him then?

Elizabeth: I don't know.

Laura: Would you marry him if he asked you?

Elizabeth: I don't know.

Laura: You'd have to be engaged first, I suppose. Do you think Mama would let you be engaged to him?

Elizabeth: I don't know.

Laura: What do you think?

Elizabeth: I think Mama might, but Papa wouldn't.

Laura: Do you think you would have to elope to marry him?

Elizabeth: Yes.

Laura: Would you?

Elizabeth: Yes.

Laura: Even if it meant Mama and Papa never would forgive you?

Elizabeth: Yes.

Laura: Don't say that.

Elizabeth: I mean it.

Laura: Fifer Ecker's Mama and Papa never forgave her for eloping and her husband deserted her and she died all alone, in New Orleans. What if that happened to you?

Elizabeth: I don't think it will happen to me. Not if I marry Horace. I don't think Horace would ever desert me. I think we will live together a long time and that we will be very happy all our married life.

Laura: How can you be sure?

Elizabeth: Because I am sure.

Laura: Suppose he doesn't love you and is just infatuated and he meets someone out on the road while he's travelling around that he likes much better than you and he never asks you to marry him? What will you do then?

Elizabeth: I don't know. I wouldn't know what I would do about that unless it happened.

Laura: Would you ever marry someone older than you like Aunt Evy and Aunt Lucy did? Just because it was the sensible thing to do?

Elizabeth: No.

Laura: What if . . . what if no one you like ever asks you to marry them? And you get to be thirty or thirty-five like Aunt Sarah? And you met a nice older man, a widower say, and you didn't love him, but you respected him and he was kind and thoughtful, would you marry him or go on being an old maid?

Elizabeth: I don't know.

Laura: I worry about that so much. Don't you worry about things like that at all?

Elizabeth: No. The other night when I was out riding with Horace he said he was not going to take out any other girls while he was away travelling this time. And I said I would not see any other young men. I said I would write to him at least three times a week, but I asked him not to write me but every ten days or so, because I didn't want Mama and Papa nagging me about it.

Laura: If you're not seeing anyone else and he's not seeing anyone else does that mean you're engaged?

Elizabeth: In a way. (*She reaches into her dress and pulls out a ring that is on a chain around her neck. She shows it to her.*) Look here. . .

Laura: What's that?

Elizabeth: It's a ring he gave me. I keep it hidden so Mama and Papa won't ask any questions.

Laura: Is that an engagement ring?

Elizabeth: I consider it so.

Laura: And he must consider it so. I bet that's why he didn't take a date to the dance tonight and why he didn't dance when he got there. Because he thinks you're engaged. Can I tell Annie Gayle?

Elizabeth: You can't tell a living soul. (LAURA *cries*.) Why are you crying?

Laura: I think it's terrible we have to deceive and slip around this way. Why can't we be like other girls and have our beaux come to the house and receive presents and go to the dances? I think we should just defy Papa and Mama and tell them right out.

Elizabeth: I did that with Syd and it does no good. It just means constant fighting. The boys won't come here because no one wants to be insulted.

Laura: Of course, with Syd it was a good thing they opposed your marrying him, because you didn't really love him.

Elizabeth: No.

Laura: Oh, my God! That worries me so. Suppose I think I'm in love with a man and I marry him and it turns out I'm not in love with him. (*A pause.*) What does being in love mean?

Elizabeth: Oh, Laura, you'll go crazy if you always think of the bad things that can happen. I don't think of that.

Laura: What do you think of?

Elizabeth: I don't think.

Laura: I wish to heaven I didn't. Everything bad that happens to a girl I begin to worry it will happen to me. All night I've been worrying. Part of the time I've been worrying that I'd end an old maid like Aunt Sarah, and part of the time I worry that I'll fall in love with someone like Syd and defy Papa and run off with him and then realize I made a mistake and part of the time I worry . . . (*A pause.*) that what happened to Sibyl Thomas will happen to me and . . . (*A pause.*) could what happened to Sibyl Thomas ever happen to you? I don't mean the dying part. I know we all have to die. I mean the other part . . . having a baby before she was married. How do you think it happened to her? Do you think he loved her? Do you think it was the only time she did? You know . . . (*A pause.*) Old, common, Anna Landry said in the girls room at school, she did it whenever she wanted to, with whomever she wanted to and nothing ever happened to her. And if it did she would get rid of it. How do women do that?

Elizabeth: Do what?

Laura: Not have children if they don't want them?

Elizabeth: I don't know.

Laura: I guess we'll never know. I don't trust Anna Landry and I don't know who else to ask. Can you imagine the expression on Mama's face, or Aunt Lucy's or Mrs. Cookenboo's if I asked them something like that? (*A pause.*) Anyway, even if I knew I would be afraid to do something like that before I got married for fear God would strike me dead. (*A pause.*) Aunt Sarah said that Sibyl's baby dying was God's punishment of her sin. Aunt Lucy said if God punished sinners that way there would be a lot of dead babies.

I WON'T DANCE
by Oliver Hailey

ACT II, SCENE 2

Dom, a paraplegic, has disappeared. His wheelchair is missing and the two women in his life are worried. One is Kay,

a prostitute (and unsuccessful actress) who was hired by
Dom's brother, Buddy, to have sex with Dom. Dom was not
supposed to know she was paid to be with him. Her assign-
ment was to convince him that she loved him and wanted to
marry him. Dom learned the truth only recently when he saw
Buddy's checkbook and all the check stubs made out to Kay.

The second woman is Lil, the sister of Buddy's wife,
Paula. Buddy and Paula took care of Dom up until yesterday
when they both were murdered. The police are questioning
everyone, including Dom, Kay, and Lil. Buddy and Paula
hated Lil—apparently so much that when Paula wrote a book
based on her family she left her sister out of it entirely. As Lil
sees it, Buddy and Paula even found a way to hurt her after
their deaths: Dom told her that they left all their money to her
and the responsibility for taking care of him. But Lil is living
happily with a man (an Indian) in New Mexico and doesn't
want her life burdened with Dom. She told him that she was
going to give him the entire inheritance and return to her
home. Dom then tried to convince her to stay with him (he has
been in love with her for years), but she refused. Shortly after
that he disappeared.

The setting is Dom's room in Los Angeles. As the scene
opens Kay is sitting in a wheelchair, crying. Lil enters.

Kay: Did you find him?

Lil: No. Where'd you find his wheelchair?

Kay: This one's not his. It's mine.

Lil: (*A beat as she stares at* KAY, *then:*) You know, I've about
had it with you.

Kay: I mean it's his extra—his spare chair. But I think of it as
mine. (*Tears in her voice.*) And I don't even care who
knows it.

Lil: I really have.

Kay: What?

Lil: *Had* it with you!

Kay: (*More tears.*) Yeh? Well, how do you suppose I feel
about me? My life reduced to a bunch of check stubs? It's
bad enough I was paid—but for everybody to know how
much? Damn, why didn't I demand cash?

Lil: Have you always done that?

Kay: He's the only one who ever *wanted* to pay by ch—
(*Beat as she realizes that she has answered the wrong
question.*) Oh. You mean have I taken money from *other*

men? (*Beat*.) Yeh, but they always made it seem more like gifts. And sometimes there *were* actual gifts. Gifts *and* cash. Or cash *in* gifts. Things like that. But nobody ever wanted a Goddamn *receipt*! Except *Buddy*! All those stubs—my God!

Lil: They showed you his checkbook?

Kay: It was so embarrassing. They asked me if I knew any of the other girls.

Lil: Did you?

Kay: Honey, L.A.'s not that big a place.

Lil: Were the others actresses, too?

Kay: That's a slur. You know that, don't you? On a very noble profession.

Lil: Why do you do it?

Kay: What?

Lil: Hook.

Kay: Honey, everybody needs to feel there's *something* they do well. Plus I never heard of anybody being fired from it. They may not ask you back—but at least nobody ever fires you while you're at it!

Lil: You shouldn't think of it as a career.

Kay: My God, I *don't*! My God, does it look like I *do*? My God. I may hook, but that doesn't make me a hooker. People sing without being singers. They dance without being dancers. They sing because they love to sing, they dance because they love to dance. The problem is *charging*. Once you start charging, there's a real stigma attached to it. I suppose you've never charged anybody for anything.

Lil: No. A couple of times I felt I should've—but no.

Kay: My mama's dead, my daddy's dead and my brother's dead. I never charged anybody 'til all three were gone. They truly rest in peace. At least that's something to be proud of. (*She sighs, glances about trying to lift her spirits, notices the Taco Bell bag on the table.*) What's in that—anything to eat?

Lil: An enchirita. Have it.

Kay: Whose is it?

Lil: I got it for Dom—but he really wanted you to have it.

Kay: (*Opening the bag.*) I'm so hungry I could eat anything.

Lil: I wonder.

Kay: That was really sweet of Dom to want me to have it. (*She unwraps the enchirita, takes a large bite—then smiles:*) Yum!

Lil: Who did this room?

Kay: Did it?

Lil: Decorated it.

Kay: Oh, Buddy. This is all Buddy's taste. He had it redone for Dom last year. Don't you just love it? (LIL *responds in silence as she surveys the room again.* KAY *takes another bite from her enchirita—then:*) You don't really think he's run away, do you?

Lil: At best he rolled. (KAY *smiles, takes another hearty bite from the enchirita.*) And would you mind climbing out of that wheelchair? I get the message—we are all *crippled*. So put it away now—okay?

Kay: You know, it used to give me the willies, too—when he first asked me.

Lil: First asked you *what*?

Kay: To *sit* in it.

Lil: Why would he do that?

Kay: It turned him on.

Lil: You in one chair and he in the other?

Kay: Right. This is his spare chair. (*Beat.*) When I think of all the wonderful times we used to have in them.

Lil: *That's* the part I'm *still* not really clear on.

Kay: The wonderful times?

Lil: Yes.

Kay: (*With a giggle.*) Well, what can I say?

Lil: I have no idea.

Kay: Have you ever seen somebody naked in one of these?

Lil: No . . . not yet.

Kay: It's a surprising turn-on. And not just for him—but for me, too. You know how as a young person, you learn not to be ashamed of your body? Well, together, we took that extra step—we learned not to be ashamed of our wheelchairs either. (LIL *stares at* KAY *for a beat, shakes her head in wonderment, halfway between laughter and tears. Finally:*)

Lil: Kay, I'm beginning to like you.

Kay: Are you really?

Lil: Finally.

Kay: Would *you* like to sit in it for awhile?

Lil: No—it's yours—you belong there.

Kay: What does that mean?

Lil: It means you're the best thing that could happen to him.

Kay: Yes, you're probably right. And I have thought about it since you said he'll be inheriting their money. But the truth is, once you get in the habit of knowing more than one man, it's hard to cut back. I find myself already looking forward to all the ones I haven't even had yet. So the thought of settling with one—of marriage—which used to be my absolute goal—now seems so limiting. Someone like you probably can't even understand that.

Lil: I really do like you. (*The buzzer sounds sharply.* KAY *hurries to the phone.*)

Kay: Maybe the police found him. (*She picks up the receiver, speaks into it.*) Yes. Oh, thank God. Where? What? (*Beat.*) How? My God, was he killed? Oh, no—no . . .

Lil: What's happened?

Kay: (*To* LIL.) He's been located—but it's just awful. (*And then into the phone again.*) What? You're kidding. But that's ridiculous. He couldn't mean it. Where is he? Well, can't you find out? Yes, I'll wait right here—thank you. (*And she replaces the receiver.*)

Lil: What is it?

Kay: It makes no sense . . . his mind must've snapped.

Lil: What?!

Kay: They found him on the Ventura Freeway.

Lil: How did he get on a freeway?

Kay: How do you think? In his wheelchair.

Lil: My God—it sounds like his dream.

Kay: He dreamed of getting on a freeway?

Lil: He dreamed of *rolling* on a freeway. He dreams everybody rolls on freeways. How'd he get up the entrance ramp?

Kay: That's the awful part. With his belt. He hooked it to some car's bumper.

Lil: He should've been killed.

Kay: Yeh—thank God it was an L.A. freeway—traffic bumper to bumper. He hadn't gone half a mile before some damn fool tailgated him.

Lil: Hit him?

Kay: Knocked him out of his chair and off the freeway.

Lil: My God—where is he?

Kay: They took him to an emergency ward.

Lil: Where?

Kay: I don't know. The policeman said he'd call back as soon as they find out.

Lil: Do they know how badly he's hurt?

Kay: Not yet—no. (*Beat.*) It's so strange about that belt.

Lil: What about the belt?

Kay: He never wears one. Why would anybody who just sits need anything to hold up his pants? So . . . since he had one with him, he must've *planned* to get on a freeway. Hooked to a bumper by a belt. It's not easy for a cripple to run away, is it? Where do you suppose he wanted to go?

Lil: You said he was on the Ventura Freeway—where is Ventura?

Kay: Oh, nobody goes to *Ventura* on the Ventura Freeway. At least I never met anybody who did. It just connects all the other freeways.

Lil: Out-of-state freeways?

Kay: (*She ponders this notion for a beat.*) You think he was headed out of state? All the way out of state on a freeway in a wheelchair? You'd really have to be fed up with California.

Lil: *Or* . . . not know you were *in* one.

Kay: Not know he's in a wheelchair? What do you mean?

Lil: I mean I'm beginning to think *he* thinks he can walk.

Kay: Walk? Walk! He better not be able to walk! As many times as I've had to haul and shove and lift and push that ass of his? We've fallen out of his damn bed a dozen times. Who the hell do you think got us back in it? (*She gestures at herself with a thumb.*)

Lil: I mean alone. When we're not here.

Kay: He walks when we're not here?

Lil: I don't mean actually. I mean in his mind. But to him it's real. He *thinks* he walks.

Kay: But what good is it to *think* it—if he can't *do* it?

Lil: I didn't say it was good. I suspect it gets him in trouble.

Kay: Ah ha! If he thinks he can walk, then he probably also thinks he could've killed them. Which explains the other dumb thing he did.

Lil: What?

Kay: When they picked him up, he confessed. He told them he killed Buddy and Paula.

Lil: I don't believe it.

Kay: (*Putting it all together.*) He probably thought he was hurt worse than he was on that freeway—so if he was dying, he sure as hell wanted credit for killing Buddy.

Lil: You've really got his number. You're terrific.

Kay: I can't seem to do anything wrong by you today.

Lil: (*Suddenly serious.*) Make it a perfect day for me. Take him. You don't have to marry him. Just take the responsibility. You've got a much better grip on life than I do.

Kay: Yes, I can see that. But what about *his* grip?

Lil: His grip is as good as anybody's.

Kay: Like hell. He just rolled onto a damn *freeway*.

Lil: Which of us doesn't go for a roll on a freeway at one time or another?

Kay: (*She takes* LIL's *hand, then:*) I sure wish I liked you as much as you like me. (*Beat.*) Why did *Paula* hate you?

Lil: She didn't hate me.

Kay: She left you out of her book, didn't she? My God.

Lil: She didn't find me interesting enough to be in a book. She never even found me interesting enough to be in the living room. Which is why I stayed in my *own* room for years. She had me convinced I wasn't interesting enough to leave it. And so when I finally did leave it, I was a shambles.

Kay: You certainly seem interesting enough now.

Lil: I'm fascinating now! But the price I've had to pay!

Kay: I'd rather have your problem than mine—the prices I've had to *charge*!

Lil: From England to New Mexico—bluebloods to redskins.

Kay: Indians? You, too? (*She giggles.* LIL *winks.*)

Lil: Kay, I can't just leave him here.

Kay: Why not? You said he inherits plenty of money. Let him *buy* who he needs.

Lil: Buy strangers?

Kay: Watch it . . .

Lil: For the rest of his life?

Kay: Lots of people have to pay. All their lives.

Lil: Yes, but *he's* never actually paid before. Even that was done for him.

Kay: Yes, but Buddy's gone now. He can't expect just anybody to take responsibility for him *and* take care of him *and* make love to him—*all* without pay? A person would have to be crazy—or in love with him. Or better, *both*.

Lil: Both? I suppose that *is* a possibility. (*The phone rings sharply. Both women turn toward it, but* LIL *is nearer. She speaks into the receiver.*) Hello . . . Dr. who?

Kay: Is that the hospital?

Lil: (*To* KAY.) Yes.

Kay: Thank God.

Lil: (*Into the receiver.*) His next of kin? My God, how bad is it? Well, no, I'm not his next of kin . . . I mean . . . well, yes . . . I am . . . I am his next of kin . . . I'm his sister—yes. What is it—tell me. What? But the—Oh, I see . . . (*There are tears.*) Yes—yes—we'll be right there—*I'll* be there right away. No, I'm fine—really. Thank you, doctor. (*She replaces the receiver.*)

Kay: What is it?

Lil: The doctor says he's in good spirits—and asking for me—but Dom felt I should know before I got there . . . in fact, he insisted the doctor tell me.

Kay: What?

Lil: The doctor thinks that somehow the fall—out there on the freeway . . . (*Suddenly between laughter and tears.*) He has just told Dom he will never walk again.

JOHNNY BULL
by Kathleen Betsko Yale

ACT II, SCENE 1

When Iris, a working-class English girl, married Joe Kovacs, an American soldier stationed in England, she expected to come to America and head straight for Hollywood to lead a life of wealth and glamour. But instead she wound up in Joe's home town, Willard Patch, Pennsylvania—an impoverished and backward mining town in Appalachia. Iris got pregnant, Joe went on welfare, and they moved in with Joe's Hungarian-born parents.

Iris's life grew more dismal with each passing day. Her relationship with Joe quickly deteriorated. Joe's father turned out to be a tyrant. And her slightly retarded sister-in-law, Katrine, resented her presence and the fact that Joe and Iris shared her room. Iris's only pleasant moments have been with Joe's mother, Marie, a stolid and hard working woman who befriends her but also drives her hard ("We get up at five. *We* fetch water . . . . Wednesday we iron.").

Just prior to the scene below Iris has tried to lift Marie's spirits by performing an English music hall song and dance. Katrine is enraged at seeing her mother laughing at Iris's antics. She reminds Marie that they are behind in their chores. Marie exits, leaving the two young women alone.

Iris: Oh, Kattie . . . . wasn't that a scream? Who needs Hollywood, eh, Duckie? We'll call ourselves the "Wild Willard Wenches" and entertain all the pickers over on the old slag heap. What d'you think?

Katrine: (*Dangerously.*) She's *my* mother. She *ain't your'n.*

Iris: I'm not going to take her away from you.

Katrine: That's right.

Iris: We can share her, Kattie.

Katrine: Leave her alone.

Iris: But I like her. What's wrong with that?

Katrine: You wouldn't like her if you knew what she done.

Iris: What do you mean?

Katrine: She done sump'n bad so you better stay away from her.

Iris: She hasn't done anything bad.

Katrine: Wanna bet?

Iris: What?

Katrine: Sump'n.

Iris: What?

Katrine: Sump'n.

Iris: Tell me!

Katrine: She killed a man.

Iris: What a terrible thing to say.

Katrine: Shot him dead.

Iris: I don't believe you.

Katrine: Ask her.

Iris: No wonder Joe smacks you. You're a naughty, jealous girl! You deserve it.

Katrine: I don't tell lies. (*She goes to the dresser and gets a yellowed newspaper, gives it to* IRIS.) It's in the paper . . . an' a picture a' Momma.

Iris: Where? (*Snatches paper. Sees photograph.*) Oh, God . . . it *is* Marie . . . it *is*!

Katrine: So better quit hangin' on her. Else she'll get you, too. (IRIS *examines paper.*) Go on . . . read it!

Iris: Mrs. Marie Kovacs is supported down the steps of the county courthouse, following her arraignment after the

shooting death of coal miner Dan Krutchik . . . Oh, God
. . . she really did. She really killed someone.

Katrine: That's why Joe went into the service. Him an'
Pishta seen it. I didn't get to see it.

Iris: But why? Why did she?

Katrine: (*Secretively.*) I got raped. Don't you tell Momma I
tol'.

Iris: You got raped?

Katrine: (*With poignant simplicity.*) Sumabitch got off
with it, Daddy said, 'cause the judge ask me was it
snowin' when it happened an' I said yes. I forgot it was
summer bein' I had my coat on. My head don't always
work too good. Daddy was mad, boy, when he seen the
blood . . .

Iris: Blood?

Katrine: It got on my Sunday apron . . . then that judge let
the Hunky go. That's why we can't go in town. Daddy
kep' sayin' he was gonna kill him . . . kep' settin' on the
porch cussin' every day, sayin' how he's gonna get that
raper if the law don't. "I'll kill him! I'll kill him!" He kep'
on sayin' it, but he didn't.

Iris: What happened?

Katrine: One day that Krutchik come offa his shift at the
mine, an' Daddy's waitin' on the porch swing to go nex'
shift, an' he's rockin' an' bangin' his dinner bucket . . . so
you could hear it clear in the house. Momma took the
bread out the oven and set it nice to cool . . . then she pick
up that rifle an' went to the screen door. "You quit that
bangin', now, Stephen." An' Daddy yell, "There goes that
no good Hunky sumbitch. One day I'll blow his head off."
(*Pause.*) So that's when Momma done it. Then she come
back an' put the lard on the bread so the crust shine . . .

Iris: (*Deeply shocked.*) That's awful.

Katrine: Well, you got to put grease on the crust else it don't
cut nice. (*Pause.*) Police let Momma take the bread over
the neighborwoman's. Momma don't like no waste. (*She
goes back to kitchen.*)

Iris: (*Follows* KATRINE.) But she's not in prison . . .

Katrine: (*Sadly.*) She got sick in the head . . . like me. They
let her go. I didn't like it when she wasn't here. (*Goes to
screen door.*) Iris, you better cover that dough with a wet
rag. (*Gently.*) She'll rise up on us, if you don't wet her

down. (*She smiles with genuine sweetness. It is the first smile she's ever given to Iris. She leaves.*)

CHEATING CHEATERS
by John Patrick

ACT I

Theresa and Angelica are nuns. Or are they? Well, actually they dress up as nuns and sit on street corners collecting money from charitable passersby who believe they are giving to a good cause. But Theresa and Angelica have used the money, first to put their niece Tania through college, and now through an expensive art school in Paris. To these oddball sisters, Tania is a very good cause indeed. During the course of the play their money-making scheme is jeopardized by some unexpected events, such as a cat burglar descending into their apartment from a skylight and a police officer who arrests Theresa for begging without a license. The scene below starts the play.

(*The hall door opens and Theresa, a diminutive nun in a traditional black habit, enters carrying a folding stool, a red pot, and a sign reading: "God Loveth A Cheerful Giver."*)

Theresa: Angelica? (*Waits.*) Angelica! (*She beams happily and puts her "accouterments" on the table. She then takes a chair and places it under the bookshelves. She mounts it and removes a book. She takes out a hidden bottle of bourbon and reads the label in joyous anticipation. Behind her, Angelica, another nun, enters unobserved. She also carries a stool, a red pot, and a sign reading: "It Is Later Than You Think." She puts these down and tiptoes up to stand behind Theresa.*)

Angelica: (*As Theresa takes a swallow.*) Theresa! (*Theresa sprays out a mouthful of bourbon.*)

Theresa: Don't do that! I've got a spastic colon!

Angelica: Hand me that bottle! (*She does, but hides the book she has removed.*) What are you hiding?

Theresa: The Bible.

Angelica: Shame on you—hiding Wild Turkey behind the Bible.

Theresa: I have a sore throat.

Angelica: Then gargle. I'll get you some salt.

Theresa: It's not the same. Lend me your hand.

Angelica: You got up there by yourself. You can jump down.

Theresa: My teeth will fall out.

Angelica: (*Extends a hand.*) I should give you the back of my hand. Sneaking drinks when I'm not here. God will punish you.

Theresa: God is going to punish both of us for pretending to be nuns. Especially since we're good Catholics . . . at least on Sunday.

Angelica: Well, He hasn't punished us for ten years. I think we're safe. (*Goes to the table and lights a cigarette.*)

Theresa: His eye is on the sparrow, that's why. Deception is a sin.

Angelica: If your conscience is bothering you after all these years—go to confession. Then you can sin again with a clear conscience.

Theresa: (*Whimpers.*) I'm running out of churches. Oh, Angelica, I hate being a fraud.

Angelica: Well, at least we're respectable frauds.

Theresa: We're sneaky, freaky frauds. We let people put their pennies in our pots thinking it's for a good cause.

Angelica: It *is* for a good cause. It's put our darling Tania through college. And it's a much nicer profession than prostitution, according to Reader's Digest.

Theresa: The Bible says, "Woe to him that buildeth his house by unrighteousness."

Angelica: It also says, "Woe to the bloody city." We live in what the Bible calls a "generation of vipers."

Theresa: And according to Job 8:13, He warns, "The hypocrite shall perish and his trust shall be a spider web." I hate spiders.

Angelica: Well, I know the Bible as well as you do, my dear. As Matthew says, "Ye hypocrite—ye can discern the face of the sky but can ye discern the sign of the times?" Well, you bet I can. It says "survive or sink."

Theresa: Yes, but Luke says, "Thou hypocrite! Doth not each one of you on the Sabbath loose his ass from the stall."

Angelica: Well, since neither one of us hustles on Sunday, I think our asses are safe.

Theresa: Matthew says, "Cursed be the deceiver."

Angelica: Will you stop hiding behind the Bible. It's bad enough that you use it to hide your Wild Turkey.

Theresa: Well, I can't help worrying. Someday one of us is going to be arrested.

Angelica: Theresa dear, stop worrying. You're life expectancy is getting shorter by the minute. Don't waste it worrying. There will be time for that when you get to Heaven.

Theresa: That's what worries me. I may never get there.

Angelica: You will if you repent. But wait until you're eighty—that will give you a happy goal to look forward to in your old age.

Theresa: Couldn't we put part of our ill-gotten gains in the poor box at the church? I'd sleep better.

Angelica: And have them stolen?

Theresa: Then why couldn't we give a percentage of what we get to the Humane Society or Wayward Girls? Then we'd really be Sisters of Charity. We're already blood sisters.

Angelica: We're going to need every cent for Tania's vacation. She wants to go back to Switzerland.

Theresa: I'll go without breakfast . . . at least butter.

Angelica: Oh, all right. How much do you want to give away to salve your conscience?

Theresa: Twelve percent.

Angelica: Why twelve?

Theresa: There were twelve Apostles in the Bible.

Angelica: We'll give ten. There are only ten Commandments. What are you doing home this early anyway?

Theresa: I had to go to the toilet.

Angelica: You could have gone down to the subway toilet.

Theresa: No! With all those dirty words on the wall. Have you ever seen a nun in a public toilet? Of course not—it's indecent.

Angelica: Come to think of it, I've never seen a nun in any toilet—maybe they just dehydrate. Now you better get back to your subway exit, or you'll miss the Bronx traffic going home. (*Sits to count money.*)

Theresa: Angelica, why can't I sit outside of Saks for a change? You meet such a better class of people.

Angelica: Because they're rich. And rich people don't give as much as poor people. That's why they're rich.

Theresa: But Bronx people going home from work look so unhappy—as if they have a toothache or hemorrhoids—it depresses me.

Angelica: That's because poverty pinches, dear. Have you forgotten?

Theresa: Why do all the working people live in the suburbs? It costs them subway fare to get there and they waste their valuable time getting home to their wives and boiled cabbage.

Angelica: Read your Bible. "The poor of the earth hide themselves together." So get back to your post and help them feel noble by taking their money. They probably cheated someone out of it anyhow.

Theresa: (*At the door.*) Couldn't I have just an itsy-bitsy bit of bourbon before I go back just to give me moral strength?

Angelica: No! (*Holds up an object.*) What's this? Someone put a Masonic button in your bucket!

Theresa: Maybe it was all some poor soul had.

Angelica: Nonsense—people just aren't honest anymore.

Theresa: Isn't that the pot calling the kettle black—begging for a living.

Angelica: We do *not* beg. We sit on our little stools and look a little sad. If people want to put their little pennies in our little pots, that's their mistake. Our little pots have put little Tania through college—and art school as well. That's all that matters.

Theresa: I guess you're right. Was there any mail from her today?

Angelica: She's probably too busy painting pictures of saints for French cathedrals.

Theresa: (*Returns from the door.*) Maybe she's sick.

Angelica: You can't expect her to write us every day.

Theresa: *We* do. We write *her* every day.

Angelica: We'll get a letter tomorrow. (*Hands back the Masonic button.*) And for God sake—will you stop taking buttons! Keep your eyes open! You could be robbed.

Theresa: Maybe she's been run over and God is punishing us.

Angelica: God wouldn't punish Tania just to punish us. That's negative thinking. Be optimistic.

Theresa: All right. Maybe she's pregnant.

Angelica: Theresa dear, you know damn well that Tania stutters. And girls who stutter rarely get pregnant. But don't ask me why.

Theresa: Why?

Angelica: I don't know, dear—maybe that's why she wanted to be an artist. Maybe it's a kind of compensation—to have her paintings speak for her. Lots of famous artists stutter. Michelangelo, Giotto, Da Vinci—

Theresa: Is that true?

Angelica: No, but it's a good argument. (*Points to an abstract picture on the wall.*) You like that beautiful painting she sent us, don't you?

Theresa: Oh, I *do* like it, but I wish I knew what it meant.

Angelica: It doesn't have to *mean* anything. Does a rose have meaning—a sunset?

Theresa: It means the day is over.

Angelica: Well, doesn't her painting make you *Think*?

Theresa: Yes. I think it's upside down.

Angelica: Oh, get back to your subway station. I'm trying to add, and I can't add anyway.

Theresa: You're mean to me. And you're bossy, too.

Angelica: I am not bossy. I'm efficient. There's a difference.

Theresa: Yes—the difference is they're spelled different.

Angelica: (*Puts her arm around Theresa.*) And I'm not mean to you, dear. Whatever I do or say is for your own good.

Theresa: Why is it that everything that's for my own good never feels good, looks good, or tastes good.

Angelica: Now you've no grounds for complaint, dear. We're doing all right.

Theresa: We're cheating people. And I hate cheaters.

Angelica: Cheating is a respectable, national practice. Ask anyone who pays income tax.

Theresa: I wish I'd married that nice boy, Otis, that was in love with me in high school. His father had the biggest turkey ranch in Pyorrhea, Texas.

Angelica: Yes, dear. You could have been Turkey Queen.

Theresa: Do you know for Christmas once, he gave me a life subscription to "Turkey World"? He said if I married him he'd give me a mink coat. Do you think, after we pay for the vacuum cleaner, I could have a mink coat?

Angelica: Nuns don't wear mink coats, dear.

Theresa: But I'm not a nun on Sundays. I could wear it to confession.

Angelica: A mink coat! I'm ashamed of you. Think of all those poor little minks, and chinchillas, and bunny rabbits that are killed and skinned just to make coats when celanese would do just as well. In my opinion, ladies who lust for mink—stink.

Theresa: Well, you don't get a chill in chinchilla, and you can freeze in celanese. As for me, I'd just as soon stink in mink.

Angelica: And just where did you read that bit of wisdom?

Theresa: "Turkey World."

Angelica: Well, I'll tell you what I'll do, dear. For Christmas I'll buy you a beautiful coat of genuine Russian burlap.

Theresa: We'll probably spend Christmas in jail.

Angelica: Nonsense. We've had a successful career, so don't be so glum.

Theresa: I can't help it! I just know one of us is going to be arrested someday—and be hanged. (*Goes to door and stops.*) Well, here I go to the gallows.

Angelica: Don't say that! Don't be negative! (*Shouts.*) Be happy!

Theresa: (*Winces.*) All right—I'm happy. (*Grimaces.*) See? And I'll be back in an hour—unless I'm arrested.

Angelica: And don't run home. Nuns don't run. I'll have dinner ready. I'll fix eggs Benedict for you. That should cheer you up. St. Benedict was a martyr, too.

Theresa: Eating an egg only depresses me. You're really eating a poor future chicken.

Angelica: Well, maybe it will rain. That should make you happy.

Theresa: Well at least it washes the doggy-doo away.

Angelica: Oh! Get back to work! You're depressing me. And for Heaven's sake, while you're sitting on your stool, don't whistle either. Nuns don't whistle.

Theresa: Yes, Angelica. (*She exits whistling with her bucket and sign.*)

Angelica: (*She sits at table and looks heavenward.*) Oh Lord, look after my dear, dumb sister. She means well. But, you know what happens to well-meaning people— they always get run over by a dump truck or ambulance. (*She begins to count coins again, singing, "I Got The Whole World In My Hands." After a moment, she rises.*)

Well, that's that . . . as the mortician said when he closed the coffin. (*Starts out, sighing.*) Oh, my aching back. I wish I were born eighty years old and grew younger as I got older. I could end my days happily back in my dear mother's womb instead of a wheelchair or the grave. Of course, by the time I got back to the womb, Mother would be a hundred and ten. Oh, well. (*She goes into the kitchen.*)

LIFE AND LIMB
by Keith Reddin

ACT II, SCENE 7

It is almost Christmas in 1954. Effie is alone in her apartment, her Christmas tree decorated and lit. Her husband Franklin is out shopping. Franklin lost an arm in the Korean War, and since his return a year ago he has not been able to find work. He is moody and depressed and critical of everything that Effie says and does. Effie's one confidante is her closest friend, Doina. Doina's family immigrated from Romania, and although Franklin considers her stupid and shallow, Effie likes her and enjoys her company. In particular they share a passion for movies and collect pictures of movie stars.

The scene starts as Doina enters, arms loaded with presents.

Doina: So a very merry Christmas.
Effie: Thank you, Doina.
Doina: Where is Franklin? Is he at home?
Effie: He's out shopping.
Doina: How nice the apartment looks. Franklin is a lucky fellow.
Effie: I guess.
Doina: In Romania, we never have a tree such as this one.
Effie: Franklin picked it out for me.
Doina: It is quite beautiful.
Effie: Thank you.

Doina: May I put the packages down? (*She dumps the packages.*)

Effie: Oh sure.

Doina: You see the movie this week?

Effie: You mean the Montgomery Clift?

Doina: Oh, yes.

Effie: Not yet. But I got it. The picture. (*She holds out envelope.*) He signed it too.

Doina: You must be very happy.

Effie: Yeah, I guess. (*Pause.*) Doina, are you and Jerome happy?

Doina: Happy. How do you mean happy?

Effie: Happy happy.

Doina: Effie, I'm married to him. (*Thinks.*) We are not happy like that. But we are happy enough.

Effie: Oh.

Doina: Are you and Franklin having difficulties now?

Effie: I guess.

Doina: Do you want to tell me?

Effie: I'm so unhappy.

Doina: That's no good.

Effie: We never talk to each other.

Doina: Yes. . . .

Effie: Franklin doesn't like to spend time with me.

Doina: I see . . . .

Effie: So, I'm dating someone else.

Doina: Yes.

Effie: It's this guy who works at the plant.

Doina: Do I know him?

Effie: Naw.

Doina: Go on.

Effie: I make love to him.

Doina: Good. (*Effie buries head in hands.*)

Effie: Oh, God!

Doina: How often do you have intercourse?

Effie: I guess at first once or twice a week, we would sneak off, but now we're doing it every day.

Doina: And is the intercourse good?

Effie: I guess.

Doina: Go on . . .

Effie: Well, that's about it. But I'm so unhappy about the whole thing. I mean, here I am cheating on Franklin, my husband.

Doina: Yes.

Effie: Doina, I'm a Catholic.

Doina: You have told me this.

Effie: But it's a sin. A very serious sin. I could go to hell.

Doina: Oh, we all go to hell. I know that.

Effie: Yeah, but like I was brought up you were only supposed to have sex to have babies.

Doina: But that's silly.

Effie: Yeah, I know but there you are.

Doina: So you have sex with this man every day?

Effie: Yeah—

Doina: Do you love him?

Effie: I don't think so.

Doina: Did you buy him a Christmas gift?

Effie: Naw.

Doina: You should have gotten him something.

Effie: I know.

Doina: You want my advice?

Effie: Yes.

Doina: You sleep with this man, and when you get tired of him, you don't sleep with him anymore.

Effie: You think so?

Doina: I have just told you this.

Effie: Okay.

Doina: I am faithful to Jerome, sometimes I don't know why, but this is the way I am. You are different.

Effie: That's true.

Doina: I want you to be happy at Christmas. It is the time of good cheer.

Effie: I'm just miserable about this.

Doina: Don't tell Franklin about this sex otherwise your holidays might be ruined.

Effie: Good thought.

Doina: So, have a good Christmas. There are my presents to you and Franklin.

Effie: Thank you. Here's my thing for you and Jerome. Franklin helped me pick it out.

Doina: Franklin, he's not crazy about me.

Effie: He's very moody.

Doina: Okay, have a happy holiday.

Effie: So we go to the movies again soon?

Doina: You bet.

Scenes for Two Men

BRIGHTON BEACH MEMOIRS
by Neil Simon

ACT I

It is 1937, and Eugene Jerome is fifteen years old and living in Brighton Beach with his parents, his older brother, his
widowed aunt and her two daughters. Today is a tough day in
the Jerome household. Eugene's father, like many fathers during those deep Depression years, barely ekes out a livelihood
for his family, even with two jobs. Today he learned that one
of the companies he worked for went bankrupt. And this
afternoon Eugene's brother, Stanley, received an ultimatum
from his boss to write an apology for his insubordination at
work, lest he be fired (Stanley spoke up for a fellow worker
who was being treated unfairly.). And earlier today, Eugene's
beautiful sixteen-year-old cousin Nora was "picked out" by a
"producer" who stopped by her dance class to hold auditions
for a road show of a Broadway musical. She is excited. Her
mother, to say the least, is not. All this (and more) is background, though, to Eugene's central concern today—let us
say, his obsession—with his cousin Nora's breasts. As Eugene
himself describes it to the audience, "What I'm about to tell
you next is so secret and private that I've left instructions for
my memoirs not to be opened until thirty years after my death
. . . I, Eugene M. Jerome, have committed a mortal sin by
lusting after my cousin Nora. I can tell you all this now because I'll be dead when you're reading it . . . If I had my
choice between a tryout with the Yankees and actually seeing
her bare breasts for two and a half seconds, I would have some
serious thinking to do."

In the scene that follows, Stanley and Eugene are in their bedroom. Stanley is lying on his bed, deep in thought, wondering how to tell his father about the letter of apology he was told to write. Eugene is sitting on his bed, banging a baseball into his glove.

Stanley: Will you stop that? I'm trying to think.

Eugene: I'm glad I don't have your problems.

Stanley: How'd you like an official American League baseball in your mouth?

Eugene: I've got to talk to you, Stanley. I mean a really serious, important talk.

Stanley: Everybody in this house has to have a talk with somebody. Take a number off the wall and wait your turn.

Eugene: I had a dream last night. It was about this girl. I can't tell you her name but she's gorgeous. We were really kissing hard and rubbing up against each other and I felt this tremendous build-up coming like at the end of *The Thirty-nine Steps*. And suddenly there was an explosion. Like a dam broke and everything rushed and flowed out to sea. It was the greatest feeling I ever had in my life . . . and when I woke up, I was—I was—

Stanley: All wet.

Eugene: (*Surprised.*) Yeah! How'd you know?

Stanley: (*Unimpressed.*) It was a wet dream. You had a wet dream. I have them all the time.

Eugene: You do? You mean there's nothing wrong with you if it happens?

Stanley: You never had one before?

Eugene: Yeah, but I slept through it.

Stanley: Didn't you ever try to do it by yourself?

Eugene: What do you mean?

Stanley: Didn't you ever diddle with yourself?

Eugene: No. Never.

Stanley: Baloney. I've heard you. You diddle three, four times a week.

Eugene: You're crazy! What do you mean, diddle?

Stanley: Whack off. Masturbate.

Eugene: Will you be quiet! Laurie might hear you.

Stanley: There's nothing wrong with it. Everybody does it. Especially at our age. It's natural.

Eugene: What do you mean, everybody? You know guys who do it?

Stanley: Every guy I know does it. Except Haskell Fleischmann, the fat kid. He does it to the other guys.

Eugene: I can't believe I'm having this conversation.

Stanley: You can't grow up without doing it. Your voice won't change.

Eugene: Where do you get this stuff from? Is it in a medical book or something?

Stanley: It's puberty.

Eugene: It's what?

Stanley: Puberty. You never heard that word before? You don't read books?

Eugene: Yeah. *The Citadel* by A. J. Cronin. He never mentioned puberty.

Stanley: Even Pop did it.

Eugene: Pop? *Our* pop? You know what, Stanley? I think you're full of shit.

Stanley: (*Sits up.*) Hey! Don't you use that language. Who do you think you are? You're just a kid. Never let me hear you say that word again.

Eugene: I don't get you. You mean it's okay for you to say "puberty" but I can't say "shit"?

Stanley: "Puberty" is a scientific word. "Shit" is for those guys who hang around the beach.

Eugene: What do you expect me to say when you tell me that Pop whacks off?

Stanley: I don't mean he still does it, because he's married now. But when he was a kid. Fourteen or fifteen. The whole world whacks off.

Eugene: President Roosevelt too?

Stanley: Rich kids are the worst. They whack off from morning till night. In college, they sit around in their dorms drinking beer and whacking off.

Eugene: Stanley, this is the most useful information you ever taught me . . . What about girls?

Stanley: Five times as much as boys.

Eugene: *Five* times as much? Is that an actual figure? Where do you know all this from?

Stanley: You pick it up. You learn it. It's handed down from generation to generation. That's how our culture spreads.

Eugene: Five times as much as boys? Some of them don't

even say hello to you and they're home all night whacking off.

Stanley: They're human just like we are. They have the same needs and desires.

Eugene: Then why is it so hard to touch their boobs?

Stanley: If you were a girl, would you like some guy jumping at you and grabbing your boobs?

Eugene: If I had boobs, I would love to touch them, wouldn't you?

Stanley: I've got my own problems to think about.

Eugene: How do girls do it?

Stanley: I can't explain it.

Eugene: Please, Stanley. I'll be your slave for a month. Tell me how they do it.

Stanley: I need a pencil and paper. I'll do it later.

Eugene: (*Quickly hands him his notebook and a pencil.*) Do you want crayons? Maybe you should do it in color?

Stanley: Hey, Eugene. I have a major problem in my life. I haven't got time to draw girls masturbating for you.

Eugene: I'll bet Nora doesn't do it.

Stanley: Boy, could I win money from you. You think she's in the bathroom seven times a day just taking showers?

Eugene: She does it in the bathroom?

Stanley: I knew two girls who used to do it in English class. I saw a girl do it during a final exam and she got a ninety-eight on her paper . . . Is she the one you were thinking about last night?

Eugene: No. It was somebody else. One of the beach girls.

Stanley: It was Nora. I see what's going on. I knew why you dropped your napkin twelve times at dinner tonight.

Eugene: She drives me crazy. I think I'm in love with her.

Stanley: Yeah? Well, forget it. She's your cousin.

Eugene: What's wrong with being in love with your cousin?

Stanley: Because it's against the laws of nature. If she was your stepsister, it would be dirty, but it would be okay. But you can't love your own cousin. Let me give you a piece of advice: When you're going through puberty, don't start with anyone in your own house.

Eugene: Who made up those rules? Franklin Roosevelt married his cousin.

Stanley: Maybe she was his second or third cousin. But you can't marry your first cousin. You get babies with nine heads . . . I wish Pop would get back. I got to talk to him tonight.

Eugene: I still would love to see her naked. Just once. There's nothing wrong with that, is there?

Stanley: No. I do it all the time.

Eugene: *You've seen Nora naked?*

Stanley: Lots of times. I fixed the lock on the bathroom door, then opened it pretending I didn't know anyone was in there.

Eugene: I can't believe it. What a pig! . . . What did she look like?

Stanley: All I can tell you is I was pretty miserable she was my first cousin.

(*He lies back on his bed.* EUGENE *turns and looks out at the audience.*)

Eugene: That was the night I discovered lust and guilt were very closely related. (*To* STANLEY.) I have to wash up.

Stanley: (*Teasingly.*) Have a good time.

Eugene: I don't do that.

ANTON CHEKHOV'S "THE DUEL"
adapted by Michael Schulman and Eva Mekler
from the translation by Ann Dunnigan

ACT I, SCENE 1

The play takes place in the 1880's in a small sea town on the fringe of the Russian Empire in the Caucasus by the Black Sea. It is early morning in the parlor of Aleksandre Davidych Samoilenko, a middle-aged army physician. Alone in the parlor is Ivan Andreich Layevsky, a young man in his late twenties.

Layevsky comes from a wealthy St. Petersburg family. He ran away to the Caucasus two years ago with his mistress (a married woman), seeking a meaningful life in which he would earn a living through his own labors. He took a position as an official in the Ministry of Finance, but quickly found his new life tedious and dull. As the scene opens, Layevsky is reading a letter. He puts it away quickly as Samoilenko enters.

(For more information see other scenes from this play in other sections of the book.)

Samoilenko: So early, Ivan Andreich? Is this for professional reasons or just to visit? Are you ill?

Layevsky: I'm sorry. I wasn't able to sleep. Is it too early for you? Shall I come back later?

Samoilenko: No, no, my friend, sit down. In fact, I've meant to tell you to come by for an examination. I've noticed that you've been nervous lately, and distracted. That's not usual for you, and quite frankly, you look rather pale to me.

Layevsky: I've been having trouble sleeping lately. Sasha, have you some vodka?

Samoilenko: Vodka? This early in the day?

Layevsky: Never mind, never mind . . . Sasha . . .

Samoilenko: Sit, sit . . . one moment, let me get my instruments.

Layevsky: Aleksandre Davidych, I'm just tired. I'm sure my physical health is sound.

Samoilenko: One should not take sleeplessness lightly. There are many physical ailments that can cause insomnia without your even suspecting they are there. It's probably nothing serious, but it certainly pays to be cautious. No arguments! Let's have a little look. Unbutton your shirt. There. Good. Does this hurt?

Layevsky: No.

Samoilenko: Here?

Layevsky: No.

Samoilenko: Good. Now turn your head sideways, take a deep breath, and hold it.

(During most of the ensuing scene, SAMOILENKO continues to examine LAYEVSKY, palpating, listening with stethoscope, checking eyes, ears, nose, throat, etc.)

Layevsky: Sasha . . .

Samoilenko: Breath . . . hold . . .

Layevsky: Aleksandre Davidych, answer one question for me. Suppose you had fallen in love with a woman, had lived with her, say for over two years, and then as often happens, fell out of love . . .

Samoilenko: One second, turn to the other side. Breath . . . hold.

Layevsky: Aleksandre Davidych . . .

Samoilenko: Wait, let me look in your mouth. Tongue out— good. Go "ah."

Layevsky: Ah.

Samoilenko: Again.

Layevsky: Ah.

Samoilenko: A little infection there. Too much smoking. I'll mix up a gargle for you, and make sure you take it. Of course, a sore throat can interfere with sleep.

Layevsky: Aleksandre Davidych, please . . . can I speak to you frankly, as a friend?

Samoilenko: Of course.

Layevsky: Things are going badly with Nadyezhda Fyodorovna and me . . . in fact, very badly! Forgive me for discussing my private life with you, but I've lived with her for two years now and have stopped loving her; or perhaps there never was any love. These two years have been a delusion. Sasha, talk to me. I know perfectly well you can't help me, but I'm desperate and I'm ineffectual, and conversation is my only comfort. I have to find an explanation and justification for my absurd life in talk, in someone else's theories, even in literary types; in the notion, for instance, that we noblemen are degenerating, and so on. Last night, for example, I kept consoling myself by thinking: Ah, how right Tolstoy was, how fundamentally right! And that made me feel better.

Samoilenko: Yes, all the other authors write from imagination, while he writes straight from nature . . .

Layevsky: My God, we have been mutilated by civilization!

Samoilenko: Yes, I'm listening to you, but turn around.

Layevsky: I fell in love with a married woman and she fell in love with me. In the beginning there were the kisses, intimate evenings, vows; there was Spencer and ideals, and common interests . . . What a deception! We lied to ourselves that we were running away from the emptiness of our lives, when we were actually only running away from her husband—it was a game, an adventure . . . an entertainment to break the tedium. What fantasies we had about our future. We would rush off here to the Caucasus and I would launch my life of usefulness by entering the civil service. Then, in time, we'd find a plot of land and with the sweat of our brows work the land: plant a vineyard, fields, and so on. If it had been you or that zoologist of yours, Von Koren, you would have lived with Nadyezhda Fyodorovna for thirty years, perhaps, and left your heirs a rich vineyard and three thousand acres of maize. As for me, from the very first I knew my ideas about farming and a life of labor were worthless and self-deceiving. I found the heat here unbearable, the town dull, barren; you go out into the country and under every bush and stone there's an insect or a scorpion or a snake ready to bite you; and beyond the fields—mountains, desert. Alien people, alien nature, a pitiful culture . . . All this, my friend, is not so easy as it seemed then in Petersburg, strolling along the Nevsky in a fur coat, arm in arm with Nadyezhda, dreaming of the sunny south. I am a misplaced person. And as for love, I can tell you that living with a woman who has read Spencer and has followed you to the ends of the earth is no more exciting than living with any other woman. There's the same smell of ironing, of powder, of medicines, the same curl papers every morning, the same self-deception . . .

Samoilenko: You can't run a household without ironing. You're out of sorts today, Vanya, I can see that. Nadyezhda Fyodorovna is a fine woman, very beautiful, well educated, and you—you're a man of the greatest intelligence . . . Of course, the two of you can't be married but that's not your fault and, besides, one must be able to rise above such outdated conventions, one must move with the times. I believe in free love, myself; yes . . . but in my opinion, once you've lived together you ought to go on living together for the rest of your lives.

Layevsky: Without love?

Samoilenko: Now let me explain something to you. Lean forward a bit . . . fine. (*Checking his eyes.*) Eight years ago we had an old fellow, an agent here—a man of the greatest intelligence. He used to say: the major ingredient in a marriage is patience. Do you hear, Vanya? Not love, but patience.

Layevsky: You may believe your old agent, but to me his advice is absolute nonsense. One can only exercise patience by treating a person you no longer love as an object, something indispensable to one's routine; but I haven't fallen that low yet. If I want to exercise patience I'll take up chess or buy an unruly horse and leave human beings in peace . . . Enough of this! Where is my vest.

Samoilenko: Wait, I haven't checked your pressure.

Layevsky: Right now, it's quite high; believe me, quite high . . .

Samoilenko: Vanya, you misunderstand what I'm saying . . .

Layevsky: Just answer one question for me—a technical question.

Samoilenko: Ask.

Layevsky: What does softening of the brain mean?

Samoilenko: It's . . . how can I explain it to you? . . . It's a disease in which the brain becomes softer . . . as if it were dissolving. Why do you ask? You don't think your sleeplessness is . . . Are you having headaches?

Layevsky: No, no, no, my friend, no . . . Sasha, can't you appreciate the position I'm in? On the one hand I can't live with her, I simply cannot. And at the same time it's impossible to leave her. She's alone, she can't work, neither of us has any money . . . What would become of her? Whom could she turn to? This awful indecision . . . How true was Shakespeare's observation, oh, how true . . . There's nothing I can think of . . . Advise me: what am I to do?

Samoilenko: Does she love you?

Layevsky: Yes, she loves me, for all that means. Given her age and temperament she needs a man. It would be as hard for her to give me up as it would be to give up her powder or her curl papers. I'm an indispensable part of her boudoir.

Samoilenko: You're not yourself today, Vanya. It's probably the lack of sleep.

Layevsky: Yes . . . altogether I feel miserable, empty, numb. I feel a kind of weakness . . . I must get away.

Samoilenko: Where to?

Layevsky: The north. To the pines, to the crisp air, to people, ideas . . . I'd give half my life to be bathing right now in some little stream near Moscow or Tula, to feel chilly, and then to stroll about for a few hours with even the worst student, talking and talking; and the scent of hay! Do you remember? And evenings, walking in a garden and hearing the sound of a piano in the house, hearing a train pass . . .

Samoilenko: I haven't been in Russia for eighteen years. I've forgotten what it's like. In my opinion, there's not a place on earth more magnificent than the Caucasus.

Layevsky: If I were offered my choice of being a chimney sweep in Petersburg or a prince here, I'd take the chimney sweep.

Samoilenko: My dear, sad friend . . . Is your mother living? Can you turn to her?

Layevsky: She's living, but we are not on good terms. She couldn't forgive me for this affair. She still fancies herself an aristocrat and insists that I've disgraced the family name by running off with a married woman. Aleksandre Davidych, there is something else, but it must remain between you and me. I'm keeping it from Nadyezhda Fyodorovna for now so don't let it slip out in front of her. I received a letter this morning telling me her husband had died of softening of the brain.

Samoilenko: May the kingdom of heaven be his. Why are you keeping it from her?

Layevsky: To show her that letter would simply mean "Let's go to the church and get married." Before I show it to her we must clarify our relations. When she understands that we can't go on living together, I'll show her the letter. It will be safe then.

Samoilenko: Do you know what, Vanya? Marry her, my dear boy.

Layevsky: Why?

Samoilenko: Fulfill your obligation to that splendid woman. Her husband has died. This is the hand of providence showing you what to do.

Layevsky: But don't you understand that this is impossible . . . deceitful . . . ?

Samoilenko: But it is your duty.

Layevsky: Why is it my duty?

Samoilenko: Because by taking her away from her husband you assumed responsibility.

Layevsky: But I'm telling you in plain Russian, I don't love her!

Samoilenko: All right, there's no love, but you can respect her, show her consideration . . .

Layevsky: Respect her, show her consideration . . . you'd think she was an abbess . . . You're a poor psychologist and physician if you think that all a woman wants from a man she is living with is respect and consideration. The most important thing for a woman is what happens in the bedroom.

Samoilenko: Vanya, Vanya . . . Shush!

Layevsky: You think like a child, you're unrealistic, and we shall never understand each other. Let's end this conversation.

Samoilenko: You're spoiled, my friend. Fate has sent you a young, beautiful, cultivated woman, and you refuse the gift; while I—if God were to give me some lopsided old woman—so long as she was kind and affectionate, I'd live with her in my own little vineyard and . . . and the old witch could at least look after the samovar for me. I am truly fond of you. We drink, we laugh together. But I simply do not understand you. You are an educated man, but you foolishly discount the many simple pleasures this life has to offer you: the pride that comes from putting on a new white tunic and freshly polished boots and then strolling down the boulevard and being greeted with respect by passing friends; the contentment that comes from feeling the warm ocean breeze and observing that the cypresses and eucalyptuses have grown taller and fuller since last you noticed them; of awakening to the smell of strong coffee and looking forward to a small glass of cognac after breakfast. For me it is doing a day's work and feeling satisfied at the end of the day knowing that the patients have been treated and the infirmary is empty. My advice to you is to marry Nadyezhda Fyodorovna, to devote yourself to her and to your work, and to open your eyes to the many small wonders that you are now blind to.

Layevsky: I can only reply to you that everything she does or says seems to me to be a lie or the equivalent of a lie, and everything unpleasant I have ever read about women and love seems to apply perfectly to myself, to Nadyezhda Fyodorovna, and to her husband. At this moment what I detest above all about her is her bare white neck with the little curls at the nape. Remember when Anna Karenina stopped loving her husband what she disliked most were his ears. Tolstoy! How right Tolstoy was! You see, my friend, I am not insensitive to the small details in life. On the contrary, they constantly remind me of my present unhappiness . . . I will go home now (*Spot on* LAYEVSKY *as he crosses away from* SAMOILENKO. *The lights fade on* SAMOILENKO *as they come up on* NADYEZHDA FYODOROVNA *seated at a table on the other side of stage*) and when I get there Nadyezhda Fyodorovna will be sitting at the window already dressed, her hair done and with a preoccupied expression on her face, drinking coffee and leafing through a thick magazine. Drinking coffee is clearly not a sufficiently remarkable event to warrant such a preoccupied expression. She will have wasted her time on such a fashionable coiffure since there is no one to attract and no occasion for it. The magazine, too, represents a lie—she will have dressed and arranged her hair in order to appear beautiful and she will be reading—not for pleasure or enlightenment—but so that she will give the impression that she is intelligent.

GLENGARRY GLEN ROSS
by David Mamet

SCENE 2

Moss and Aaronow are real-estate salesmen and both are having a hard time making sales. They have just finished their meal at a Chinese restaurant and are venting their frustrations about their business.

(For more information see other scenes from this play in "Monologues for Men" section of this book.)

Moss: Polacks and deadbeats.

Aaronow: . . . Polacks . . .

Moss: Deadbeats *all*.

Aaronow: . . . they hold on to their money . . .

Moss: All of 'em. They, *hey:* it happens to us all.

Aaronow: Where am I going to work?

Moss: You have to cheer up, George, you aren't out yet.

Aaronow: I'm not?

Moss: You missed a fucking sale. Big deal. A deadbeat Polack. Big deal. How you going to sell 'em in the *first* place . . . ? Your mistake, you shoun'a took the lead.

Aaronow: I had to.

Moss: You had to, yeah. Why?

Aaronow: To get on the . . .

Moss: To get on the board. Yeah. How you goan'a get on the board sell'n a Polack? And I'll tell you, I'll tell you what *else*. You listening? I'll tell you what else: don't ever try to sell an Indian.

Aaronow: I'd never try to sell an Indian.

Moss: You get those names come up, you ever get 'em, "Patel"?

Aaronow: Mmm . . .

Moss: You ever get 'em?

Aaronow: Well, I think I had one once.

Moss: You did?

Aaronow: I . . . I don't know.

Moss: You had one you'd know it. *Patel.* They keep coming up. I don't know. They like to talk to salesmen. *(Pause.)* They're *lonely*, something. *(Pause.)* They like to feel *superior*, I don't know. Never bought a fucking thing. You're sitting down "The Rio Rancho *this*, the blah blah blah," "The Mountain View—" "Oh yes. My brother told me that. . . ." They got a grapevine. Fuckin' Indians, George. Not my cup of tea. Speaking of which I want to tell you something: *(Pause.)* I never got a cup of tea with them. You see them in the restaurants. A supercilious race. What is this *look* on their face all the time? I don't know. *(Pause.)* I don't know. Their broads all look like they just got fucked with a dead *cat*, *I* don't know. (*Pause.*) I don't know. I don't like it. Christ . . .

Aaronow: What?

Moss: The whole fuckin' thing . . . The pressure's just too great. You're ab . . . you're absolu . . . they're too important. All of them. You go in the door. I . . . "I got to *close* this fucker, or I don't eat lunch," "or I don't win the *Cadillac* . . . ." We fuckin' work too hard. You work too hard. We all, I remember when we were at Platt . . . huh? Glen Ross Farms . . . *didn't* we sell a bunch of that . . . ?

Aaronow: They came in and they, you know . . .

Moss: Well, they fucked it up.

Aaronow: They did.

Moss: They killed the goose.

Aaronow: They did.

Moss: And now . . .

Aaronow: We're stuck with *this* . . .

Moss: We're stuck with *this* fucking shit . . .

Aaronow: . . . *this* shit . . .

Moss: It's too . . .

Aaronow: It is.

Moss: Eh?

Aaronow: It's too . . .

Moss: You get a bad month, all of a . . .

Aaronow: You're on this . . .

Moss: All of, they got you on this "board . . ."

Aaronow: I, I . . . I . . .

Moss: Some *contest* board . . .

Aaronow: I . . .

Moss: It's not right.

Aaronow: It's not.

Moss: No. (*Pause.*)

Aaronow: And it's not right to the *customers*.

Moss: I know it's not. I'll tell you, you got, you know, you got . . . what did I learn as a kid on Western? Don't sell a guy one car. Sell him *five* cars over fifteen years.

Aaronow: That's right?

Moss: Eh . . . ?

Aaronow: That's right?

Moss: Goddamn right, that's right. Guys come on: "Oh, the blah blah blah, *I* know what I'll do: I'll go in and rob everyone blind and go to Argentina cause nobody ever *thought* of this before."

Aaronow: . . . that's right . . .

Moss: Eh?

Aaronow: No. That's absolutely right.

Moss: And so they kill the goose. I, I, I'll . . . and a fuckin' *man*, worked all his *life* has got to . . .

Aaronow: . . . that's right . . .

Moss: . . . cower in his boots . . .

Aaronow: (*Simultaneously with* "*boots.*") Shoes, boots, yes . . .

Moss: For some fuckin' "Sell ten thousand and you win the steak knives . . ."

Aaronow: for some *sales* pro . . .

Moss: . . . sales promotion, "You *lose*, then we fire your . . ." No. It's *medieval* . . . it's wrong. "Or we're going to fire your ass." It's wrong.

Aaronow: Yes.

Moss: Yes, it is. And you know who's responsible?

Aaronow: Who?

Moss: You know who it is. It's Mitch. And Murray. 'Cause it doesn't have to be this way.

Aaronow: No.

Moss: Look at Jerry Graff. He's *clean*, he's doing business for *himself*, he's got his, that *list* of his with the *nurses* . . . see? You see? That's *thinking*. Why take ten percent? A ten percent comm . . . why are we giving the rest away? What are we giving ninety per . . . for *nothing*. For some jerk sit in the office tell you "Get out there and close." "Go win the Cadillac." Graff. He goes out and *buys*. He pays top dollar for the . . . you see?

Aaronow: Yes.

Moss: That's *thinking*. Now, he's got the leads, he goes in business for *himself*. He's . . . that's what I . . . that's *thinking*! "Who? Who's got a steady *job*, a couple bucks nobody's touched, who?"

Aaronow: Nurses.

Moss: So Graff buys a fucking list of nurses, one grand—if he paid two I'll eat my hat—four, five thousand nurses, and he's going *wild* . . .

Aaronow: He is?

Moss: He's doing *very* well.

Aaronow: I heard that they were running cold.

Moss: The nurses?

Aaronow: Yes.

Moss: You hear a *lot* of things. . . . He's doing very well. He's doing *very* well.

Aaronow: With River Oaks?

Moss: River Oaks, Brook Farms. *All* of that shit. Somebody told me, you know what he's clearing *himself*? Fourteen, fifteen grand a *week*.

Aaronow: Himself?

Moss: That's what I'm *saying*. Why? The *leads*. He's got the good leads . . . what are we, we're sitting in the shit here. Why? We have to go to *them* to *get* them. Huh. Ninety percent our sale, we're *paying* to the *office* for the *leads*.

Aaronow: The leads, the overhead, the telephones, there's *lots* of things.

Moss: What do you need? A *telephone*, some broad to say "Good morning," nothing . . . nothing . . .

Aaronow: No, it's not that simple, Dave . . .

Moss: *Yes.* It *is*. It *is* simple, and you know what the hard part is?

Aaronow: What?

Moss: Starting up.

Aaronow: What hard part?

Moss: Of doing the thing. The dif . . . the difference. Between me and Jerry Graff. Going to business for yourself. The hard part is . . . you know what it is?

Aaronow: What?

Moss: Just the *act*.

Aaronow: What act?

Moss: To say "I'm going on my own." 'Cause what you do, George, let me tell you what you do: you find yourself in *thrall* to someone else. And we *enslave* ourselves. To *please*. To win some fucking *toaster* . . . to . . . to . . . and the guy who got there first made *up* those . . .

Aaronow: That's right . . .

Moss: He made *up* those rules, and we're working for *him*.

Aaronow: That's the truth . . .

Moss: That's the *God's* truth. And it gets me depressed. I *swear* that it does. At MY AGE. To see a goddamn:

"Somebody wins the Cadillac this month. P.S. Two guys get fucked."

Aaronow: *Huh.*

Moss: You don't *ax* your sales force.

Aaronow: No.

Moss: You . . .

Aaronow: You . . .

Moss: You *build* it!

Aaronow: That's what I . . .

Moss: You fucking *build* it! Men come . . .

Aaronow: Men come *work* for you . . .

Moss: . . . you're absolutely right.

Aaronow: They . . .

Moss: They have . . .

Aaronow: When they . . .

Moss: Look look look look, when they *build* your business, then you can't fucking turn around, *enslave* them, treat them like *children*, fuck them up the ass, leave them to fend for themselves . . . no. (*Pause.*) No. (*Pause.*) You're absolutely right, and I want to tell you something.

Aaronow: What?

Moss: I want to tell you what somebody should do.

Aaronow: What?

Moss: Someone should stand up and strike *back*.

Aaronow: What do you mean?

Moss: *Somebody* . . .

Aaronow: Yes . . . ?

Moss: Should do something to *them*.

Aaronow: What?

Moss: Something. To pay them back. (*Pause.*) Someone, someone should hurt them. Murray and Mitch.

Aaronow: Someone should hurt them.

Moss: Yes.

Aaronow: (*Pause.*) How?

Moss: How? Do something to hurt them. Where they live.

Aaronow: What? (*Pause.*)

Moss: Someone should rob the office.

Aaronow: Huh.

Moss: That's what I'm *saying*. We were, if we were that kind of guys, to knock it off, and *trash* the joint, it looks like robbery, and *take* the fuckin' leads out of the files . . . go to Jerry Graff. (*Long pause.*)

Aaronow: What could somebody get for them?

Moss: What could we *get* for them? I don't know. Buck a *throw* . . . buck-a-half a throw . . . I don't know. . . . Hey, who knows what they're worth, what do they *pay* for them? All told . . . must be, I'd . . . three bucks a throw . . . *I* don't know.

Aaronow: How many leads have we got?

Moss: The *Glengarry* . . . the premium leads . . . ? I'd say we got five thousand. Five. Five thousand leads.

Aaronow: And you're saying a fella could take and sell these leads to Jerry Graff.

Moss: Yes.

Aaronow: How do you know he'd buy them?

Moss: Graff? Because I worked for him.

Aaronow: You haven't talked to him.

Moss: No. What do you mean? Have I talked to him about *this*? (*Pause.*)

Aaronow: Yes. I mean are you actually *talking* about this, or are we just . . .

Moss: No, we're just . . .

Aaronow: We're just "*talking*" about it.

Moss: We're just *speaking* about it. (*Pause.*) As an *idea*.

Aaronow: As an idea.

Moss: Yes.

Aaronow: We're not actually *talking* about it.

Moss: No.

Aaronow: Talking about it as a . . .

Moss: *No.*

Aaronow: As a *robbery*.

Moss: As a "robbery"?! No.

Aaronow: *Well*. Well . . .

Moss: *Hey.* (*Pause.*)

Aaronow: So all this, um, you didn't, actually, you didn't actually go talk to Graff.

Moss: Not actually, no. (*Pause.*)

Aaronow: You didn't?

Moss: No. Not actually.

Aaronow: Did you?

Moss: What did I say?

Aaronow: What did you say?

Moss: Yes. (*Pause.*) I said, "Not actually." The fuck *you* care, George? We're just *talking* . . .

Aaronow: We are?

Moss: Yes. (*Pause.*)

Aaronow: Because, because, you know, it's a *crime*.

Moss: That's right. It's a crime. It is a crime. It's also very safe.

Aaronow: You're actually *talking* about this?

Moss: That's right. (*Pause.*)

Aaronow: You're going to steal the leads?

Moss: Have I said that? (*Pause.*)

Aaronow: Are you? (*Pause.*)

Moss: Did I say that?

Aaronow: Did you talk to Graff?

Moss: Is that what I said?

Aaronow: What did he say?

Moss: What did he say? He'd *buy* them. (*Pause.*)

Aaronow: You're going to steal the leads and sell the leads to him? (*Pause.*)

Moss: Yes.

Aaronow: What will he pay?

Moss: A buck a shot.

Aaronow: For five thousand?

Moss: However they are, that's the deal. A buck a throw. Five thousand dollars. Split it half and half.

Aaronow: You're saying "me."

Moss: Yes. (*Pause.*) Twenty-five hundred apiece. One night's work, and the job with Graff. Working the premium leads. (*Pause.*)

Aaronow: A job with Graff.

Moss: Is that what I said?

Aaronow: He'd give me a job.

Moss: He would take you on. Yes. (*Pause.*)

Aaronow: Is that the truth?

Moss: Yes. It is, George. (*Pause.*) Yes. It's a big decision. (*Pause.*) And it's a big reward. (*Pause.*) It's a big reward. For one night's work. (*Pause.*) But it's got to be tonight.

Aaronow: What?

Moss: What? What? The *leads*.

Aaronow: You have to steal the leads tonight?

Moss: That's *right*, the guys are moving them downtown. After the thirtieth. Murray and Mitch. After the contest.

Aaronow: You're, you're saying so you have to go in there tonight and . . .

Moss: *You* . . .

Aaronow: I'm sorry?

Moss: *You.* (*Pause.*)

Aaronow: Me?

Moss: *You* have to go in. (*Pause.*) *You* have to get the leads. (*Pause.*)

Aaronow: I do?

Moss: Yes.

Aaronow: I . . .

Moss: It's not something for nothing, George, I took you in on this, you have to go. That's your thing. I've made the deal with Graff. I can't go. I can't go in, I've spoken on this too much. I've got a big mouth. (*Pause.*) "The fucking leads" et cetera, blah blah blah ". . . the fucking tight ass company . . ."

Aaronow: They'll know when you go over to Graff . . .

Moss: What will they know? That I stole the leads? I *didn't* steal the leads, I'm going to the *movies* tonight with a friend, and then I'm going to the Como Inn. Why did I go to Graff? I got a better deal. *Period*. Let 'em prove something. They can't prove anything that's not the case. (*Pause.*)

Aaronow: *Dave.*

Moss: Yes.

Aaronow: You want me to break into the office tonight and steal the leads?

Moss: Yes. (*Pause.*)

Aaronow: No.

Moss: Oh, yes, George.

Aaronow: What does that mean?

Moss: Listen to this. I have an alibi, I'm going to the Como Inn, why? Why? The place gets robbed, they're going to come looking for *me*. Why? Because I probably did it. Are you going to turn me in? (*Pause.*) George? Are you going to turn me in?

Aaronow: What if you don't get caught?

Moss: They come to you, you going to turn me in?

Aaronow: Why would they come to me?

Moss: They're going to come to *everyone*.

Aaronow: Why would I *do* it?

Moss: You wouldn't, George, that's why I'm talking to you. Answer me. They come to you. You going to turn me in?

Aaronow: No.

Moss: Are you sure?

Aaronow: Yes. I'm sure.

Moss: Then listen to this: I have to get those leads tonight. That's something I have to do. If I'm not at the *movies* . . . if I'm not eating over at the inn . . . If you don't do this, then *I* have to come in here . . .

Aaronow: . . . you don't have to come in . . .

Moss: . . . and *rob* the place . . .

Aaronow: . . . I thought that we were only talking . . .

Moss: . . . they *take* me, then. They're going to ask me who were my accomplices.

Aaronow: *Me?*

Moss: Absolutely.

Aaronow: That's ridiculous.

Moss: Well, to the law, you're an accessory. Before the fact.

Aaronow: I didn't ask to be.

Moss: Then tough luck, George, because you are.

Aaronow: Why? *Why,* because you only *told* me about it?

Moss: That's right.

Aaronow: Why are you doing this to me, Dave. Why are you talking this way to me? I don't understand. Why are you doing this at *all* . . . ?

Moss: That's none of your fucking business . . .

Aaronow: Well, well, well, *talk* to me, we sat down to eat *dinner,* and here I'm a *criminal* . . .

Moss: You *went* for it.

Aaronow: In the abstract . . .

Moss: So I'm making it concrete.

Aaronow: Why?

Moss: Why? Why *you* going to give me five grand?

Aaronow: Do you need five grand?

Moss: Is that what I just said?

Aaronow: You need money? Is that the . . .

Moss: Hey, hey, let's just keep it simple, what I need is not the . . . what do *you* need . . . ?

Aaronow: What is the five grand? (*Pause.*) What is the, you said that we were going to *split* five . . .

Moss: I lied. (*Pause.*) Alright? My end is *my* business. Your end's twenty-five. In or out. You tell me, you're out you take the consequences.

Aaronow: I do?

Moss: Yes. (*Pause.*)
Aaronow: And why is that?
Moss: Because you listened.

ORPHANS
by Lyle Kessler

ACT II, SCENE 4

Treat and Phillip are brothers living in Philadelphia. Treat has always taken care of Phillip—*taken care* of him to the point of virtually becoming his keeper. Phillip is never allowed out. Treat has told him that he is allergic to the air outside the house and that he'd get lost and never find his way home. Treat keeps Phillip like a child, even playing tag with him (with Phillip always winding up "it"). Phillip spends his days staring out the window, hiding in the hall closet that contains his deceased mother's coats, and watching Errol Flynn adventure movies on television. Secretly, he tries to learn new words from the newspaper and from some old books he found in the house and keeps hidden from Treat. Once, when Treat found a word underlined in the newspaper, he flew into a rage and Phillip pretended that someone who looked like Errol Flynn had sneaked into the house and marked the paper.

Phillip also prizes a woman's high-heeled shoe that he found in the house. Treat, unable to accept anything unusual in Phillip's routine, anything that might weaken his control over his brother, threw the shoe out the window in anger.

Treat spends his days robbing people at knifepoint. One day he brings home a well-dressed man named Harold. Harold is drunk and obviously rich and from out of town—from Chicago. Treat's scheme is to hold him for ransom. But Harold has a scheme of his own. He has a fondness for what he calls "Dead End Kids." He quickly overpowers Treat and befriends Phillip and turns their lives around. He moves in with the brothers, hires Treat to be his bodyguard (he has enemies from Chicago), and helps Phillip gain confidence in himself.

Even Treat comes to admire Harold, but flees the house in a panic when Harold tries to comfort him physically (by stroking his shoulder). Harold then takes Phillip out with him in order to help him escape his life of confinement. When Treat returns home it is clear that he has been drinking. He soon discovers that the red high-heeled shoe that he threw out is back under the couch cushion. He checks the closet for Phillip, but quickly realizes he is gone. Treat comes out of the closet calling out his brother's name and carrying "almost absentmindedly" one of his mother's coats. When Phillip returns two hours later (carrying flowers), Treat is still holding the coat.

Phillip: What's the matter, Treat? You look pale. (*No answer.*) You look white as a ghost. You want an aspirin? (*No answer.*) I'll get you a Bayer aspirin. (*He starts into the kitchen.*)

Treat: I don't want a Bayer aspirin.

Phillip: What about Excedrin?

Treat: I don't want any fucking aspirins! (PHILLIP *notices the coat.*)

Phillip: Wadaya doing with that coat? (TREAT *looks down and realizes he is holding the coat.*) That's Mom's coat, Treat. How come you're holding Mom's coat. (TREAT *drops the coat on the floor.*)

Treat: Where were you?

Phillip: I was out. I took a walk, Treat. I walked all the way over to Broad and Olney.

Treat: Where's Harold?

Phillip: I don't know, Treat. One moment he was with me and the next moment he was gone.

Treat: Where is the son of a bitch!

Phillip: He seen these fellows from Chicago, Treat. They were walking right behind us, and he said, "You keep walking, Phillip, I'll see you later," and then I seen him walk to the corner and he disappeared.

Treat: Wadaya mean disappeared?

Phillip: He wasn't there.

Treat: He didn't disappear, Phillip, he just turned the corner!

Phillip: Oh.

Treat: He was just out of sight!

Phillip: Anyway, I ain't seen him. (PHILLIP *walks into the kitchen.*)

Treat: I WANT HIM OUT OF HERE, PHILLIP! I WANT HIM THE FUCK OUT! (TREAT, *upset, tries to compose himself. He takes a swig from the liquor bottle. He calls off to* PHILLIP.) I seen a friend of yours.

Phillip: (*Off.*) What?

Treat: I SAID I JUST NOW SEEN A FRIEND OF YOURS! (PHILLIP *returns with an empty large bottle of Hellman's Mayonnaise. He places the flowers inside.*)

Phillip: Who'd you see?

Treat: I seen an old re-run of the "Charge of the Light Brigade," starring none other than your old buddy, Errol Flynn.

Phillip: He's not my buddy. I hardly know him.

Treat: He's a handsome son of a bitch though, isn't he?

Phillip: He's handsome, all right.

Treat: Did you see the film?

Phillip: Yes.

Treat: I bet there's not a goddamn film you haven't seen. I mean, I bet you're a fucking walking encyclopedia of the film industry.

Phillip: I seen every one of his films.

Treat: That's what I'm saying. I'm also wondering what a famous movie star like him is doing hanging around North Philly, sneaking into people's houses, underlining words, underlining sentences, even phrases.

Phillip: I wouldn't know.

Treat: Here I am sitting watching Errol Flynn on horseback, leading the famous Charge of the Ten Thousand, when suddenly I hear something. Wadaya think I heard?

Phillip: I don't know, Treat.

Treat: I'm watching Errol Flynn on TV and at the same time out of the corner of my eye I see the bastard sneaking around my house. The fucker is a glutton for punishment, Phillip. I mean, the last time he was here he hadda jump out a second story window. He could've broken his neck, could've ruined his career. Hollywood ain't interested in no leading man with a broken neck. What kinda parts is he gonna play . . . broken neck parts! Corpses!

Maybe even the Hunchback of Notre Dame! He must have been hanging around here for years, Phillip! Look! (*Pulls out the books from under the couch.*) Life on the Mississippi, by Mark Twain! The Count of fucking Monte Cristo! The Arabian Nights! Books, books, everywhere and in each of these books, underlined words, thousands of underlined words. And look what else I found! (*Pulls out the red shoe.*) Imagine that! All this time we was thinking she was some kind of one-legged tramp when all along she had two legs. She does have an unusual problem though. This is a shoe for a right foot and the shoe we threw out that window was for another right foot, which leads me to believe that this woman has two right feet. What the fuck does she look like, Phillip, some kind of awful monster roaming the Philadelphia streets, leaning to the right. (*He hurls the shoe against the wall. He fixes himself a drink.*) I think that's the last of Errol Flynn, though, Phillip.

Phillip: Wadaya mean?

Treat: I caught him dead to rights. He's not gonna bother us ever again.

Phillip: What did you do?

Treat: I cut off his hands. (*Pause.*) I had no choice. You didn't happen to see him on the way home, did you?

Phillip: No.

Treat: Let me give you a fuller description . . . a handsome looking fellow with a pencil thin mustache, a movie star, running along Camac Street with two bloody stumps.

Phillip: I didn't see him, Treat.

Treat: You didn't see no trail of blood?

Phillip: I didn't see no trail of blood, but I seen other things.

Treat: What other things you seen?

Phillip: Plenty of other things. (*Faces him.*) He's got rights, Treat.

Treat: What rights you talking about?

Phillip: He's got certain unalienable rights. He's got the right to Life, Liberty and the Pursuit of Happiness.

Treat: Who told you that? Harold!

Phillip: It's in the Declaration of Independence, Treat! (*Pause.*) I took a walk tonight. I walked over to Broad and Olney.

Treat: I'm not interested.

Phillip: I was breathing okay, Treat. I didn't have no allergy reaction like you said I would.

Treat: I was watching out for you.

Phillip: I took the subway, Treat.

Treat: I don't want to hear no more!

Phillip: Harold told me the secret. You can stand all day at the turnstile putting in nickles and dimes, you can say Open Assasime and all kinds of words, but it won't do any good unless you have one of these magical coins. (PHILLIP *pulls out a coin. He hands it to him.*)

Treat: That's a token!

Phillip: If Harold hadn't given me one I never would have been able to take that ride.

Treat: It's a fucking Philadelphia subway token! (*Throws it away.*)

Phillip: I know that.

Treat: Anyone can buy one of those lousy tokens. All you gotta do is walk up to any token booth.

Phillip: You never told me about them token booths! You never told me about nothing!

Treat: I had other things on my mind. I was making us a living. I had the responsibility.

Phillip: You told me I would die if I went outside.

Treat: Don't you remember what happened last time? Your face swelled up, your tongue was hanging outta your mouth. You couldn't breath! (PHILLIP *runs to the pantry window and throws it open. He runs across the living room to the window seat and throws open that window. He flings the door open wide.*)

Phillip: I can breathe, Treat. Look! My tongue ain't hanging out. My face ain't swollen! (*Pause.*) I walked over to Broad and Olney tonight, Treat. I seen people walking, and I heard children laughing.

Treat: I told you I wasn't interested.

Phillip: I wasn't scared no more 'cause Harold gave me something. (PHILLIP *takes out the map.*) He gave me this! (*Opens the map.*)

Treat: It's a map! It's a map of fucking Philadelphia!

Phillip: You never gave me no map, Treat. You never told me I could find my way!

Treat: I didn't want us separated. I didn't want anything happening to you.

Phillip: Nothing's gonna happen to me, Treat, 'cause I know where I am now. I know where I am, and you ain't ever gonna take that away from me.

Treat: Where are you?

Phillip: I'M AT SIXTY-FORTY NORTH CAMAC STREET, IN PHILADELPHIA, TREAT! I'M ON THE EASTERN EDGE OF THE STATE OF PENNSYLVANIA IN THE UNITED STATES OF AMERICA! I'M ON THE NORTH AMERICAN CONTINENT, ON THE PLANET EARTH, IN THE MILKY WAY GALAXY, SWIMMING IN THE GREAT OCEAN OF SPACE! I'M SAFE AND SOUND AT THE VERY EDGE OF THE MILKY WAY! THAT'S WHERE I AM, TREAT! (*A long pause.* PHILLIP *picks up the map and tags* TREAT.) And you're it, Treat.

Treat: No.

Phillip: You're fucking it. Game's over. (PHILLIP *crosses to the stairs, closes the door, and begins to walk up the stairs.* TREAT *calls to him.*)

Treat: PHILLIP! PHILLIP! (PHILLIP *stops.*) How come Harold never mentioned that there are people out there who might just walk right up to you and . . . (*Walks up to* PHILLIP, *pulls map out of his hand.*) steal your map.

Phillip: Give me that, Treat!

Treat: Malicious people.

Phillip: I'm warning you, Treat!

Treat: Terrible people. (TREAT *begins to tear the map up into little pieces.* PHILLIP *grabs him from behind and wrestles with him.* TREAT *continues to rip the map.*) People who got no scruples.

Phillip: Stop that! (TREAT *and* PHILLIP *wrestle.* TREAT *grabs* PHILLIP'*s head and throws him to the floor.*)

Treat: (*On top of him.*) How come he didn't warn you! (TREAT *is strangling* PHILLIP. *He stops suddenly and pulls away in horror. He backs up against the wall and turns and faces it.* PHILLIP, *on the floor, moves to the torn pieces of the map.*)

Phillip: You shouldn't've done that, Treat. You shouldn't've touched my map.

Treat: (*Facing wall.*) He should have warned you. (PHILLIP *grabs the torn pieces of the map and stuffs them into his pockets. He crosses to his jacket at the table and puts it* *on, moving to the closet.* TREAT *turns and sees him.* PHIL-LIP *takes a small satchel from the closet. He begins to shove the books and the shoe into it.*) I guess you don't need me anymore, then, Phillip, huh? I guess you can get along without me? (PHILLIP *is packing.*)

Phillip: (*On floor.*) I'm gonna travel, Treat. I'm gonna visit places.

Treat: I guess you don't need your big brother Treat no more.

Phillip: I'm gonna go wherever I wanna go. (*Runs to window-seat, gets tape, comes back, tries to tape the map together.*)

Treat: Your big brother Treat who stole so we could have food on the table, so you could have them tuna fish sandwiches spread thick with Hellman's mayonnaise. And then when they came for you, your brother Treat who stood in the door blocking the way. Do you remember?

Phillip: I remember!

Treat: You were crying. You hid in the closet.

Phillip: Yes!

Treat: They tried to come in, but I stopped them. I bit the man's hand. I was only a little boy, but I bit his hand. Remember!

Phillip: I remember!

Treat: They never bothered you again. I took care of you all these years, but you don't need me anymore. Is that right!

Phillip: I'm leaving! (TREAT, *stunned, moves back. He wanders around the room in a daze.* PHILLIP *on the floor is trying to put the map together.* TREAT *walks into the open closet. He pulls down the mother's coats. He crosses over to the coat that is on the floor. He drops to his knees and begins slamming it against the floor. He stops.*)

Treat: Where was he all those years I was raising you. Where was he?

BENT
by Martin Sherman

ACT I, SCENE 6

Max and Horst are prisoners in Dachau, the German concentration camp. They are imprisoned because they are homosexual. Horst was arrested because his name was on a petition to legalize homosexuality. Max was arrested with his long-term lover, Rudy, because the authorities became aware of their homosexual activities when Max picked up and brought home (for a threesome) a man the Nazis were looking for.

Before his arrest, Max, who came from a wealthy family, led an open and flamboyant homosexual life among Berlin's sophisticates. After he learned the authorities were looking for him, Max could have escaped from Germany through the use of family connections, but he would not abandon Rudy.

On the train to Dachau Rudy was brutally beaten by the Nazi guards. It was on the train that Max first met Horst, who saved his life by advising him not to come to Rudy's aid. Max listened to Horst and sat silently—in terror and anguish—as he heard Rudy screaming. When the Nazi guard told Max to hit Rudy, he complied over and over again, and Rudy soon died from his beatings.

Horst told Max that the Nazis treated homosexuals even worse than they treated Jews, so Max managed to get himself categorized as a Jew and was given a yellow star to wear on his uniform instead of a pink one.

Just prior to the scene below, Horst complained to the prisoner in charge of doling out the soup that he had not received any meat or vegetables in his bowl, only water. The prisoner pushed Horst away and called him a "fucking queer." Max saw the incident and after getting his soup, followed Horst into the barracks.

Max: Hi.

(HORST *looks at him; says nothing;* MAX *holds up his bowl.* MAX *looks at* HORST's *bowl. He gives him some vegetables.*)

Here.

Horst: Leave me alone.

Max: I got extra. Some vegetables. Here. (*Drops some vegetables from his bowl in* HORST's *bowl.*)

Horst: (HORST *looks in his own bowl.*) Thanks.

(*They eat quietly.*)

(HORST *looks up. Stares at* MAX's *uniform.*)

Horst: (HORST *does not look at* MAX.) Yellow star?

Max: What?

Horst: Jew?

Max: Oh. Yeah.

Horst: I wouldn't have figured it.

(*Silence.*)

I'm sorry about your friend.

Max: Who?

Horst: Your friend.

Max: Oh.

(*Silence.*)

Horst: It's not very sociable in these barracks. (*Laughs.*) Is it?

Max: (MAX *slides into* HORST *and indicates the triangle.*) How'd you get the pink?

Horst: I signed a petition.

Max: And?

Horst: That was it.

Max: What kind of petition?

Horst: For Magnus Hirschfield.

Max: Oh yeah. I remember him. Berlin.

Horst: Berlin.

Max: He wanted to . . .

Horst: Make queers legal.

Max: Right. I remember.

Horst: Looked like he would too, for a while. It was quite a movement. Then the Nazis came in. Well. I was a nurse. They said a queer couldn't be a nurse. Suppose I had to touch a patient's penis! God forbid. They said rather than be a nurse, I should be a prisoner. A more suitable occupation. So. So. That's how I got my pink triangle. How'd you get the yellow star?

Max: I'm Jewish.

Horst: You're not Jewish, you're a queer.

(MAX *looks right and left to see who might have heard.*)

(*Silence.*)

Max: I didn't want one.

Horst: Didn't want what?

Max: A pink triangle. I didn't want one.

Horst: Didn't *want* one?

Max: You told me it was the lowest. So I didn't want one.

Horst: So?

Max: So I worked a deal.

Horst: A deal?

Max: Sure. I'm good at that.

Horst: With the Gestapo?

Max: Sure.

Horst: You're full of shit.

(*Silence.*)

Max: I'm going to work a lot of deals around here. They can't keep us here forever. Sooner or later they'll release us. I'm only under protective custody, that's what they told me. I'm going to stay alive.

Horst: I don't doubt it.

Max: Sure. I'm good at that.

Horst: Thanks for the vegetables. (HORST *starts to rise. He haunches over.*)

Max: Where are you going?

Horst: (HORST *pauses in movement.*) To sleep. We get up at four in the morning. I'm on stone detail. I chop stones up. It's fun. Excuse me . . .

(HORST *starts again to rise.* MAX *stops him with his right hand.* HORST *sits back on haunches.*)

Max: Don't go.

Horst: I'm tired.

Max: I don't have anyone to talk to.

Horst: Talk to your lansmen.

Max: I'm not Jewish.

Horst: Then why are you wearing that?

Max: You told me pink was the lowest.

Horst: It is, but only because the other prisoners hate us so much.

Max: (MAX *holds out and indicates bowl.*) I got meat in my soup. You didn't.

Horst: Good for you. (HORST *rises and crosses left of* MAX.)

Max: Don't go.

Horst: (HORST *goes into deep knee position.*) Look, friendships last about twelve hours in this place. We had ours on the train. Why don't you go and bother someone else.

Max: You didn't think I'd make it, did you? Off the train?

Horst: I wasn't sure.

Max: I'm going to stay alive.

Horst: Yes.

Max: Because of you. You told me how.

Horst: Yes. (*Pause.*) I did. (*Pause.*) I'm sorry.

Max: About what?

Horst: I don't know. Your friend.

Max: Oh.

(*Silence.*)

He wasn't my friend.

(*Silence.*)

Horst: You should be wearing a pink triangle.

Max: I made a deal.

Horst: You don't make deals here.

Max: I did. I made a deal.

Horst: Sure. (HORST *rises and crosses left corner of right wall. Starts to leave again.*)

Max: They said if I . . . I could . . . they said . . .

Horst: (HORST *takes a step in toward* MAX.) What?

Max: Nothing. I could prove . . . I don't know how . . .

Horst: What? (*Stops, sits next to* MAX.)

Max: Nothing.

(*Silence.*)

Horst: (HORST *moves in to* MAX *and kneels to him.*) Try.

(*Silence.*)

I think you better.

(*Silence.*)

Try to tell me.
Max: Nothing.

(*Silence.*)

Horst: O.K. (HORST *stands to leave. Moves away.*)
Max: I made . . .

(MAX *pulls* HORST *down. The next lines do not relate to* HORST. *He finds it exceptionally difficult to tell.*)

they took me . . . into that room . . .
Horst: (*Stops.*) Where?
Max: Into that room.
Horst: On the train?
Max: On the train. And they said . . . prove that you're . . . and I did . . .
Horst: Prove that you're what?
Max: Not.
Horst: Not what?
Max: Queer.
Horst: How?
Max: Her.
Horst: Her?
Max: They said, if you . . . and I did . . .
Horst: Did what?
Max: Her. Made . . .
Horst: Made what?
Max: Love.
Horst: Who to?
Max: Her.
Horst: Who was she?
Max: Only . . . maybe . . . maybe only thirteen . . . she was maybe . . . she was dead.
Horst: Oh.
Max: Just. Just dead, minutes . . . (MAX *indicates a gun at the temple.*) bullet . . . in her . . . they said . . . prove that

you're . . . and I did . . . prove that you're . . . lots of them, watching . . . laughing . . . drinking . . . he's a bit bent, they said, he can't . . . but I did . . .

Horst: How?

Max: I don't . . . I don't . . . know. I wanted . . .

Horst: To stay alive.

Max: And there was something . . . (MAX *holds his head in his hands.*)

Horst: Something . . .

Max: Exciting . . . (MAX *raises his head.*)

Horst: Oh God.

Max: I hit him, you know. I kissed her. Dead lips. I killed him. Sweet lips. Angel.

Horst: God.

Max: Angel . . . She was . . . like an angel . . . to save my life . . . little breasts just beginning . . . her breasts . . . just beginning . . . they said he can't . . . he's a bit bent . . . but I did . . . and I proved . . . I proved that I wasn't . . .

(*Silence.*)

And they enjoyed it.

Horst: Yes.

Max: And I said, I'm not queer. And they laughed. And I said, give me a yellow star. And they said, sure make him a Jew. He's not bent. And they laughed. They were having fun. But . . . I . . . got . . . my . . . star . . . (MAX *fingers his star.*)

Horst: (*Gently.*) Oh yes.

Max: I got my star.

Horst: Yes. (HORST *reaches for* MAX.)

Max: *Don't do that!* (MAX *pulls away right.*) You mustn't do that. For your own sake. You mustn't touch me. I'm a rotten person.

Horst: No . . .

(HORST *reaches for* MAX *again.* MAX *strikes out at and crawls right.*)

Max: Rotten.

(HORST *stares at* MAX.))

Horst: No.

(HORST *pauses then stands. He exits between walls and out U.C. There is a silence.* MAX *leans against wall. He closes his eyes, takes a deep breath.*)

Max: One. Two. Three. Four. Five. (MAX *takes another breath.*) Six. Seven. Eight. Nine. Ten.

FOXFIRE
by Susan Cooper and Hume Cronyn

ACT I

Annie Nations lives alone in a farmhouse on a hill in Rabun County, Georgia. She is seventy-nine years old. Her husband Hector (whose father first cleared the land for farming) died five years ago, but she has "brought him back" in her mind. She talks to him, argues with him, and loves him.

Real-estate developers have bought most of the land surrounding Annie's property; the other farms have all been replaced by vacation-home developments. Now one developer, Prince Carpenter, is offering Annie $100,000 to sell her property, twice what he offered Hector when he was alive. But she doesn't want to sell and tells him to talk to Hector, up in the apple orchard. He knows Hector is dead, but he goes anyway. The authors describe Prince as a "shrewd but not unprincipled operator; he likes people and is genuinely likeable." When he returns from the orchard (eating an apple), he encounters another man who he assumes is another developer (from Florida) out to buy the land. But, in fact, it is Dillard Nations, Annie and Hector's son, who has come for a visit. Dillard is a guitarist and singer and is performing at a nearby fair.

Dillard worries about his mother living alone and wants her to come and live with him and his children in Florida. But he understands her attachment to her house and land and doesn't try to encourage her to sell them. He also knows about her conversations with Hector and handles it sensitively. It's a tough time in Dillard's life. His wife left him recently for another man, and now she wants their two children.

As Prince comes around the corner of the house, Dillard is putting some oranges away for his mother.

Prince: Hi.

Dillard: Hi.

Prince: These are great. Hey—fruit salad! You got oranges, I got apples. Fruit salad—get it?

Dillard: I got it.

Prince: Mrs. Nations told me to help myself.

Dillard: Yeah, I know.

Prince: You don't get 'em this good in the city.

Dillard: Sure don't.

Prince: I sure ain't dressed for farmin'—look at these shoes! You live around here?

Dillard: Nope.

Prince: (*Indicating oranges.*) Bring them with you?

Dillard: Yep.

Prince: Real cheap down there, ain't they?

Dillard: Pebbles on the beach.

Prince: Well, we never 'preciate what we got. How about this, huh? (*He waves his apple at the scenery.*) Beautiful!

Dillard: Sure is. (*He takes the oranges into the cellar.*)

Prince: Florida, huh?

Dillard: (*Off.*) That's right.

Prince: You boys really movin' in up here, ain't you?

(DILLARD *reappears.*)

You interested in this place?

Dillard: (*Warily.*) Yeah, I'm interested.

Prince: (*Putting out his hand.*) Well, meet the competition. I'm Mountain Development. Prince Carpenter. Pleased to meetcha. I've had my eye on this place for a long time now. But it's no sale. You ever talk to the old man?

Dillard: Who d'y' mean?

Prince: Hector Nations. Tough old bird. (*Pause; munch.*)

Dillard: Sure, I've talked to him.

Prince: How'd you do?

Dillard: I haven't spoken to him in quite a while.

Prince: Won't budge. Ain't no way in this world t' reach him. (*Pause.*) Ain't *never* goin' t' sell.

Dillard: He told you that?

Prince: Sure did. Right up there in the orchard.

Dillard: How'd you manage that?

Prince: Weren't easy.

Dillard: I guess not. Pa's been dead five years.

Prince: Come again?

Dillard: My pa. Dead.

(*Pause, then* PRINCE *picks up unabashed.*)

Prince: You're absolutely right! Five years ago—August '77. You must be the son in show business—Dillard.

Dillard: I sure ain't in real estate.

Prince: No, a' course not. (*He laughs it away.*) Got a mite ahead a' myself there. Smart man, your pa. I talked to him just before he passed over.

Dillard: You did, huh?

Prince: Absolutely! Your ma remembers. Offered him fifty thousand dollars for this place and he wouldn't touch it. He knew values'd go up.

Dillard: You think that's th'only reason he wouldn't sell?

Prince: (*Casually.*) Offered your ma a hundred.

Dillard: Y' ain't gonna budge Ma neither. (*Pause.*) Look, Mr. Carpenter—

Prince: Call me Prince.

Dillard: My grand-daddy cleared this land. My pa worked it—I worked it—an' my ma *lives* here.

Prince: Well, we all move on sometime. Take *my* ma—we got her a nice little place near us in Greenville. TV, dishwasher, everythin'—an' I'm right there if there's trouble.

Dillard: Ma's got good neighbors.

Prince: Had, Dillard, had. You're outa touch. Must get mighty lonely up here—guess that's why she's brought back y'r pa, huh?

Dillard: You knew about that?

Prince: Hell, Dillard, this is my territory.

Dillard: You didn't call her on it.

Prince: What d'you take me for? I wasn't about to spoil anythin' for a fine old lady. I like these people, an' everybody likes ol' Prince.

Dillard: This place ain't for sale.

Prince: You won't get a better offer. We can't use all the land anyway. There's about six acres of swamp—plus your old burial ground up there. Law won't let us touch that. Don't just piss on it, Dillard—think it over.

Dillard: You're wastin' y'r breath, Mr. Carpenter. It ain't my land—it ain't my life.

Prince: It's your mother. Face it, Dillard—everythin's changed since you an' me grew up in these mountains. The kids with any get up an' go have got up an' went— jus' like you did. The old ones are jus' hangin' on like fox-fire on rotten wood.

ANOTHER COUNTRY
by Julian Mitchell

ACT II, SCENE 6

The scene begins just after Guy Bennett, a seventeen-year-old student at an upper-class English "public school," has received six strokes with a cane from fellow students who are the "house prefects" in charge of monitoring the activities of lower-level students. Guy's offence: he sent a love note to another student, a young man named James, and it was intercepted by Fowler, one of the prefects. Fowler has always despised Guy for failing to take the school rules and rituals seriously and, most recently, for causing their unit to lose a competition. He has also despised Guy for his homosexuality, and has been looking for a legitimate way to punish him. Guy's note, with its open homosexual content, was all he needed to get permission for the beating from the senior student governing council (called "Twenty Two").

In an earlier episode in which Fowler tried to get permission to cane him, Guy threatened the other prefects with blackmail. He would reveal to the school administration ("Farcical") the names of all of his homosexual contacts during his three years at the school—the other prefects were on that list. Homosexual contacts were common at the school, but most of the young men "grew out of it" and eventually sired families and took their place among the English elite. Not Guy. And apparently not another young man named Martineau, who killed himself after being caught, literally, with his pants down.

As the scene begins Guy enters the library. His classmate and friend, Tommy Judd, is there alone, working. Tommy, too, is an outsider in this school of budding British aristocrats—but not for the same reason as Guy. Tommy is an avowed Communist. It is the early 1930's, and Stalin is rebuilding Russia into his version of the Marxist ideal state. Few of the English upper class are inclined to give up their privileges to join the proletariat, but Tommy is an exception. Ultimately, he and Guy become spies for Russia—Tommy, out of his belief; Guy, out of his desire for revenge. The story and characters are derived from actual events. (For clarification, Barclay, Delahay, Menzies, and Sanderson are student officers, and Delahay actually did the caning of Guy.)

(*It is evening.* JUDD *is working. The door is flung open and* BENNETT *rushes in, throws himself on the window-seat and hides his face.* JUDD *gets quietly up and shuts the door, then goes back to the table. Pause.*)

Judd: Didn't the blackmail work this time?

Bennett: (*Muffled.*) I couldn't use it.

Judd: I don't see why not.

Bennett: (*Still hiding his face.*) Because. (*Pause.*)

Judd: Because what?

Bennett: (*Turning his tear-stained face.*) Because James has two more years here! And if I'd gone to Farcical they'd have reported him too!

Judd: So what?

Bennett: I couldn't do that! I *love* him!

Judd: Guy—

Bennett: (*Sitting up.*) You still don't believe me, do you?

Judd: I think you may *think* you're in love with him.

Bennett: Look—I'm not going to pretend any more. I'm sick of pretending. I'm— (*He can't find a suitable word.*) —I'm never going to love women.

Judd: Don't be ridiculous. (*Pause.*)

Bennett: It's why Martineau killed himself. He'd known since he was ten, he told me. I didn't know. Well—I wasn't sure. Till James.

Judd: You can't possibly know a thing like that at ten. Or now.

Bennett: Oh, yes you can. (*Pause.*) It doesn't come as any great revelation. It's more like admitting to yourself—what you've always known. Owning up to yourself. It's a great relief. In some ways. (*Pause.*) All this acting it up—making a joke of it even to myself—it was only a way of trying to pretend it wasn't true. But it is.

Judd: Of course it's not.

Bennett: Tommy, when you come down to it, it's as simple as knowing whether or not you like spinach.

Judd: I can never make up my mind about spinach.

Bennett: Then perhaps you're ambidextrous.

Judd: No, I am *not*!

Bennett: You see? You know. (*Pause.*)

Judd: You can't trust intuitions like that.

Bennett: What else is there? Are you a communist because you read Karl Marx? No. You read Karl Marx because you know you're a communist. (*Pause.*)

Judd: Well—I'm very sorry.

Bennett: Thanks! If that's how friends react—

Judd: What do you want me to do? Get a horsewhip?

Bennett: (*Standing and feeling himself.*) Not after Delahay, thanks.

Judd: Why Delahay?

Bennett: Barclay's lost his nerve. And Delahay has a very whippy wrist. (*Pause.*)

Judd: I apologise. You're quite right. It was patronising and unforgivable.

Bennett: But you couldn't help it, could you? In your heart of hearts, like Barclay and Delahay and Menzies and Sanderson—in spite of your talk about equality and fraternity—you really believe that some people are better than others because of the way they make love.

Judd: There's complete sexual freedom in Russia.

Bennett: That's not a lot of comfort at the moment, actually. (*Pause.*) Martineau killed himself because he simply couldn't face a lifetime of *that*.

Judd: But you said it was a great relief, knowing.

Bennett: Oh, don't you ever listen? I said in some ways. It's also a life sentence. (*Pause.*) Poor Martineau! He was just the sort of pathetic dope who'd've got caught the whole time. Spent his life in prison, being sent down every few months by magistrates called Barclay and Delahay. (*Pause.*)

Judd: I'm sorry, but I don't see how you can be so sure about it.

Bennett: Because I *love* him!

Judd: Come on!

Bennett: You've never been in love. You don't understand. (*Pause.*) Everything seems different. Everything seems possible. You can really believe life could be—it's so obvious! It's madness what we have now. Strikes and beating and Twenty Two and—how many unemployed are there?

Judd: Three million, seven hundred and fifty thousand.

Bennett: God, are there really?

Judd: Yes.

Bennett: Well—there must be a better way to run things. And when you're in love, it all seems so easy. (JUDD *looks disapproving.*) Don't cluck at me, Tommy. You don't know what I'm talking about. (*Pause.*) We've been meeting every night. In Girdley Field pavilion. We don't just—actually we don't more often than we do. We just—hold each other. And talk. Or not talk. Till dawn last night. (*Pause.*) Maintaining ecstasy.

Judd: Is he getting beaten, too?

Bennett: No, no. He never got the note. They couldn't pin anything on him. And after Martineau and Robbins—Barclay doesn't want anyone in Longford's even suspecting. (*Pause.*) I understand all about Martineau now. He was in love with Robbins, but Robbins wasn't with him.

Judd: Don't let your imagination run away with you.

Bennett: For Robbins it was just a game. Assignation—excitement—hands fumbling with buttons in the dark—all perfectly normal! School practice! But then poor Martineau—he went and told him. And Robbins was revolted—disgusted! He shoved him away. *That's* not what he'd come for! And Martineau knocked something over and Nickers came in to see what was happening and—

Judd: Yes.

Bennett: Robbins furiously buttoning. Martineau—sobbing and sobbing with his trousers down. (*Pause.*) Think of that for a lifetime. (*Pause.*) Think of the names. Pansy. Nancy. Fairy. Fruit. (*Pause.*) Brown nose. (*Pause.*)

Judd: Do I detect just a touch of self-pity?

Bennett: Probably.

Judd: Fight it. Every time someone calls you a name—thump him.

Bennett: Thanks! And spend my whole life locked up?

Judd: The suffragettes didn't get the vote by whining.

Bennett: Suffragettes!

Judd: You have to change the fundamental social attitudes, Guy. You have to make people *see*. It always comes down to that.

Bennett: It does with you.

WELCOME TO THE MOON
by John Patrick Shanley

In a "lowdown Bronx bar," Vinnie, a New York Italian in his early thirties, nurses a beer and waits for his old friend Stephen. It's been three years since they've seen each other and it's not been the best of times for either of them.

(*For scene-study purposes, slight adjustments can be made in the dialogue to eliminate the character of Artie, the bartender.*)

Vinnie: Steve?

Stephen: Vinnie! How are you?

Vinnie: Good! Good! How you been, man?

Stephen: Alright.

Vinnie: You look like shit. It's been three years, man. I've been sitting here counting.

Stephen: Too long.

Vinnie: Damn right it's too long. Artie, give Steve a beer. (ARTIE *silently does so.*)

Stephen: Thanks. So where is everybody? This used to be the big hangout.

Vinnie: Everybody split a long time since. The Bronx is dead.

Stephen: Where'd they all go?

Vinnie: Upstate.

Stephen: How come you didn't go?

Vinnie: Guess I'm lazy. Got the job at the Post Office. It's good. And I just don't like upstate. Fuckin' Poughkeepsie. Fuckin' Nanuet. Gimme a break.

Stephen: You like the Bronx.

Vinnie: That's right.

Stephen: I like the Bronx, too.

Vinnie: Now that does not compute.

Stephen: What d'you mean?

Vinnie: You were the first one to go.

Stephen: It just worked out that way. I went in the army, and by the time I got out . . .

Vinnie: Yeah, I know. By the time you got out, time and tide had you by the balls, and you were on your way to who knows where. Anyway, why would you come back to the Bronx? The Bronx is dead.

Stephen: There's still some neighborhoods that seem okay.

Vinnie: The Bronx is like one a those moon craters, man. Another couple of years, they're gonna be sendin astronauts up here. Guys from Houston 'ill be collecting rocks on Tremont Avenue. So how's Manhattan?

Stephen: Manhattan's all right. It's good. Exciting. Always a lot going on.

Vinnie: Uh-huh.

Stephen: Good museums.

Vinnie: Museums. Yeah, they're electrifying.

Stephen: I can walk to school.

Vinnie: Still in school! Ain't that some shit!

Stephen: Well, I wasn't in right along. There was the service. And then a lot of shitty jobs.

Vinnie: And then you got married.

Stephen: Yeah.

Vinnie: What is she again?

Stephen: A Speech Pathologist.

Vinnie: A Speech Pathologist. It sounds fuckin' hideous. I live with a Speech Pathologist.

Stephen: Very nice.

Vinnie: Sorry. I'm hungry. Artie, what do you got to eat?

Artie: Canadian bacon and cheese.

Vinnie: Gimme one. You want one?

Stephen: All right.

Vinnie: Two.

Artie: (*Puts sandwiches in a little oven.*) It'll take twelve minutes.

Vinnie: We're not going nowhere.

Stephen: Vinnie . . .

Vinnie: Yeah?

Stephen: Vinnie . . . It's good to see you, man. (*Starts to cry.*)

Vinnie: It's good to see you, too, man. Time goes by, and everybody goes away, and you see what you had.

Stephen: It's true.

Vinnie: You went out and stood on the corner, and everybody you ever knew was hanging there with you.

Stephen: You know . . .

Vinnie: It was your neighborhood. It was something to be inside of. You could do anything because you knew the fuckin' rules.

Stephen: You know, I think I left my wife.

Vinnie: What d'you mean, you think you left your wife?

Stephen: Things have been bad for a long time. I don't know why. School is driving me up the wall. I can't seem to . . . I can't seem to find . . . There's nothing left that I enjoy.

Vinnie: I'm sorry.

Stephen: Nothing happened. That's the really strange thing. I just told her I felt like going . . . coming to the Bronx, you know, the old neighborhood, and she said okay. And I walked out.

Vinnie: Don't sound final to me. You can go back.

Stephen: I don't think I can. I don't want to.

Vinnie: It's your life.

Stephen: We were . . . We're friends, Vinnie. I know I didn't call you for three years, and I know I didn't keep in touch much for years before that, but, we're friends.

Vinnie: Yeah.

Stephen: I don't really have any friends in Manhattan. I know people, but . . .
Vinnie: Shut up.
Stephen: Yeah.
Vinnie: Look, Steve. How do you feel?
Stephen: I'm all right.
Vinnie: Yeah?
Stephen: Yeah.
Vinnie: Cause when I got your call, I thought you might like to see some of the old crowd. So I phoned around. A couple of the folks should be here in a minute. Is that gonna be okay?
Stephen: Who?
Vinnie: Ronny.
Stephen: Ronny. Yeah, I'd like to see Ronny. How's he doing?
Vinnie: Bad. Ronny's always doing bad. Tried to kill himself.
Stephen: No!
Vinnie: Three times.
Stephen: Really?
Vinnie: Yeah. I make him come around. He comes to my house sometimes. A few beers. Whatever. To keep him from thinking.
Stephen: About what?
Vinnie: I don't know. But whenever he starts thinking about it, he goes right down the tubes.
Stephen: Who else?
Vinnie: Shirley.
Stephen: Shirley.
Vinnie: Shirley Dunbar.
Stephen: She's coming here?
Vinnie: Yeah. She should be here now.
Stephen: Bartender!
Vinnie: His name's Artie.
Stephen: Artie!
Artie: The sandwiches aren't ready yet. A little bell rings when the sandwiches are ready.
Stephen: Gimme a big glass of tequila.
Vinnie: What are you doing?
Artie: How many shots?

Stephen: Five.

Vinnie: Five!

Artie: Okay. One. Two. Three. Four. Five.

Vinnie: What are you doing?

Stephen: You don't know what you've done.

Vinnie: I guess not.

Stephen: Shirley's coming here.

Vinnie: So?

Stephen: You know she was my girlfriend.

Vinnie: She was your girlfriend when you were seventeen. Hey, you been seeing her on the sly?

Stephen: I haven't laid eyes on her since the day we broke up.

Vinnie: That was fourteen years ago.

Stephen: So?

Vinnie: So what are you doing?

Stephen: I'm trying to drink enough tequila to hold myself together.

Vinnie: What the hell are you talking about?

Stephen: Don't you understand? That's why my marriage is breaking up! That's why I can't make it through college! That's why I can't gain any weight! Can't sleep! Can't . . . live. I'm still in love with Shirley Dunbar! (VINNIE *bursts out laughing.*)

Vinnie: You're kidding me?

Stephen: I can't joke about it.

Vinnie: But it was fourteen years ago!

Stephen: Five thousand, one hundred and twenty-three days ago.

Vinnie: Wow.

Stephen: The day we broke up, I knew it wasn't over. I knew we'd have to meet at least one more time. I was crying. I could see that she didn't understand, didn't want to understand. The thing we had was big. I joined the service to get away. I couldn't stand seeing her walking down the street, knowing that she wasn't mine anymore. That's why I never came back to live in the Bronx! That's why I hardly ever called you! Why I hardly ever called anybody from the old days. You were all part of that time, the time Shirley and I were together. The only time in my life I was ever really alive! (STEPHEN *downs the tequila at one*

> *toss, throws himself down on the bar, and begins to sob*
> *violently. The sandwich bell rings.*)

Artie: (*Serving sandwiches, apparently unfazed.*) Two Canadian bacon and cheese. You want mustard with those? (*Getting no answer, he shrugs and goes back to his paper.*)

Vinnie: I am impressed. Here I thought you were just another nice shaky guy looking for his roots, and you turn out to be Heathcliff. "I cannot live without my love, I cannot die without my soul!" Welcome to the moon. (*Spots something outside.*) Oh shit. Steve, Ronny's coming down the block. I know it's a lot to ask, but can you pull yourself together? It's just that Ronny is real easy to get depressed, and he is always trying to do himself in, and . . . Can you hear me? (STEPHEN's *crying has continued unabated.*) Oh well. Fuck it.

SPLIT SECOND
by Dennis McIntyre

ACT II, SCENE 3

Val is a black cop in New York City. On duty on a hot July 4th evening, he shot a white man he caught trying to steal a car. He had the white man handcuffed and had called for a car to pick him up when the man, a petty criminal with a number of previous arrests, launched into a string of racial slurs. Val drew his revolver and shot him in the chest. After the shooting Val planted the man's knife in his hand and reported that the man had tried to stab him and that he shot him in self-defense. As is standard when an officer shoots a suspect, a departmental hearing was scheduled.

Val's wife Alea wants him to stick to his story at the hearing and not ruin his career and their lives by admitting that he didn't shoot in self-defense. Val's father, Rusty, a retired police officer, wants him to tell the truth. Val, who had never shot anyone before—not even in Vietnam—is troubled over the killing and confused about what to say at the hearing.

In the scene below, he meets his friend and fellow officer, Charlie, in the park. Charlie is sitting on a bench and is drinking beer from a can wrapped in a paper bag. He has a second can for Val, who enters and sits next to him. Both men are dressed in civilian clothes.

(For more information see other scenes from this play in "Monologues for Men" section of this book.)

Charlie: What's happening? (VAL's *beer*.) Better cover it up. Cop might come along. (CHARLIE *sips his beer. He watches* VAL *twist the beer can in his hands*.) What's up, man? You still got that asshole on your mind? (VAL *nods*.) It'll be a breeze. You'll be in and out in ten minutes. Don't eat. I'll buy you breakfast.

Val: (*Looks up.*) You ever kill anybody, Charlie? Nam? Here? I never asked you.

Charlie: Nam. "Bach Ma." I got a guy up close, like you did, except I used a knife. He slipped under the wire—four satchel charges—a special delivery. It took two guys to get my hand off the handle. I must have been standing there, maybe twenty, thirty minutes, holding this "Charlie" up. My namesake. So, I know what you're going through, man. I've been there.

Val: What about here?

Charlie: I haven't had the chance. But I haven't been looking for it either.

Val: One "Charlie"? That's it? (CHARLIE *stares down at his beer. He drinks*.) That's it?

Charlie: (*Looks up.*) I knocked off a Corporal. Saigon. White. A real prick, this guy. He was dealing scag, low-grade stock, the pits, skipping all the directions, lacing it—No, man, you don't want to hear this—(VAL *stares at* CHARLIE. CHARLIE *sips his beer*.) See, the word got around, guys were getting themselves into deep shit. Convulsions, that kind of stuff. One guy, brain damage. Another guy, a kid from Alabama, real competent—a real good pool player. He O.D.ed on it. Threw himself out a window. Landed on a motorcycle. A lot of the black guys, this Corporal, he was their contact. Sold it to them cheap. Maybe ten bucks. A big bag. Made it seem like you could get through a whole tour on one bag. The white dudes, the ones into the heavy stuff, this Corporal, he took care of their bags, too. Except it was a hundred percent for them. Real Asian bliss. So, this dude, this Corporal, he was dealing two bags. A white bag, and a black bag. And the "brothers" were getting "schizo," while the whites were off dreaming the good dream. Well, we decided to take him out, this Corporal, and I got the low card. (CHARLIE *sips his beer.*)

Val: How'd you do it?

Charlie: We grabbed him off the street. Two in the morning. He was making his rounds. We'd been following him for five hours.

Val: You shot him? (CHARLIE *shakes his head "no."*) Then what?

Charlie: You sure you want to hear this?

Val: I want to hear it.

Charlie: Put a wire around his neck. The idea was—he should go out slow. And he did. I don't know what they did when they found him. We never heard anything. I don't think they gave him a Bronze Star. He had a reputation.

Val: What if he'd been black, Charlie?

Charlie: Wouldn't have happened. Everybody takes care of their own. At least we did over there. You know that.

Val: You didn't give him a chance?

Charlie: No, I didn't.

Val: No explanation?

Charlie: None. We had the facts.

Val: Murder?

Charlie: "Euthanasia," that's what I like to call it. I lost maybe a night's sleep over it. The "Charlie" I gutted, he stayed with me a lot longer. But wasting that Corporal, it saved a lot of black boys. It saved them a lot of pain.

Val: It was still murder, Charlie.

Charlie: Look, man, what do you think?! The world runs on flowers?! He was dealing bad scag to the "brothers"— turning whites into fucking lotus blossoms! There comes a time you don't take it anymore! And that's not "murder one"! No way! That's just getting it on and doing what's right when everybody else is looking the other way! (*The park*.) What are you staring at, shithead?!

Val: You took him from behind. You didn't give him a chance.

Charlie: He didn't deserve a chance! Certain people, they don't belong here! They don't have the credentials! And that scumbag, he happened to be one of them! All right, it wasn't pretty. It wasn't neat. It wasn't by the book. It wasn't like your caper. He didn't have a knife on me. He wasn't coming at me. I didn't have to warn him. But he was a killer, baby, just like your customer! Except he didn't need a knife. He had a chemistry set, and you tell me, what's the fucking difference?! I came out tonight—I figured you needed help. I figured I'd help you out!

Val: I do need help.

Charlie: How come?

Val: I need help, that's all—

Charlie: The dude from Detroit, it wasn't clean enough for you? He maybe should have stuck it in you a couple of times before you pulled the trigger? Is that what's bothering you?

Val: It wasn't three feet—

Charlie: No?

Val: It was nine feet—Maybe ten—I wasn't close—

Charlie: Three feet, and you could dream at night, right?

Val: Right!

Charlie: Shit, I would have smoked the motherfucker at fifteen feet—I even saw the tip of a blade!

Val: But he wasn't—He wasn't—

Charlie: He wasn't "what?!"

Val: I didn't—

Charlie: What are you talking about, man?

Val: I didn't—I didn't have him cuffed—

Charlie: Let me get this straight. It wouldn't have happened, you had him cuffed. He couldn't have reached for his knife, right?

Val: No!

Charlie: What do you mean "no"?!

Val: That's not how it happened! I put it in him!

Charlie: You sure as shit did! The cat's dead!

Val: (*Stands, grabs* CHARLIE *by the shirt.*) I put it in him—

cuffed! (VAL *releases* CHARLIE *and backs away from him.*)

Charlie: No knife coming out, right?

Val: No knife.

Charlie: No fancy footwork? (VAL *shakes his head "no."*) But they don't know that, do they?

Val: No.

Charlie: Then that makes us just about equals, doesn't it? How'd it go off?

Val: The guy was a "lip," so I pulled it out. I figured it might impress him.

Charlie: You should have rapped on his neck. That's all it takes.

Val: Radio car was around the corner. I didn't start out to mess him up.

Charlie: So you put a bullet in him instead?

Val: It was an accident. (*They stare at each other.*)

Charlie: (*Crosses S.L. of* VAL.) If that's what it was, then fuck them. It's "street." They don't know anything about it. And the less they know, the better. (CHARLIE *rubs* VAL*'s shoulder, but the affection is gone. As he does so.*) But they've got a shovel for people like you. My advice—don't let the mothers use it. I left it in Saigon. No regrets.

Val: Did you?

Charlie: You leave it on 28th. You play good-guy cop, Johnson, you won't have a friend left in the world. Guaranteed. That's just the way it is, brother. (CHARLIE *exits. Music.* VAL *stares straight ahead. The lights slowly fade on* VAL.)

K2
by Patrick Meyers

The setting is "a ledge, eight feet wide and four feet deep, located on a six hundred foot ice wall at 27,000 feet on K2, the world's second highest mountain." Harold and Taylor reached the top of the mountain, then fell to the ledge on their descent. Harold broke his leg in the fall. Both men slept through the night on the ledge. When they awake they are covered with snow.

Taylor is a cynical lawyer working as a district attorney. Harold is a radiation scientist filled with wonder about the universe and the meaning of life. As the play proceeds and they realize that one or both of them are likely to die on the mountain, their mutual plight leads them to assess their friendship and what they really value in life.

The time is a morning in September, 1977.

(There is a beat of complete stillness, and then slowly the mound of snow on the ledge begins to move and break up. A man's head, and then torso, rises from the mound. Taylor sits looking into the sun for a long moment, a sleepy smile growing on his face. He looks up and then begins to giggle softly. Suddenly he is digging into the mound around him feverishly.)

Taylor: Harold wake up. Harold . . . morning . . . Harold. Made it . . . Harold . . . alive . . . alive Harold! *(He has uncovered a body which he yanks to a sitting position, wiping snow from the face and shaking it.)* HAROLD BE ALIVE!

Harold: Hu . . . Tay . . . lor . . .

Taylor: *(Hugging HAROLD to him.)* Yeah . . . yeah, Taylor. Made it Harold . . . alive. *(Turning HAROLD's face to the sun.)* Feel buddy . . . Oh Jesus . . . it feels . . . Oh Jesus . . . feel buddy.

Harold: Yeah . . . Yeah.

Taylor: Gonna make it now buddy. Gonna make it off this mother. *(Hugging HAROLD again.)* WE'RE ALIVE!

Harold: Uh . . . huh.

Taylor: *(Propping HAROLD up against the wall.)* History . . . history buddy! *(He begins digging in what's left of the mound, pulling out various pieces of equipment.)* History! . . . Hornbein . . . Unsoeld . . . Jerstad . . . and Bishop . . . 28,000 feet on Everest . . . no tent . . . no bags . . . one night. We didn't break that record buddy but we got second place. We have now definitely got second place—Poor old Buhl standing on that ledge all alone, all night on top of Nange Parbat, he is from this day forward relegated to a lowly third . . . You and me Harold, no tent, no bags, one night . . . You and me Harold . . . (TAYLOR *sticks a piece of beef jerky he has taken from a pocket into* HAROLD's *mouth.*) History Harold . . . at 27,000 feet.

Harold: (*Chewing dreamily.*) Uh . . . huh.

Taylor: (*Chewing on his piece of jerky for awhile.*) Now we gotta get off this fuckin' mountain. (TAYLOR *looks at* HAROLD's *leg.*) How's the leg?

Harold: Huh? (TAYLOR *takes off his down filled mittens to reveal black silk gloves. He rummages in a pack.*)

Taylor: Here! (*He takes a small green cylinder with a black hose and mask attached out of the pack and places the mask over* HAROLD's *mouth. He turns the nozzle.*) Breathe. Breathe deep buddy and come back to me . . . Earth to Harold, Earth to Harold. (TAYLOR *starts to giggle.*) Oh Christ. (HAROLD *begins to wake up from the oxygen and see the view. He lets the oxygen mask drop away as he stares in wonder.* TAYLOR *puts it back over his mouth.*) Breathe! If we don't wake up we're gonna be in a lot of trouble. Here. Hold it. (TAYLOR *places* HAROLD's *hands on the cylinder and mask.*) Got it? (HAROLD *nods.*) Good. Breathe. (TAYLOR *gropes in the pack until he finds another cylinder.*) Hypoxia won't cut it now. Maybe three hours before it starts snowin' again . . . enough . . . they'll be comin' up to six. They know we're in trouble . . . they hafto. (TAYLOR *puts the mask from the second cylinder over his mouth and turns the nozzle. They sit breathing the oxygen in deeply for awhile, then* TAYLOR *shuts off his nozzle and does the same for* HAROLD.) Not too much . . . we're gonna need it goin' down . . . Harold? (HAROLD *smiles dreamily.*) You gonna be alright?

Harold: Yeah . . . hunky-dory.

Taylor: Let's see the leg. (*He gently straightens* HAROLD's *left leg and puts it in his lap. Then* TAYLOR *slowly unzips his left overboot.*) You wanna take a look? (HAROLD *nods and* TAYLOR *unzips the leg of* HAROLD's *suit.*) Thank god for E.H.A.'s. Wearin' these fuckers for the summit was your idea Harold. (*Slapping* HAROLD's *face.*) You saved our miserable lives . . . you realize that? (HAROLD *smiles.*)

We'd've froze for sure last night without these babies. You ready?

Harold: Yeah. (TAYLOR *delicately peels back the heavy woolen sock from* HAROLD's *leg and pulls the leg of the suit open. We can see that the leg is badly broken.*)

Taylor: . . . Holy shit . . . we gotta get off this fuckin' mountain.

Harold: Stupid. (TAYLOR *puts the sock back on, then the overboot, and zips the pant leg up again, talking rapidly while he works.*)

Taylor: Can't do anything for it now. Have to get you off fast as possible. They might be able to save it. The quicker we get to base, better chance you've got. So just hang in there . . . Harold . . . just hang in there . . . all right?

Harold: I'm okay. It's just stupid. I should have known you were still on the rope.

Taylor: What the hell's it matter now? Right now we got to get off this mountain. Right?

Harold: Right.

Taylor: Okay. Equipment inventory, situation assessment.

Harold: (*Shaking his head.*) Water.

Taylor: Dehydration! Good. Very good. Water first. Yes. We are gonna help each other beat this mother. Good. (TAYLOR *unzips the top of his suit still further and reaches inside.*) Shouldn't be frozen, it's been layin' on my belly all night. (TAYLOR *pulls an insulation wrapped canteen out and takes off the cap. He drinks.*) Yeah, oh yeah. Drink. Not too much. (HAROLD *drinks.*) Not too much. (TAYLOR *takes the canteen away from* HAROLD, *screws the cap on and gives it back.*) Okay. Now, equipment inventory, situation assessment. (TAYLOR *grabs a pack and starts taking things out of it.*) Two ice axes . . . two oxygen bottles . . . climbing rope, 120 feet . . . Ice screws . . . Three . . . Ice hammer . . . thank god. Mine's gone. I threw it right off the fuckin' mountain when we went. (*Holding up a small tube.*) Sun screen . . . (*He takes* HAROLD's *mittens off and hands him the tube of sun screen.*) Save enough for me . . . Nylon tubing, thirty feet. These are thirty feet right?

Harold: Right.

Taylor: That should be enough if we need a sling. Two meat bars! You dirty fucker . . . holding out again. A little piggy to the end. We'll eat 'em before we go. One Pentax. You didn't use this on the summit did you?

Harold: No. Just back up, in case you screwed up your roll.

Taylor: (*Tossing the camera into space.*) Fat fucking chance.

Harold: We get back Cindy's going to kill you.

Taylor: We get back it's going to be because we carried us . . . and as little else as possible down this bastard. (TAYLOR *takes the other pack.*) Okay. What I got? Ice screws . . . two. Good. (*He rummages awhile, then all at once he is frantic, muttering to himself.*) Oh no . . . oh no . . . oh fuck, no . . . (*Totally frantic.*) oh holy fuck, no . . . no, no, no, no.

Harold: What is it?

Taylor: (*In utter disbelief.*) No rope . . . there's no rope in here. (*Howling.*) I forgot my back up rope! Oh . . . God Damn Mother fucking Son of a Bitch! (*He suddenly loses his breath and grabs the oxygen, turns the nozzle and puts the mask over his face. After a moment he puts it down.*) Mistake. Can't get upset about anything. We just have to work with what we've got. (*Pause.*) Harold, we've only got one rope.

Harold: Put some sun screen on.

Taylor: (*Taking the tube from* HAROLD.) Right. Sun screen. (*He puts some on his neck and face.*) Okay. We still got only one rope.

Harold: See what else is in the pack.

Taylor: I'll see what else is in the pack. Alright! Four carabiners. With the two on my rack and . . . (*He checks* HAROLD'*s belt.*) You've got one . . . that's seven beaners. Enough. Enough if we have to take you down in a sling . . . And I really can't see any other way we're gonna get you off this wall. Unfortunately, we don't have half the rope we need to run through the little buggers but we've got plenty of beaners . . . Yes! Well if nothing else, we can play horseshoes with the little fuckers.

Harold: Maybe I could make it on the rope.

Taylor: Yeah, sure Harold. I'd rather not repeat yesterday's experience if you don't mind. You need a sling. You're a wreck. You NEED a sling.

Harold: How's your shoulder?

Taylor: (*Rubbing his shoulder absently.*) Great. Fine. Does wonders for the deltoids—havin' somebody stomp on 'em with crampons. Yeah. They're just wonderful.

Harold: Yeah . . . well . . . I broke my leg.

Taylor: Right. That makes 'em feel a lot better. (*Noticing holes in the fabric on his shoulder.*) Look at those holes . . . brand new, state of the fuckin' art, expedition parka, and you punch fuckin' holes all through it.

Harold: I thought you were off the rope.

Taylor: Forget it. (*A beat, and then* TAYLOR *starts laughing.* HAROLD *joins in. They stop.*)

Harold: What are we laughin' at?

Taylor: We've only got one rope.

Harold: Maybe we can still make a sling and use just one rope.

Taylor: Come on, Harold! We're gonna be lucky to find one more ledge between here and the bottom of this wall that'll hold both me and you all trussed up in a sling, let alone three!

Harold: See what else is in the pack.

Taylor: I'll see what else is in the pack. One camera containing records of a triumph that others may never see . . . one rain poncho. You've got yours under you. They'll come in handy to make the sling that can't be used BECAUSE we've only got one fucking rope. It's no good. (TAYLOR *puts the pack down and stares into space for a moment.*) It's no good. I gotta go back and get the other rope. (*He takes the ice screws and carabiners, and puts them on his gear sling.*)

Harold: Taylor, you can't go up this wall. We're both half frozen! We're exhausted. Your shoulder's racked up. We can't go up this monster!

Taylor: Speak for yourself John . . . we're gonna go down the god damn wall aren't we?

Harold: That's different and you know it! It's a lot easier goin' down on a rappell than it is tryin' to . . .

Taylor: RIGHT! RIGHT! YOU TELL ME HOW EASY A RAPPELL IS HAROLD!!! Let me explain this to you all right? SITUATION ASSESSMENT! We've got one one hundred and twenty foot rope. The wall we are on is 600 feet if it is a fucking inch! We are maybe half way down it

. . . if we are lucky. We couldn't have fallen more than twenty, twenty-five feet to this ledge. We'd've bounced right off the motherfucker if it'd been any farther than that. That's three hundred feet to go—one more ledge if we are lucky! The rope will be doubled using a beaner as a pulley for the sling . . . one one hundred and twenty foot rope will become just sixty feet long. One ledge Harold, if that . . . We need two ropes to be in striking distance of that ledge. God help us if it's not there. Do you understand now Harold? Do you understand? (*We hear the wind.* TAYLOR *looks up, then down at the ledge they are on.*)

Harold: I thought you had a ledge. I thought you were off the rope. I couldn't see you in the snow. There wasn't any tension!

Taylor: I had a crack. I was takin' a little breather. You should've called down to me.

Harold: . . . I know.

Taylor: Wait a minute . . . Harold . . . what would you say the odds are of two climbers on a six hundred foot, ninety degree ice wall coming off their rope . . . and then surviving the night with a temperature somewhere between forty and fifty degrees below zero in nothing but Emergency High Altitude suits, overboots, and a couple of fucking ponchos . . . what would you say the odds are of that happening?

Harold: No odds. Too improbable.

Taylor: No odds . . . no odds. I'm goin' up there and get the rope. With the luck we've had so far, I may dance up the son of a bitch. On belay.

Harold: Belay on. (TAYLOR *taps the R. ledge with his ice axe.*) Rotten! Yep! Rotten ice . . . oh no you don't baby, you've won all the rounds you're gonna get from me. Cruise on the crack. (TAYLOR *moves over to the L. side of the ledge.*)

Taylor: She's up there, probably just beyond that overhang. I can't climb up and tie this rope off to it, cause with it doubled I'd still be about eighty feet short of this ledge and that's too big of a jump even for me . . . I'm just gonna have to pull the bastard free. It's our only chance. (TAYLOR *puts his ice axe and ice hammer in his tool belt,*

then he begins testing the face of the wall for hand holds.)
Harold: Take care.

HOOTERS
by Ted Tally

SCENE 1

Clint and Ricky, two nineteen-year-olds, have come to Cape Cod for the weekend in the hope of "scoring" with some women. They were buddies in high school. Clint, who is shy and inexperienced with women, has gone on to college. Ricky, who acts the great stud, has gone to work for his father selling cars.

The play opens with the young men arriving at their motel room near the beach. Ricky is excited—he has spotted a "ten" in the parking lot.

(*Clint enters, struggling with the weight of a large styrofoam cooler. He drops it with a gasp on one of the beds. He sits, opens the cooler, takes out a beer. He opens it and drinks.*)

Ricky: (*Offstage.*) Did you *see* that?
Clint: See what?
Ricky: (*Off.*) Incredible!
Clint: See what?
Ricky: (*Off.*) Parking lot! Jesus!
Clint: See *what*? (RICKY *enters, carrying two suitcases, an airline bag, and a suit bag.*)
Ricky: Right after we pulled in!
Clint: Where?
Ricky: The window!
Clint: Where?
Ricky: Hurry up! (RICKY *is dropping bags in a wild flurry as*

he races for the "window," D.C. Clint tries to catch a
falling suitcase and misses it.)

Clint: Hey, watch it!

Ricky: (*Looking out.*) Where are you, I know you're out
there, come *on* . . .

Clint: My binoculars are in here!

Ricky: (*Points.*) There, right there! Peace on earth, good
will to men. (*The next two lines overlap.*)

Clint: Just throw my goddam binoculars down next time
like they were made out of rubber why don't you?

Ricky: Will you shut up already and just come over here and
take a *look* at this?

Clint: Jerkwad.

Ricky: And bring the binoculars! (CLINT *fumbles in his suitcase, pulls out binoculars, hurries to the "window."*)

Clint: What's the big deal?

Ricky: That! Will you look at that? Un-be-lievable.

Clint: Where?

Ricky: Behind the green *Camaro*! What are you, blind?
Hurry up, it's on the hoof!

Clint: Where's the *Camaro*, for Christ's sake?

Ricky: Big tree—left side—over a little—

Clint: I see it! I see the green *Camaro*! (*Pause.*) I don't see
anything else.

Ricky: (*Stares out, relaxes.*) Skip it.

Clint: That's *it*? A green *Camaro*?

Ricky: Skip it, it's gone. You'll never see it again for the rest
of your life.

Clint: I never saw it the first time! (RICKY *crosses, sprawls
out on a bed.*)

Ricky: You had your chance and you blew it.

Clint: (*Still peering through binoculars.*) Where? (*Pause.*)
You mean that fat number in the sweatshirt?

Ricky: *Wrong.*

Clint: You broke my Swiss binoculars just to show me some
fat broad in a Snoopy sweatshirt?

Ricky: Idiot! I'm talking masterpiece and all you can see is
the livestock. Throw me a beer.

Clint: Well, I don't see anything.

Ricky: Throw me a beer.

Clint: Throw yourself a beer!

Ricky: C'mon sport. (CLINT *opens cooler, gets a beer and tosses it to* RICKY. *Then he sits on the other bed and examines his binoculars.*)

Clint: If you'll pardon me saying so, I think you're full of it. And I don't even believe there *was* anything.

Ricky: (*Pause.*) Well?

Clint: I think they're okay.

Ricky: Will you forget the stupid binoculars?

Clint: These things are *Zeiss*, buddy, in case you never heard of that.

Ricky: No, I never heard of that.

Clint: Well maybe if you were still in school you'd hear about a few things for a change.

Ricky: Oh yeah? Sure. What are you, *ma*joring in binoculars? Look, you want to hear about this or not, cause you know you do, only you just can't stand to be too *inter*ested, cause that's not cool for college types or something.

Clint: I really don't give a flying fart.

Ricky: Course not.

Clint: (*Pause.*) It's not as if I even did, cause I don't.

Ricky: Sure. (*Pause.*) Five foot ten.

Clint: Get out.

Ricky: I swear to God. Twenty-five or twenty-six years old.

Clint: (*Whistles.*) Jesus. I never made it with an older woman. Have you?

Ricky: Plenty of times.

Clint: And?

Ricky: And, maybe you weren't aware, but there's a very interesting statistic that women that age and up are just be*gin*ning to hit their sexual potential.

Clint: I know how they feel.

Ricky: Ha! For you it was fourteen. You're five years over the hill already.

Clint: What color hair did she have?

Ricky: Well—brown.

Clint: Boring, in other words.

Ricky: Hair okay, but nothing to write home about.

Clint: What color eyes?

Ricky: I don't know—big! What's all this color business?

Clint: Physique?

Ricky: Now you're talking. *Great* physique—A minus on the lungs.

Clint: Good knockers, huh?

Ricky: Very good hooters.

Clint: *Hooters!*?

Ricky: Honk honk!

Clint: Jesus, I haven't heard that word since high school.

Ricky: Well it's only been a year. You make it sound like World War II or something. (*They have begun unpacking their suitcases.*)

Clint: What about her legs?

Ricky: Endless.

Clint: What about her ass?

Ricky: Clint, try not to be so crude. You're talking about the woman I love.

Clint: In other words, she's got a *great* ass.

Ricky: Hey hey hey!

Clint: Whattya say?

Ricky: Okay, hold it a minute: Her face. Clint, I can't even find the words. Never before seen in our galaxy.

Clint: Yeah?

Ricky: *Overall* rating—including the face—are you ready?

Clint: Overall.

Ricky: (*Takes a breath.*) A Ten.

Clint: (*Pause.*) Are you out of your mind?

Ricky: A definite Ten.

Clint: Are you crazy?

Ricky: From the Russian judge, a nine-point eight, but I gotta say an All-American Ten.

Clint: With boring hair and A minus hooters?

Ricky: I'm talking overall effect. The sum is more than the parts.

Clint: Ricky, there is no such thing. Tens are only in your mind.

Ricky: Nadia Comaneci was a Ten. This is a Ten.

Clint: You're just saying that because I didn't see her.

Ricky: One-Oh.

Clint: You're making it up.

Ricky: I stand by my judgment.

Clint: You must mean a Nine. Surely you mean a high Nine, which in itself is unbelievable.

Ricky: I think we ought to recognize perfection when it floats by us.

Clint: You're delirious!

Ricky: Ah, *now* he wakes up. Don't get too many Tens around the dorm, huh? But I saw one here. You're just pissed you didn't.

Clint: Nobody's *ever* seen a Ten! (*Pause.*) The whole idea of Tenhood loses its meaning if anybody ever sees one!

Ricky: I not only saw her.

Clint: What do you mean?

Ricky: I more than just saw her.

Clint: What?

Ricky: I nodded to her.

Clint: You did *what*?

Ricky: You heard me, ace.

Clint: (*Pause.*) Did you—talk to her?

Ricky: What do you think, I wanted to scare her off? Jesus!

Clint: Okay!

Ricky: We looked. I nodded. (*Pause.*) Then I gave her the eye.

Clint: Get out of here!

Ricky: No, man.

Clint: You gave her the eye?

Ricky: Well, I sort of squinted. The sun was in my eyes. I was carrying all our junk.

Clint: You didn't do that thing with your tongue, did you?

Ricky: No!

Clint: If you did that tongue thing I'll murder you.

Ricky: I didn't!

Clint: Because you may think that's cool, but it makes you look like a rattlesnake.

Ricky: Will you grow up? I just gave her the eye.

Clint: What did she do?

Ricky: She sort of smiled.

Clint: Are you kidding? She was *nice*?

Ricky: It's true. I swear to God she's got the hots for me.

Clint: Oh man, now I know you're full of it! (*Pause.*) Did she *say* anything? What did she say?

Ricky: She was playing it a little cool, but a guy can tell.

Clint: Well what did she say?

Ricky: This and that.

Clint: No, man, *c'mon*!

Ricky: Just stuff. Excuse me, could you move your car you're blocking me in and stuff. But *nice*.

Clint: Oh God, I can *hear* her! She's got this voice like hot maple syrup in February . . .

Ricky: Yeah. So then I moved the car and—

Clint: She opens her mouth, her beautiful gorgeous twenty-five-year-old mouth, and out comes this—*sound*—

Ricky: Whatever. So then—

Clint: Like a cool breeze when you've worked up a sweat— like a—

Ricky: Who's telling this?

Clint: Promise me she's not a c.t.

Ricky: No way, Renee. This girl puts out, I can tell.

Clint: Cause if she's a Ten and a c.t., I'm going to go in*sane*. There won't be any reason to go on living.

Ricky: I'm telling you, she puts *out*.

Clint: Are you crazy? A Ten that puts out?

Ricky: The mind boggles, doesn't it?

Clint: (*Grabbing binoculars, hurrying back to window.*) A Ten that puts out—and is staying right here in this motel?

Ricky: Hey man, it's the Cod, right? What'd I tell you? We're here five minutes and a Ten is trolling her ass through the goddam parking lot.

Clint: The Cape, Ricky. Not "the Cod." And a real Ten wouldn't troll her ass through any parking lot. She'd be too nice.

Ricky: Well maybe there's two kinds of Tens, Mr. Coolness, did you ever stop to think about that? Maybe there's the nice girl kind, sort of the skinny wispy model, and then maybe there's another kind that will chew through you like a Black and Decker chainsaw. And maybe—I say just maybe—what we've got here is the kind with teeth.

Clint: A minus on the hooters, right?

Ricky: Like she got hit in the back by a pair of bazooka shells.

Clint: Jesus.

Ricky: Jesus H.

Clint: This is it, huh? A Ten. Oh wow . . .

Ricky: Hey—hey Clint—just like old times, huh?

Clint: You said it, pal.

Ricky: All *right*! Only this time with a Ten!

Clint: And how many of *those* were there at Dwight D. Eisenhower Senior High?

Ricky and Clint: (*Together.*) Zilch!

Ricky: A Ten!
Clint: A Ten!
Ricky: An Ab-so-lute Ten . . .

MUSEUM
by Tina Howe

It is the last day of an art show in a major museum of modern art. The guard has just turned on the lights and prepares himself for the crowds: "He rocks on his heels, sucks his breakfast out from between his teeth, picks fuzz off his uniform, hoists up his underwear, and then waits."

Michael Wall enters "carrying an arsenal of photographic equipment including a camera attached to a tripod." He walks up to a painting, studies it, takes a reading with his light meter, and prepares to photograph it—"all with enormous concentration, energy, and flair." But just before he snaps . . .

The Guard: It's against museum regulations to photograph the art works.
Michael Wall: (*Whirling around, furious.*) You're kidding!
The Guard: It's against museum regulations to photograph the art works.
Michael Wall: Thanks alot for waiting to tell me until I was all set up . . .
The Guard: I'm surprised they even let you in with all that stuff . . .
Michael Wall: (*Shaking his head.*) Too much!
The Guard: The attendant downstairs is supposed to see that all photographic equipment is left in the check room . . .
Michael Wall: I don't believe this . . .
The Guard: . . . and that includes binoculars, telescopes, folding . . .

Michael Wall: You wait until I'm all set up, tripod locked, camera attached, "f" stop set . . .

The Guard: I've seen the attendant downstairs refuse visitors admittance who were just carrying . . . film!

Michael Wall: . . . AND WHEN ALL OF THAT IS DONE, THEN YOU TELL ME IT'S AGAINST MUSEUM REGULATIONS TO PHOTOGRAPH THE ART WORKS!

The Guard: And not just film either, but radios, tape-recorders, typewriters and sandwiches . . .

Michael Wall: Who do I see to get permission?

The Guard: I've seen the attendant downstairs stop visitors who had bulging pockets.

Michael Wall: (*Detaching his camera from the tripod.*) The Head of Public Relations? The Administrative Assistant?

The Guard: The public has no respect for "place" anymore.

Michael Wall: The Curator? The Chairman of the Board?

The Guard: They wear tennis shorts to church. They drink soda at the opera. They bring flash cameras to museums. . . .

Michael Wall: (*His camera in hand, walks up to* THE GUARD *and starts snapping his picture.*) Come on, who do I see for permission to photograph the art works? (*Taking a picture with each guess.*) The Cinematic Representative? The Acting President of the Exhibition? The Liason for Public Information? (*Pause.*) You have an interesting profile.

The Guard: I've caught men exposing their genitals in this room!

Michael Wall: (*Getting involved with* THE GUARD *as a model.*) Good cheek bones!

The Guard: Certain shows . . . inspire that!

Michael Wall: . . . strong chin . . .

The Guard: 19th Century French Academy nudes encourage . . . flashing.

Michael Wall: (*Adjusts* THE GUARD's *head for a shot.*) Hold it . . .

The Guard: (*Voice lowered.*) You'd be surprised, the shortest men have the most swollen genitals . . .

Michael Wall: Nice . . . nice . . .

The Guard: (*Flattered, shyly poses for him.*) And there don't even have to be women in the room in order for these . . . shorter men to expose their swollen genitals. . . .

Michael Wall: (*Still snapping.*) Come on, give me a hint. Do I see the curatorial staff or the administrative staff?
The Guard: Very few women expose themselves.
Michael Wall: (*Taking closeups.*) Nice, very nice. . . .
The Guard: Though I *have* seen a few younger women lift their skirts and drop their panties.
Michael Wall: Please! Who do I see to get permission to photograph the art works?

RESPONSIBLE PARTIES
by Jeffrey Sweet

Scene 3

As the lights come up on the lobby of a "seedy motel" in Los Angeles, Randolph, the owner, enters looking exhausted. He buys a Coke from the machine, sits down and closes his eyes. Cornell, the hotel manager, enters carrying a small suitcase. He notices Randolph and puts the suitcase to the side, hoping Randolph will not notice it. Cornell has spent time in prison.

Randolph can't help but intrude himself into other people's lives. He has just returned from the hospital where he took a guest—a young man—who had received a serious head gash. The gash was inflicted by a young woman who invited him to her hotel room and then changed her mind about having sex with him. The girl is Cornell's former girlfriend, and she came to the hotel to resume their relationship. When Cornell rejected her, she began her seduction of the other young man, but couldn't go through with a sexual encounter because she realized she only really wanted Cornell.

Earlier in the day Randolph put pressure on a couple (the Reeses) to pay him the money they owed him. Mr. Reese went out in his car (which he calls Tammy) and held up a bar to get the money. Randolph wouldn't take the money after he learned how it was obtained and insisted that it be left with him and returned to the bar. He also offered Mrs. Reese the opportunity to stay with him when her husband left.

Cornell: You look bushed.

Randolph: (*Opening his eyes.*) What a fucking night.

Cornell: Where's Marshall?

Randolph: I just tucked him in. He was half asleep on the way back anyway. They doped him up with something. Twenty-three stitches.

Cornell: Really.

Randolph: Reminded me when my mother used to sew up Thanksgiving turkey.

Cornell: The Reeses left.

Randolph: Yeah, I saw Tammy was gone. What did you do with the money?

Cornell: It's in the safe. Nine hundred forty-three dollars.

Randolph: Almost don't deserve to get it back.

Cornell: Hunh?

Randolph: What's the name of that place? Lucky Lindy's. Letting themselves get robbed, schmuck like that.

Cornell: You're giving it back?

Randolph: Of course I am. You think I should keep it?

Cornell: No. I was just wondering how you plan on doing it.

Randolph: I'll just give it back.

Cornell: You can't just drop by and hand it to them, say "Here's some money was stolen from you last night." They'll naturally be curious about where you got it.

Randolph: I could say I found it.

Cornell: Yeah, but how would you know where it came from?

Randolph: Oh, right.

Cornell: They don't have their name stamped on it, "Property of."

Randolph: So, you got any ideas?

Cornell: Find out the name of the owner of the place and mail it to him anonymously.

Randolph: I don't like sending cash through the mail. This is a pain in the ass. Maybe I should just call the cops after all. What am I sticking my neck out for? For what? For someone pulled a gun on me, called me names? I mean, this is turning out to be more trouble than it's worth. What do you think?

Cornell: I think it depends.
Randolph: On what?
Cornell: On what it's worth. What *is* it worth?
Randolph: You're asking me?
Cornell: You're the one that's doing it.
Randolph: I can't call the cops.
Cornell: Why not?
Randolph: She doesn't need any more trouble.
Cornell: Mrs. Reese?
Randolph: She should have taken me up on my offer. (*A beat.*) Fuck it. I'll mail the damn money. I'll put on rubber gloves, address it with letters cut out from the *L.A. Times,* do the whole number.
Cornell: Secret agent time.
Randolph: Sure. And if it gets there, it gets there. (*A beat.*) I'm so fucking tired I have not got the energy to yawn.
Cornell: Why don't you go home, get some sleep?
Randolph: Sounds like a good idea. You, too.
Cornell: Yeah.
Randolph: I don't want you getting sick.
Cornell: OK.
Randolph: OK. (*Sees the suitcase.*) What's that?
Cornell: It's a suitcase.
Randolph: Isn't that your suitcase?
Cornell: Yes.
Randolph: That's your suitcase.
Cornell: It's mine.
Randolph: What's it doing out?
Cornell: I'm leaving.
Randolph: And you weren't going to tell me?
Cornell: I was afraid it would get complicated.
Randolph: So it was just going to be you gone—no explanation, no nothing?
Cornell: I wrote you a letter.
Randolph: Let's see. (CORNELL *gives him the letter.* RANDOLPH *reads it.*) What's this about?
Cornell: Like I say in the letter . . .
Randolph: All you say in the letter is goodbye. That much I can tell from seeing you walk out the fucking door with a suitcase in your hand. What I'm asking is . . . (*Frustration rising to a peak.*) What did I *do*?
Cornell: You didn't do anything.

Randolph: You're leaving here.

Cornell: It doesn't have anything to do with you.

Randolph: I'm being left in the lurch. I'd say that has a lot to do with me. (*A beat.*) Did I put too much pressure on you? Is that it?

Cornell: No.

Randolph: Or do you have some complaint how I treated you?

Cornell: No.

Randolph: I tried to treat you fair.

Cornell: You treated me fair.

Randolph: Then *what*?

Cornell: It isn't you, it's her.

Randolph: Talk, for Christ's sake! Tell me. You're blipping and blopping like you expect I know what you . . . Her. What about her?

Cornell: I used to know her. We used to have a thing. I had to break it off.

Randolph: That was before you got put away?

Cornell: (*Nods.*) Anyway, she heard I was out. She heard I was here.

Randolph: So she came to say hi.

Cornell: More than that. To start things again.

Randolph: Which you don't want.

Cornell: I don't want.

Randolph: So tell her to go.

Cornell: I did. She won't.

Randolph: You want *me* to tell her to go?

Cornell: She'd only find another place close by and keep showing up.

Randolph: All right, say that happens. She wants you, you don't want her. You keep saying no, eventually she gives up. All you've got to do is keep saying no.

Cornell: Except after you took Marshall away . . .

Randolph: What?

Cornell: I don't know. She started crying. Something happened.

Randolph: There you go blipping and blopping again. Say it. What? What is this something that happened?

Cornell: (*A flash of irritation.*) What do you want me to say? I fucked her. Is that what you want to hear?

Randolph: You're really brilliant, you know that?

Cornell: She was crying. I didn't know what else to do.

Randolph: Of course. What else could you *possibly* do. She got parents?

Cornell: A father. I tried calling him. He doesn't want her.

Randolph: Did you explain to him about what happened? Did you explain the way she is?

Cornell: I didn't have to explain to him. She's his daughter. He knows.

Randolph: But he's her *father*.

Cornell: He doesn't care he's her father. She's of age and he's tired.

Randolph: Tired. Who *isn't* tired? So you're leaving her in my hands.

Cornell: No.

Randolph: Who you trying to kid? You leave her here, her father doesn't want her. Whose hands does that leave?

Cornell: She's not your responsibility.

Randolph: Bet your sweet life she's not.

Cornell: And she's not mine.

Randolph: So you go, and here she is, and what happens to her?

Cornell: I don't know.

Randolph: Don't you care?

Cornell: I care.

Randolph: I see how much you care.

Cornell: I do. But maybe I'm afraid of drowning.

Randolph: If you drown, it'll be in your own bullshit.

Cornell: (*Flaring.*) Well, it's better than drowning in yours.

Randolph: What?

Cornell: Jesus Christ, between the two of you . . .

Randolph: What two of us?

Cornell: You, her. You want this, she wants that.

Randolph: I don't want anything. I just want to help.

Cornell: Who asked you? Man, you want a hobby, you go build model airplanes. Sorry, but I'm just not here to make you happy. That is not my job.

Randolph: And what is? Do you know?

Cornell: That's for *me* to figure out. Hey, you want to help someone, you take a look at yourself. All the advice, the opinions. Pouring out as if you had answers. As if you knew dick about anything. (CORNELL *stops. A beat.* RANDOLPH *turns to the desk, his back to the audience. He's* *deeply upset.* CORNELL *sees he's hurt him.*) Ah shit, Randolph . . .

Randolph: I'm an idiot.

Cornell: No . . .

Randolph: Jesus, the next thing you know, I would've tried tossing footballs with you. (*A beat.*) No, it's good you're going. You didn't even keep the john stocked with toilet paper.

Cornell: I know.

THERE ARE NO SACHER TORTES IN OUR SOCIETY
by Murray Schisgal

SCENE 1

Things haven't been going so well for Alex. His wife Janice's psychoanalysis (five days a week at seventy-five dollars a session) is driving him crazy *and* to the poorhouse. And today his boss at Dunfee's Department Store, Mr. Tarkis, died of a coronary right before his eyes.

But then his older brother Max showed up. Max, who disappeared years ago, has returned with a full beard, a canary in a cage, a cowboy outfit, and stories about how wonderful life can be when you drop out of the "rat-race" and live as a free man "traveling around this great country of ours." But even as his spirit is ignited by Max's presence, he is irritated over and over again by Janice's refusal to get out of her bathrobe and into some clothes that are suitable for welcoming their special guest. He does not take much comfort from her explanation that all her clothes, including her underwear, are out at the dry cleaners.

As the scene below starts, Alex has just sent Janice back to the bedroom to "please. . . . Get into something . . . . Anything." He returns from the bedroom, wipes his face with Janice's apron and starts to sweep up some glass that Max broke when he smashed the window to "let some air in here, for cryin-out-loud."

(For scene-study purposes the section from Janice's entrance to her exit may be omitted.)

Alex: So what's happening, Max? How long can you stay?

Max: Got plenty of time, Al. Not going back to Chicago anyway.

Alex: What about your job?

Max: Quit. I couldn't take it anymore. Too suffocating. They paid me peanuts. I've been traveling around this great country of ours, learning for myself what's what and who's who. I lived in Sante Fe, Boulder, Jackson Hole, San Francisco . . .

Alex: What did Doris say?

Max: Doris?

Alex: Your wife.

Max: Oh, Doris. My wife. Divorced her, Al.

Alex: Is that so?

Max: Oh, yeah. About two years ago. She got the house, the car, the bank account, the insurance policies and I got the canary.

Alex: The children stayed with her?

Max: *(Looking up.)* The . . . ?

Alex: The children. The last time I saw you you had five of them: two from your first marriage with Rosemarie and three more with Doris.

Max: Oh, the kids. You mean the kids I had with Doris when she was my wife. Oh, we had plenty of them, Al. Kids all over the place. There was one big fellow, our oldest, and then we had another boy . . . No . . . it was a girl. Was it a girl? *(Slight pause.)* One second, Al. Let me figure this out. There was a girl about eleven or twelve living in the bedroom next to the bathroom . . .

Janice: *(Sticks her head out of the bedroom.)* Alex, I'd like to see you for a minute. (ALEX *puts broom aside, takes off apron and moves to bedroom.)*

Max: I think it was a girl. Long hair, small behind, didn't do much talking, a real weirdo; used to scare the shit out of me.

Alex: I'll be right out, Max. (*He exits to bedroom, closing door.*)

Max: All I can tell you is if that kid living next to the bathroom isn't a girl, he's in plenty of trouble, oh, boy, is he in trouble. (*He rises, finds a bottle of whiskey, unscrews cap.*) I can't keep up with the kids nowadays. They got too many crazy ideas. Dope, sex, living together for the fun of it. I don't know what the hell's the matter with them! (*He lifts bottle to his mouth and drinks noisily.*)

Alex: (*Offstage.*) What is it? What are you doing standing there naked? (*Max gags on a mouthful of whiskey, turns to bedroom door in astonishment.*)

Janice: (*Offstage.*) I told you. I don't have anything to wear.

Alex: (*Offstage.*) Janice, how much more of this do you think I can take? (*MAX picks up as many glasses as he can carry, sits on sofa and fills them all with whiskey.*)

Janice: (*Offstage.*) What do you want me to do?

Alex: (*Offstage.*) I don't have any patience left, I swear. This has been absolutely the worst day of my life. First Mr. Tarkis . . . I come home . . . My brother's here . . . My only brother . . . I have to stand and sweep the floor. (*He starts sobbing loudly.* MAX *turns to bedroom door again.*) And I ask you . . . Get into a dress . . . And I have to go through this . . . The whole thing is ridiculous . . . (*He blows his nose heartily.*) Ridiculous . . . Now, please . . . Get into something . . . Anything . . . Please, Janice. (*ALEX enters from bedroom, closing door. He blows his nose again and wipes his eyes, using half-apron which he then pushes into his pocket. He picks up broom and starts sweeping.*)

Max: So what's new, kid?

Alex: It's been a . . . a hectic day for me. So much has been happening . . . (*He pulls out apron and blows his nose again.*) All at once . . . (*MAX rises, takes apron and broom from him, forcing him to sit down on sofa.*)

Max: Okay. Let's hear it. Come on, baby brother. Spit it out.

Alex: We . . . we had a terrible, an incredible tragedy at the office. Mr. Tarkis, my supervisor at the department store where I work . . . one minute I was talking to him and the next . . . he had a major coronary. They took him away in an ambulance. The ambulance driver said, "You're not seeing this guy again, Sucker!" Sucker, he called me. It all happened so quickly.

Max: Al, listen to me; look at me. Do you have to wait for somebody to drop dead before you wise-up and know what life's all about? Why do you think I quit my job, huh? Why do you think I left . . . left . . . (*He snaps his fingers.*)

Alex: Rosemarie? (MAX *shakes his head, snapping his fingers.*) Doris?

Max: Doris! That's the one. Why do you think I left her, huh? I left her because I know what you don't know. I know that life's here, now, this second. Time flies and before you know it you're too decrepit to do what you should have done when you had the chance or they put you away, six feet under, it's over! done with! forever! "No," I said to myself that day I quit my job at Winniker's Hoisery House. "You're getting out of this rat-race," I said to myself, "and you're gonna swing, baby, you're gonna bust out and up their's with their crummy time-clocks and their forty hours a week of torture and their rotten money-grubbing jobs!"

Alex: Max, I can't . . .

Max: (*Sarcastically.*) You can't. I know you can't, baby brother. You don't have the guts to break free and enjoy the good things that are outside that window. Laugh at the idiots, kid. They sold their ratty souls for pension-plans and insurance dividends and a couple of lousy martinis. Cut away from that crap. Fill your lungs with fresh air and feel the sun on your face for a change. Drink to the sun, baby brother. (*Rises; lifts glass.*) Drink to every two-legged stiff who has the guts to be his own man and yell out at the top of his lungs, "I have a right to happiness, too!" (*He swallows his drink and hurls the empty glass against wall, smashing it.* ALEX *pauses a beat, perplexed, then rises, picks up broom and starts sweeping together broken glass.* MAX *follows him.*) Your job, Al, are you happy with it? Do you get up every morning and say to yourself, "Hot-diggity-dog, this is it. If I drop dead this second I have no regrets, no complaints, no bad feelings." Do you get up every morning and say that to yourself, baby brother?

Alex: (*Feebly.*) It's not . . .

Max: How much do they pay you at . . . (*He snaps his fingers.*)

Alex: Dunfee's.

Max: Dunfee's.

Alex: Fifty-six thousand.

Max: (*Eyes popping out.*) Fifty-six . . . They pay you that much?

Alex: I'm one of the top buyers in sportswear.

Max: Then how come you're living in this chicken-coop?

Alex: (*Softly so as not to be overheard, puts broom down, leads* MAX *to sofa.*) That's what I have to speak to you about, Max. You see, it's . . . (*The bedroom door opens and* JANICE *enters. She is wearing her creased wedding gown and carries a very dry, pressed-flat bouquet of flowers.*)

Janice: We're both very glad you came, Max. Really. It's a pleasure having you here. You know, we were both very hurt when you didn't come to our wedding, but we never thanked you for your thoughtful gift of two wooden lobster-crackers and a stainless set of escargot holders which I do on this happy occasion. (*She picks up drink.*) Cheers. (*She gulps down whiskey, smashes empty glass against wall, sits down in armchair.*)

Alex: Janice, come with me, please.

Janice: (*Rises; shrugs to* MAX, *follows* ALEX.) What is it, Alex?

Alex: (*Moving to bedroom, holding* JANICE's *arm.*) I want to speak with you privately.

Janice: (*At bedroom door; whispers.*) He broke his glass. I thought it was expected of me.

Alex: (*Whispers.*) Janice . . . Will you please go into the bedroom and put on whatever it was you were wearing before? Will you please do that for me?

Janice: (*Slight pause.*) What was I wearing before?

Alex: Janice!

Janice: All right. All right. Have it your way. But if I go to Doctor Courtney again today you have no one to blame but yourself. Remember I said it first. (*She exits, closing bedroom door.*)

Alex: You have to help me, Max. You have to. I can't take anymore. It's Janice. She . . . (*Looks back to bedroom, lowers voice.*) I'm walking on a box of eggs here. I have to be careful. If I do one thing wrong, if I say one word wrong, off she goes to her analyst and it costs me another seventy-five bucks! And I can't afford it. I can't! When Grandpa and Grandma Kaminski came as refugees from Lithuania ninety-four years ago with a salami and a cardboard suitcase they had more than I have now . . . Does that make sense to you, Max? How do you explain it? What's the . . . ?

Max: (*Leads him to sofa.*) Here, here, sit down, Al. (*They both sit on sofa.* MAX *puts his arm around* ALEX *and presses his head down on his shoulder.*) What you must have gone through. All these years. And I wasn't around. (*Wipes his own tearing eyes.*) I could start crying myself. Finding you like this . . . In such misery . . . What does that woman want from you? What's she after? I don't get it.

Alex: She isn't well, Max. She's not at all well. She needs constant care and attention. She visits a doctor five times a week.

Max: (*Tapping his temple.*) Not a . . . ? (ALEX *nods solemnly.*) Has it been for long?

Alex: Three and a half years.

Max: But that's when you married her, Al.

Alex: That's when it started, Max. (*Head cuddled on* MAX's *shoulder.*) She . . . She just couldn't adjust. When she was single she worked at Dunfee's, everything was fine, terrific, but when we married, she gave up her job and she couldn't stand doing housework, so I said, "Go back to your job, who's stopping you?" So she said, "A married woman should keep house for her husband, she shouldn't be working." So I said, "So keep house for your husband, who's stopping you?" So she said, "I hate housework. I'm lonely." So I said, "Let's have children. They'll keep you company." So she began to scream and holler and she said she didn't want children, that if I ever mentioned the word children to her again, she'd jump out the window.

Max: She didn't.

Alex: She did. Once she was nearly out the window. I had to grab her and bring her back and . . . She was kicking . . . I got a shot in the eye—I couldn't see for a week!

Max: Al, you're my brother, right? (ALEX *nods.*) You're my flesh-and-blood, right? (ALEX *nods.*) I'll say this straight to your face: you're a schmuck! And I'll say it to you over and over. Schmuck, look how you're living! (*He rises.*) How can you let one precious second pass without getting up and yelling, "Enough! I had enough of this miserable life! I want more. More happiness! More fun! More sun! More love! More everything before it's over and done with! (*Finger across throat.*) Kaput!" Get off your fat behind, baby brother. What are you destroying yourself for? A woman who walks around naked and sends her underwear to the dry cleaners? For these crummy sticks of furniture? Then break them. Bust them up! Get rid of them! (*And as he speaks he wildly smashes furniture, lamps, etc.*) Smash them! They're not worth your life, kid! None of this junk is worth your life! None of it! Not a piece of it! Not a lousy . . . rotten . . . stick of it! (*From bedroom we hear* JANICE *smashing furniture. Both men turn to each other, dumbfoundedly.*)

Alex: (*Rises.*) You're right, Max. You're a hundred . . . a million percent right! I had it. I want more . . . Before it's too late, before I end up like Mr. Tarkis! (*He swallows a drink of whiskey, pulls back his arm and swings it to throw empty glass but it refuses to leave his hand: he looks at it in his hand with great surprise.*) I'm getting out. From here. From Dunfee's Department Store. From now on it's life, to the brim! to the hilt! you bet! (*He hurls empty glass against wall, but it bounces back across room—it is made of plastic. He stomps on it brutally.*)

Max: Stay with it, baby brother.

Alex: All the things I've ever dreamed of doing, I'm doing. I can't help that woman. I can't do it. No more. (MAX *takes off* ALEX's *bathrobe, puts his own tasseled jacket on* ALEX.) I'll never be able to thank you, Max. Never. I put up with so much. I took so much. Like Mr. Tarkis. Only it's too late for him. (*He turns to* MAX.) Max, you're not offended because I'm leaving . . .

Max: Don't think it, kid.

Alex: This is your first night with us and here I am running off . . .

Max: (*Puts his cowboy hat on* ALEX's *head.*) We'll get together. But I want to give you a word of advice before you go.

Alex: Please.

Max: Don't fool around with anyone under seventeen.

Alex: Under seventeen. Right.

Max: Or over eighty-five.

Alex: Eighty-five?

Max: Eighty-five, eighty-four, see how you feel about it. See what gives you the most kicks. You'll be running into all kinds of women, all kinds of weirdos. You'll find yourself in some plush hotel room with some beautiful broad and before you know it she'll rip off all her clothes and say, "Beat me."

Alex: Beat me?

Max: Beat me!

Alex: What do I do?

Max: Beat her! Beat her! Beat the living shit outta her. She'll love you for it.

Alex: (*Grins.*) She'll love me?

Max: (*Puts his own suitcase in* ALEX's *hand.*) And, Al, I advise you to stay away from drugs. But if you have to take drugs, don't take them near a drugstore.

Alex: Don't take drugs near a drugstore. Got it. (*Shakes his hand gratefully.*) Thanks. Thanks, Max.

Monologues for Women

EDUCATING RITA
by Willy Russell

ACT I, SCENE 2

Rita is twenty-seven years old and has just started college. She attends the "Open University" at a school in the North of England. She is a hairdresser who has never taken education seriously before. But now it has become extremely important to her. She wants to know "everything." She is bright and curious, and feels like a misfit among her friends and family.

Her tutor, Frank, ponders why she never pursued college before. She replies, "What? After going to the school I went to?" "Was it bad?" Frank asks. She replies with the following speech (while sharpening pencils from her pencil case "one by one into perfect spikes, leaving the shavings on the desk").

(*To use her speeches as a monologue, omit Frank's lines.*)

(*You can find more information on this play in the section of this book containing "Scenes for One Man and One Woman."*)

Rita: Nah, just normal, y' know; borin', ripped-up books, broken glass everywhere, knives an' fights. An' that was just in the staffroom. Nah, they tried their best I suppose, always tellin' us we stood more of a chance if we studied. But studyin' was just for the whimps, wasn't it? See, if I'd started takin' school seriously I would have had to become different from me mates, an' that's not allowed.

Frank: By whom?

Rita: By your mates, by your family, by everyone. So y'

never admit that school could be anythin' other than use-less.

(FRANK *passes her the ashtray but she ignores it and continues sharpening the pencils on to the table.*)

Like what you've got to be into is music an' clothes an' lookin' for a feller, y' know the real qualities of life. Not that I went along with it so reluctantly. I mean, there was always somethin' in me head, tappin' away, tellin' me I might have got it all wrong. But I'd just play another record or buy another dress an' stop worryin'. There's always somethin' to make you forget about it. So y' do, y' keep goin', tellin' yourself life's great. There's always another club to go to, a new feller to be chasin', a laugh an' a joke with the girls. Till, one day, y' own up to yourself an' y' say, is this it? Is this the absolute maximum I can expect from this livin' lark? An' that's the big moment that one, that's the point when y' have to decide whether it's gonna be another change of dress or a change in yourself. An' it's really temptin' to go out an' get another dress y' know, it is. Cos it's easy, it doesn't cost anythin', it doesn't upset anyone around y'. Like cos they don't want y' to change.

Frank: But you—erm—you managed to resist another new dress?

Rita: Can't y' tell? Look at the state of this; I haven't had a new dress in twelve months. An' I'm not gonna get one either, not till—till I pass me first exam. Then I'll get a proper dress, the sort of dress you'd only see on an educated woman, on the sort of woman who knows the difference between Jane Austen an' Tracy Austin. (*She finishes sharpening the last pencil, and arranges it in line with the others. She gathers the pencil shavings into her hand and chucks them in the waste-bin.*) Let's start.

QUARTERMAINE'S TERMS
by Simon Gray

ACT I, SCENE 2

The setting is the staff room of the Cull-Loomis School of English for foreigners in Cambridge, England. During the course of the play we follow the lives of the faculty members and the principal for about a year and a half. Melanie is the school's "Elementary Conversation specialist." Besides her teaching, Melanie takes care of her ailing mother. Her mother, a domineering woman who used to teach philosophy at Cambridge University, has had a stroke that has left her partially paralyzed.

In the following monologue Melanie is talking to Henry Windscape, a fellow teacher who once, years ago, asked her to marry him. She followed her mother's advice and said no, and has regretted her decision ever since. Henry is now married and has two children. Melanie, who is usually successful at keeping her feelings in, reveals to Henry that her mother hates her. Henry tries to be reassuring, but Melanie is convinced of her mother's ill feelings toward her.

(*To use Melanie's speeches as a monologue, omit Windscape's lines.*)

Melanie: She hates me, you see.
Windscape: Who?
Melanie: Mother.
Windscape: Oh Melanie, I'm sure she doesn't.
Melanie: When I get home in the evenings—do you know what she does? She sits there for hours refusing to speak— then when I get her supper on the table—she refuses to eat. I know she can only work one side of her face now, but she can eat perfectly well. And when I try to feed

her—she lets the food fall out of her mouth, and—and stares at me with such malevolence, until suddenly she'll say something—something utterly—Last night she said "It's not my fault you've spent your life in my home. I've never wanted you here, but as you're too stupid and too unattractive to make any reasonable man a wife, I accepted the responsibility for you. And now I need you at last, you refuse to pay your debt." And coming out of the side of her mouth like a—like a gangster in one of those films you used to take me to. And she wets herself. She wets herself all the time.

Windscape: Oh Melanie, I'm so sorry. Of course I realised that last attack must have left her more—more incapacitated—and—possibly even a little incontinent—

Melanie: She's not incontinent, Henry. She does it on purpose. Out of spite. She never does it with Grimes. Only with me. She says that as I'm behaving like a neglectful parent, she'll behave like a neglected child. The only child I'll ever have. Of course, she adores Grimes—or at least she pretends to. And she's started giving her things—things that belong to me she knows I love. The buttons from Daddy's uniform or, the other day, a silly lithograph of a donkey that's hung in my room all my life almost—of course Grimes gives them back but—but—the worst thing is I'm beginning to hate her. To hate going home or when I'm there have such dreadful feelings. Because the thought of years—it could be years apparently—years of this—and so wishing she would have another attack and die now—dreadful—too dreadful—almost imagining myself doing something to—get her out of the way.

DEMIGOD
**by Richard LaGravenese
from "A . . . My Name Is Alice"
by Joan Micklin Silver and Julian Boyd**

ACT III

The play is "a musical review" for five actresses dealing with various issues in the lives of contemporary women. In the following piece a woman "enters and crosses to center stage." She addresses Frank.

Woman: I know you're gonna go. . . . I know it. I've been thinking a lot about what you said and I believe that you love me too. . . . And I understand that she gives you something else, something you need I guess is what you said. I wanted to apologize for yesterday. I was so confused, you know. I didn't know what to do with myself. . . . I mean, two years . . . what does a person do? Do I have a nervous breakdown? Do I start a new career? Do I go and have an affair with Alan Bates? I mean what do I do? I felt so ugly, Frank, and I don't mean just looks, I mean ugly . . . you know? Then you held me and touched the back of my neck and kissed me and said the things you said, and I felt a lot better. So, I did our laundry, like I always do on Sundays. And in the middle of folding our bedspread, I noticed your jock strap in the washing machine. Drowning in the wash cycle. It was twisting and turning, being mangled and manipulated into all sorts of painful positions. It looked as if it were crying out for help, poor little thing. Then the strangest thing . . . I imagined you were still in it . . . the jock strap I mean. I got hysterical. I mean I couldn't stop laughing. I thought it was the funniest thing I ever thought of. . . . People started staring at me. . . . A woman came up to me and said I should be careful not to inhale too much of that fabric softener. . . . Then all of a sudden I heard your voice. So I ran over to the machine, lifted the lid, and I could hear you in there, choking on the Clorox 2 and the Lemon Fab. But I couldn't make out what you were saying, so I yelled, "Frank, what is it, what are you saying?" And the manager of the laundromat yelled back, "I'm gonna call the police if you don't stop screamin' at your wash, lady!" It made me think, Frank. It made me think that maybe I'm not handling this too well. I can't drop two years of being lovers and go back to being friends. We never were friends, Frank. We slept together on the first date, remember? And I know you wanted to leave on good terms, like telling me you still love me and all, but I really think it'll be easier for me if we break up as enemies. It'll be better for me just to hate you openly instead of being so adult about it, don't you think? I mean, why be adult about it? So we can meet for lunch and laugh about all this? So you can tell me about your lovers and I can tell you about my lovers? So we can sleep together for old times' sake? I don't want to be your friend, Frank. I loved you, but I never said I liked you. And if being adult means throwing *me* away for that slut-rag you picked up on the goddamned train platform, then the most mature thing I could do for you would be to rip your face off. (*She mimes doing so.*) Oh, yes! That feels much better!

(*Blackout.*)

SAVAGE IN LIMBO
by John Patrick Shanley

It is Monday night in Scales, a bar in the Bronx. Linda Rotunda, "a done-up, attractive, overripe Italian girl" enters, sits down, and starts to cry. Why? "It's my boyfriend, Anthony. Something's gone wrong with him. . . . He wants to see ugly women." A young woman at the bar, Denise Savage, who knows Anthony, tries to set Linda straight: "They may look that way to you, honey, but I guess he sees 'em different . . . . A guy like Tony Aronica would never end up with an ugly woman." Linda replies:

(For more information about this play, see other monologues in this and other sections of this book.)

Linda: What are you tellin me? You're tellin me nothin. I tell you what's goin on, and you tell me it ain't goin on. It's goin on. Anthony wants to see ugly girls cause I don't know why, but that's the fuckin news and don't tell me otherwise. Every Monday night I go to his place and we spend time together, and this night I go and he's got this look in his eye. Like he knows somethin, and like he never seen me before. I got a scared feelin right away. I touch him but he puts my hand away. He says he wants to talk. What's he wanna talk about before we go to bed? What's there to talk about? When a woman wants to talk to a man, it's cause she wants the man to see her better. When it's the other way, when the man stops you from touchin to talk, what's there to talk about? It's gotta be bad. I tried to keep him from talkin. I turned myself on. But there was somethin in his mind. Even my mother sees what Anthony's got. Even my mother. She'd like a taste. She knows where I'm goin on Monday nights. I don't come home till late, the mornin sometimes, but she don't say anything. Any other time she would. But she knows where I go, and she wants it for me. Once I was goin, and she whispered to me so's my father wouldn't hear, Take it, Linda. That's all. Take it, Linda. And I did. And now he don't wanna see me cause he wants to see ugly women. I said I'd be ugly for him, but he said no. It didn't work that way. I'm so ashamed. I feel ugly. I feel fat. Anthony don't want me no more.

ANTON CHEKHOV'S "THE DUEL"
adapted by Michael Schulman and Eva Mekler
from the translation by Ann Dunnigan

ACT I, SCENE 4

Nadyezhda Fyordorovna was a young married woman in St. Petersburg when she met Layevsky and fell in love with him. They read poetry together, dreamed of a better world and a more meaningful life for themselves, and ran off together to a small village on the Black Sea in the Caucasus. It didn't take long for both Nadyezhda and Layevsky to tire of their new life and each other.

Their relationship has grown cold, but neither can speak aloud about their changes of heart. Neither wants to openly betray the dreams they wrought together. So Layevsky expresses his trapped feelings in petty criticisms of Nadyezhda, and Nadyezhda expresses hers by having brief and not very satisfying affairs.

At a picnic, Nadyezhda reveals some of her frustrations and longings to the Deacon, a young man who was recently assigned to the local parish.

(To form Nadyezhda's conversation with the Deacon into a monologue, the Deacon's lines have been omitted and slight adjustments were made in Nadyezhda's speeches.)

(*For more information about these characters, see other scenes from this play in other sections of the book.*)

Nadyezhda: Vanya's become cold, even insulting at times, but I don't mind anymore. On the contrary, I find it preferable this way now. At first . . . oh, at first I reacted with tears, reproaches, and even threatened to leave him. But no longer. Now I respond to his indifference with silence. I withdraw. Yes, in fact I'm glad he no longer treats me with affection. . . . Because I've disappointed him. In what way? you wonder. By no longer sympathizing with his dreams. He gave up Petersburg to come here to the Caucasus for a life of meaningful work, and I thought I would find a little cottage on the shore, a cozy little garden, birds, a stream, a place where I could entertain neighbors, nurse the poor peasants, and distribute little books among them. But the Caucasus turned out to be nothing but mountains, forests and huge stifling valleys. There are no interesting neighbors of any kind and one has even to worry about being robbed. As it turned out there seems to have developed between us a tacit agreement never to mention farming and the life of labor. He is silent, I believe, because he is angry with me for being silent. I know I still love Vanya since I get jealous of him and miss him when he is away. But life is so tedious here. One day is so much like the next. When I see the foreign steamers and the sailors in white, I remember . . . I remember a vast ballroom . . . and music mingled with the sound of French; a waltz strain begins to throb in my ears and my heart races with joy. I want to dance, I want to dance, I want to speak French . . . (*She has begun to cry and runs off.*)

IT HAD TO BE YOU
by Renée Taylor and Joseph Bologna

Act I

Theda Blau is "an out of work, ex-B movie actress who has no money and has been struggling desperately for three years to write a play for herself." As the play opens, Theda tells the audience, "This is a very important day in my life because this is the day of my love story." What kind of love story? "Like out of a Fairy Tale, because if it isn't, I'm not sure, but I think I might have a major nervous breakdown." She goes on to tell us that she needs a miracle: "Actually, I need two miracles. A man to love and success in my career."

In the scene that follows, Theda is at a TV studio for an audition. The auditioner has just told her that there is no script for her to read from. "We're looking for a spokeswoman for a cocktail mix and we just want to see your quality," he tells her.

(For more information on this play, see the section of the book containing "Scenes for One Man and One Woman.")

Theda: My quality? . . . This is the wrong day to have quality. I didn't get any sleep because I was working all night. See, I've been writing a play for myself for three years and I can't finish it. I don't know if I'm blank because I'm desperate or if I'm desperate because I'm blank . . . why am I telling you this? (*She starts crying.*) Uh . . . look, I'm sorry. I'm under a lot of duress. I had to get up early to go to a funeral this morning. (*She touches her black armband.*) I loved him so much. He really believed in me . . . Harold Steinman. I finally had a good agent and he died. And I hadn't even signed with him yet . . . gee, thanks for letting me start again. I need to support myself while I finish my play. I owe my psychiatrist, Maria Birnbaum, three thousand dollars . . . I shouldn't have told you that. Alright, I'm going to tell you the reason I need therapy so badly. I have been rejected so much in this business I have a list of people who almost killed me . . . NBC, CBS, Paramount . . . I try to have humor about it . . . look, let's face it. I know I'm not conventionally uptight like the women you normally see doing these commercials. But I can do them . . . "Oh Sue, your bathroom smells so much fresher than mine. I can see myself in your bowl." . . . uh . . . maybe I should talk about the movies I've been in. "A Cop's Gun," "The Monday Mugger," "Four Boys Who Hate" . . . See, I went to Hollywood about eight years ago. Nobody sent for me. I just went. See, I was going to be a sex symbol but I got a late start. But I'm a late bloomer. I know I am. Because I'm getting sexier. I'm getting better looking. It's not like I had something and I lost it. I never had it. But I'm getting it now. I love that quality in a woman. I've often wondered why there were so many women movie stars that committed suicide and not one of them ever thought of shooting one of the studio heads instead . . . (*Stage hands remove a lamp, more sandbags, and waiting room chairs.*) I can do it all. I've done it all. I've been a hit. I've bombed out. I would dare to be me on your commercial. I can sing, not good, not bad. (*She sings "Old Man River" to a fast tempo.*) "Ol Man River, that 'ol man river, he don't know phrum, phrum, he don't say phrum, phrum . . ." See, I forget the words but I just go right on. So what, it's real, it's what I would like to see on television. You very rarely see humming on TV . . . if I were selling your product, I would stand in front of the camera and say, "Look, it's a cocktail mix, it's not going to kill you." You're lucky, you got me at the right time because I'm on the come now. (*She pantomimes shooting dice.*) Success is a series of small steps. Well, this commercial is the first one. I'm getting good vibes from you people. "Ask and ye shall receive." So I'm asking . . . no, I'd better demand it! It's mine, it's mine to take. I insist that you hire me. And I swear if you don't, I'm going to go home and finish my play and that's it for all of you . . . I have the power to change my life . . .

SAVAGE IN LIMBO
by John Patrick Shanley

Denise Savage, wearing a dress and her best black pumps, enters Scales, a bar in the Bronx on a Monday night and says, "Where is everybody? Where is somebody? Where is any fuckin body? . . . I wanna have a good time."

But Savage won't have a good time tonight; nor does she have a good time most other times in her life. The good things in life are always just beyond her grasp. She leads a lonely existence, living with and taking care of her ailing mother. She is thirty-two years old and she confesses that she is still a virgin. "How does it feel?" she is asked. Her response:

(For more information see other monologues in this and other sections of this book.)

Savage: I feel strong. Like I'm wearin chains and I could snap 'em any time. I feel ready. I go to work and I feel like I could take over the company, but I just type. I go home and I see my mother in her chair and I feel like I could pick her up with one hand and chuck her out the window and roll up the rug and throw a big party. Everybody's invited. I go to the library and I wanna take the books down off the shelves and open all the books on the tables and argue with everybody about ideas. I wanna think out loud. I wanna think out loud with other people. You know what's wrong with everybody? Too smart. I know it sounds crazy. I know. But it's true. Everybody's too smart. It's like everybody knows everything and everybody argued everything and everything got hashed out and settled the day before I was born. It's not fair. They know about gravity so nobody talks about gravity. It's a dead issue. Look at me. My feet are stuck to the fuckin floor. Fantastic. But no. That's gravity. Forget it. It's been done it's been said it's been thought, so fuck it. It's not fair. I've been shut outta everything that mighta been good by a smartness around that won't let me think not one new thing. And it's been like that with love, too. You're a little girl and you see the movies and maybe you talk to your mother and you definitely talk to your friends and then you know, right? So you go ahead and you do love. And somethin a what somebody told ya inna movie or in your ear is what love is. And where the fuck are you then, that's what I wanna know? Where the fuck are you when you've done love, and you can point to love, and you can name it, and love is the same as gravity the same as everything else, and everything else is a totally dead fuckin issue?

TO GILLIAN ON HER 37TH BIRTHDAY
by Michael Brady

Act II, Scene 4

Gillian died at the age of thirty-five. It is now two years later, and her husband David still feels her loss acutely and is haunted by her memory. After her death in a boating accident David left his job as a college English professor and has spent his time lost in thought about Gillian and their life together. Indeed, he still speaks to her as if she were alive. Gillian was a successful anthropologist and an exceedingly bright and dynamic woman. The monologue that follows is taken from a scene in which David is remembering back to the early years of their marriage and to Gillian's reaction upon learning that she was pregnant. David wanted a child. But Gillian was determined to pursue her career. So she offered David "a bargain."

Gillian: We've got to strike a bargain tonight. No games, no jokes. Just a real bargain between you and me. All I have worked for, every dream, every hope, is in this grant. I have it in my hand, David, twenty-one and published in the field. And let's face it, even though you're good at it, Hawthorne and Melville won't ever do much more than pay the rent. So, please, don't ask me to do it all. Now I will have this child, since you're so set on it. Oh, I know that when it's here and I hold it in my arms, it will be a miracle and a wonder, and a thousand other things. But right now . . . Oh, David, I'm just not ready to be a mother. So here's the bargain. Once the kid is here, it's yours. You feed it, you do the baths, the diapers, all of it. And starting next summer, I get to do my work, no questions asked. And if you can't accept this, if this isn't good enough, then I will get in the car, drive to the city, and take care of this tonight. So, lover, we have our bargain, don't we?

SEA MARKS
by Gardner McKay

Act I, Scene 5

Timothea has just made love to Colm for the first time. He is a fisherman from a remote island off the coast of Ireland and had never been with a woman before. They met over a year and a half ago at a wedding. She stayed on Colm's mind and he began to write to her. His letters were surprisingly sensitive and poetic, and Timothea found her interest in him growing, although she couldn't remember their having met.

They met a second time at another wedding—this time on Colm's island. Timothea then invited him to visit her in Liverpool. When he asked "And where would I stay in Liverpool?" she replied, "With me."

Timothea works for a publishing house in Liverpool. Colm is not the first man she has made love to. As he sleeps she tells him of her first lover when she was a girl living on a farm in Wales.

(*For more information see other monologues in "Monologues for Men" section of this book.*)

Timothea: Colm? Colm? (*She crosses to the foot of the bed and tugs his leg, making sure that he's asleep; when she's certain he is, she talks to him.*) And *you* are the first boy who had *me*. It was you, Colm. You're the boy. (TIMOTHEA *becomes Welsh, once again, speaking in an accent.*) He was always trying something with me in the barn, grabbing at me and so forth. Always trying to show me what he had for me. Waiting for me places. You're that same boy. All of him you.

The boy and me had been delivering a calf, see?, and it was not a good birthing, you see? It was a bloody, bloody mess. It wasn't raining, but there was mist coming in through the cracks in the great door of the barn. The boy and me had been working at it a long time. The boy said she was to die but the good cow would *not* die. And when the calf came, it was weak, but fine. Oh, Jesus, fine, fine, fine.

(*Perhaps she takes his jacket and holds it around her.*)

It stood up and the boy cut it off from its ma, see? She tried to turn around to look at her calf for the first time but she couldn't get up, so much had been taken out of her. She tried to lick her calf but she couldn't get her legs under her. So the calf toddles over to its mother's face so it could be licked.

(TIMOTHEA *gets up, looks again at* COLM, *and goes to the hearth and lights it; warms herself, front and back.*)

There was blood all around. We didn't know which was to live or die. There's nothing to do with a cow—you must let cows decide how much they want to live. We were so tired.

(*She pauses.*)

I let the boy have me then. It was up in the hay loft—you might have expected that—and he seized me. (*Pause.*) You're the boy. That boy was you. And all the time we was doing it up there, there was blood on us from the cow. Blood on his arms he was pinning me down with. Then there was my blood. Too.

I just wanted to tell you that.

(COLM *has awakened and is quietly watching her.*)

And do you know what? *That* boy couldn't even write his name.

THE DAY THEY SHOT JOHN LENNON
by James McLure

On the day John Lennon is murdered, Fran Lowenstein stands across the street from his apartment building to pay her last respects to the slain singer. Fran is a native New Yorker who was part of the "Woodstock generation." Before long she finds herself talking to Brian Murphy, an attractive businessman who also came to pay tribute to Lennon. They talk about the power of love and the electrical charges one's body gives off during sex. He compliments her on her skin and asks her if she likes art. She answers that she *loves* art and tells him about the Edward Hopper exhibit she has just seen at the Whitney Museum. She describes the significance she finds in Hopper's paintings.

(*For more information read the introductory notes to the scene between Fran and Brian in the section of the book with "Scenes for One Man and One Woman."*)

Fran: There's a very melancholy strain in the work of Edward Hopper. A lack of detail in the faces. He captures the mundane quality of existence. And that desperate quality within that mundaneness. I mean, his people look at each other but they don't see each other. Most of the times they don't even look at each other. They don't reach out and touch each other. They just wait. With that awful blankness. In nighthawk diners, in quiet Sunday roadside windows, forgotten gas station, over chop suey they wait. There's this one where there are no people, just the trees and the grass, and it seems to rustle as if a disturbing wind were passing by. And there's a great sense of urgency and expectancy in the woods. Something is about to happen. The woods are waiting, waiting. Waiting. Just waiting for the answer. But waiting quietly and darkly in a woodsy sort of way. There's this other one where a group of people are waiting in like reclining deck chairs like at a resort only they're facing mountains, like Arizona mountains, with a vast desert that sweeps before them and they're all dressed up as if they were waiting to be beckoned, to be called, to be taken across this vast lunar landscape By who? By what? By death? By God? By flying saucers? What power will take them? What power are they waiting for? I don't know. Who knows? (*With significance.*) But this much I do know. They're very placid as they wait. They are not disturbed, show no anxiety, they are placid. (*Pause.*) And here we are. A group of strangers looking at this building where he lived. Waiting for an answer. Waiting for understanding. Waiting for forgiveness? Waiting for something. That's for damn sure.

SEASCAPE WITH SHARKS AND DANCER
by Don Nigro

SCENE 5

The play takes place in "a small decrepit house on Cape Cod." The owner of the house is a young man named Ben, a writer in his late twenties. One night he fishes Tracy, an attractive young woman, out of the ocean. She is naked and clearly trying to kill herself—although she denies it (she says she was dancing). Tracy is a drifter who, as she puts it, is "a very bright little girl, and rather wicked (who has) wandered all over the country hitching rides and shacking up until she'd been just about everything and done almost everywhere, although she (is) in fact only twenty and a half years old."

During their very first moments together Tracy begins heaping a torrent of abuse on Ben. She almost breaks his nose, kicks him in the groin, and calls him every insulting name she can think of. But Ben sees something worthwhile in her and understands the depth of her pain. Over the next few months he continues to care for her—and continues to endure her insults. After Tracy discovers that she is pregnant she tells Ben she intends to have an abortion. He demands that she not do it. "It's my baby. . . . If you do that you can forget all about me," he threatens.

Tracy does have the abortion. She returns, looking tired, and crosses to the couch where Ben is sitting. She sits, "not close to him." She asks him if he hates her. He responds by asking her why she tries to make him hate her. She denies that she does, but he pushes her for an answer. She replies with a story about her childhood.

Tracy: When you were little did your parents always keep giving you these animals and things, like they thought you looked like you had to have something to be grabbing onto all the time or you'd fall over or blow away or something? Well, don't look at me like that. Listen, if you don't want to hear this I can just leave, if you think this is stupid or something. I mean, you asked me a question and now I'm going to answer it, whether you like it or not. So my parents kept giving me these animals, see, not just like cats and dogs but also a pregnant racoon and two ducks named Mickey and a deflowered skunk and a chicken named Arnold and all kinds of things like that. They were really dumb. Not the animals, my parents. Well, you know how dumb they are. And the house we lived in was too close to the road, and what happens when you live too close is that all of your animals get splattered always on the road, and your brothers are always having to go out with a shovel and scrape them off and take them someplace to bury. And sometimes if they're all squashed but not quite dead your brother has to hit them with the shovel until they stop screaming or quacking or squawking or whining or meowing as the case may be. And giving them names makes it worse but I loved to and I couldn't help it and I did and when they got squashed then it wasn't just the cat or the duck it was somebody with a name that you'd lived with and slept with and talked at and listened to and fussed over and took care of and accepted you and then it was the mess that was left on the road. And after the last one was squashed which was a small bowlegged Persian kitten named Clarence aged six months who was sort of dumb and loved me a lot and never wanted any more than to just be alive and play with some piece of string or something, after that last one I made my stupid parents promise me they would never get me another thing that was alive because I had figured out what was true and still is true that there is no excuse and no way ever to make up for the millions and millions and millions of innocent betrayed and squashed up dead, and nobody's parents and nobody's God was ever going to be able to explain that to me and make it all right, and the only way not to go crazy if you had the misfortune to be a compulsive namer and lover was if you never hooked yourself up with splatterable things then it can never be your fault for needing them and having them because if you don't give you can't hurt and you don't get guilty because you can't betray if you never gave to begin with. Doesn't that make sense to you? It does make sense. It does.

RAINDANCE
by M. Z. Ribalow

ACT I

Wicked Falina is a "Mexican saloon girl . . . somewhere in the mythical American southwest." She is "sultry, passionate, generous, shrewd, tempestuous, craves attention (and is) in general a knockout." She serves drinks at the bar and, for a price, takes her men upstairs for a good time. As the play opens, a light comes up on her. "She smiles warmly at the audience and starts to talk to them . . . having a wonderful time and meaning every word she says."

Falina: Hello, all you blue-eyed devils out there, waiting to break a poor girl's heart. I am Wicked Falina, the Mexican saloon-girl. You remember me. I live a lot, I love a lot, just like they say in the movies, eh? I take your money and I take your hearts. I spit in your eyes and make you love it, oh, how I make you love it. You may marry your blond toothpicks but you crawl on the floor for a chance to taste my toes. You love to hear me moan, you love to tie me to the brass bed and tickle me with your spurs, and when you leave I stay in your blood and burn your brains to ashes. I am Eve, I am woman, I am an epidemic in your empty lives. I can make you light a match and hold it until your hands catch fire. I can make you beg for more when you thought you wanted to watch the football game. I am the Queen of Paradise, the magical witch of the west, Snow Black the virgin whore, every man's brightest dark dream. I cannot heal, but I can make your wound attractive. And I will. Oh, how I will. I am the sun, the moon, the flying carpet. I can solve nothing, but I can do it all. I am Wicked Falina. So hello. It's so good to see you. I can't tell you just how good it is.

Monologues for Men

GLENGARRY GLEN ROSS
by David Mamet

SCENE 3

Glengarry Glen Ross is a tract of real estate and Roma is a real-estate salesman. The scene takes place in a Chinese restaurant. Roma is sitting alone in a booth, talking to Lingk, seated at the next booth.

(For scene-study purposes, Roma's speeches may be joined into a monologue.)

(*For more information see another scene from this play in "Scenes for Two Men."*)

Roma: . . . all train compartments smell vaguely of shit. It gets so you don't mind it. That's the worst thing that I can confess. You know how long it took me to get there? A long time. When you *die* you're going to regret the things you don't do. You think you're *queer* . . . ? I'm going to tell you something: we're *all* queer. You think that you're a *thief*? So *what*? You get befuddled by a middle-class morality . . . ? Get *shut* out of it. Shut it out. You cheated on your wife . . . ? You *did* it, *live* with it. (*Pause.*) You fuck little girls, so *be* it. There's an absolute morality? May *be*. And *then* what? If you *think* there is, then *be* that thing. Bad people go to hell? I don't *think* so. If you think that, act that way. A hell exists on earth? Yes. I won't live in it. That's *me*. You ever take a dump made you feel you'd just slept for twelve hours . . . ?

Lingk: Did I . . . ?

297

Roma: Yes.

Lingk: I don't know.

Roma: Or a *piss* . . . ? A great meal fades in reflection. Everything else gains. You know why? 'Cause it's only food. This shit we eat, it keeps us going. But it's only food. The great fucks that you may have had. What do you remember about them?

Lingk: What do I . . . ?

Roma: Yes.

Lingk: Mmmm . . .

Roma: I don't know. For *me*, I'm saying, what it is, it's probably not the orgasm. Some broads, forearms on your neck, something her *eyes* did. There was a *sound* she made . . . or, me, lying, in the, I'll tell you: me lying in bed; the next day she brought me café au lait. She gives me a cigarette, my balls feel like concrete. Eh? What I'm saying, what is our life? (*Pause.*) It's looking forward or it's looking back. And that's our life. That's *it*. Where is the *moment*? (*Pause.*) And what is it that we're afraid of? Loss. What else? (*Pause.*) The *bank* closes. We get *sick*, my wife died on a plane, the stock market collapsed . . . the house burnt down . . . what of these happen . . . ? None of 'em. We worry anyway. What does this mean? I'm not *secure*. How can I be secure? (*Pause.*) Through amassing wealth beyond all measure? No. And what's beyond all measure? That's a sickness. That's a trap. There is no measure. Only greed. How can we act? The right way, we would say, to deal with this: "There is a one-in-a-million chance that so and so will happen. . . . *Fuck* it, it won't happen to *me*. . . ." No. We know that's not the right way I think. (*Pause.*) We say the *correct* way to deal with this is "There is a one-in-so-and-so-chance this will happen . . . God *protect* me. I am powerless, let it not happen to me. . . ." But no to *that*. I say. There's something else. What is it? "If it happens, AS IT MAY for that is not within our powers, I will *deal* with it, just as I do *today* with what draws my concern today." I say *this* is how we must act. I do those things which seem correct to me *today*. I trust myself. And if security concerns me, I do that which *today* I think will make me secure. And every day I *do* that, when that day *arrives* that I need a reserve, (a) odds are that I have it, and (b) the *true* reserve that I have is the strength that I have of *acting each day* without fear. (*Pause.*) According to the dictates of my mind. (*Pause.*) Stocks, bonds, objects of art, real estate. Now: what are they? (*Pause.*) An opportunity. To what? To make money? Perhaps. To *lose* money? Perhaps. To "indulge" and to "learn" about ourselves? Perhaps. *So fucking what*? What *isn't*? They're an *opportunity*. That's all. They're an *event*. A guy comes up to you, you make a call, you send in a brochure, it doesn't matter, "There're these *properties* I'd like for you to see." What does it mean? What you *want* it to mean. (*Pause.*) Money? (*Pause.*) If that's what it signifies to you. Security? (*Pause.*) Comfort? (*Pause.*) All it is is THINGS THAT HAPPEN TO YOU. (*Pause.*) That's all it is. How are they different? (*Pause.*) Some poor newly married guy gets run down by a cab. Some *busboy* wins the lottery. (*Pause.*) All it is, it's a carnival. What's special . . . what *draws* us? (*Pause.*) We're all different. (*Pause.*) We're not the same. (*Pause.*) We are not the same. (*Pause.*) Hmmm. (*Pause. Sighs.*) It's been a long day. (*Pause.*) What are you drinking?

Lingk: Gimlet.

Roma: Well, let's have a couple more. My name is Richard Roma, what's yours?

Lingk: Lingk. James Lingk.

Roma: James. I'm glad to meet you. (*They shake hands.*) I'm glad to meet you, James. (*Pause.*) I want to show you something. (*Pause.*) It might mean *nothing* to you . . . and it might not. I don't know. I don't know anymore. (*Pause. He takes out a small map and spreads it on a table.*) What is that? Florida. Glengarry Highlands. Florida. "Florida. *Bullshit.*" And maybe that's true; and that's what *I* said: but look *here:* what is this? This is a piece of land. Listen to what I'm going to tell you now:

FOOL FOR LOVE
by Sam Shepard

Eddie and May are half brother and sister, but they didn't meet till they were teenagers. Their father, as Eddie explains, "had two separate lives. . . . He'd live with me and my mother for a while and then he'd disappear and go live with her and her mother for a while."

One night Eddie went with his father to May's house. There he met her mother and saw May for the first time. "That very second," he says, "we knew we'd never stop being in love."

The play takes place years later, when both characters are in their thirties. They have had a tempestuous, on again, off again relationship throughout those years. Now May wants to call it quits. She has accepted a date with a man named Martin, but Eddie shows up unexpectedly. He wants to take May away with him, but she won't go. When Eddie learns that she has a date, he stays to meet this new man and do what he can to undermine their relationship. Martin is a little slow and "square" and Eddie pokes fun at him (although Martin doesn't appear to realize it). May storms out of the room in exasperation, leaving the two men alone. Eddie then shocks Martin by telling him that May is his sister and that they "fooled around" in high school.

He then goes on to describe how they met and fell in love before he knew she was his sister. He describes how his father would disappear at times and be gone for a while. "Then, suddenly, one day it stopped. He stayed home for a while. . . . Then he started going on these long walks. . . . He'd walk out across the fields. In the dark. I used to watch him from my bedroom window."

(*For more information see scene from this play in "Scenes for One Man and One Woman" section in this book.*)

Eddie: But one night I asked him if I could go with him. And he took me. We walked straight out across the fields together. In the dark. And I remember it was just plowed and our feet sank down in the powder and the dirt came up over the tops of my shoes and weighed me down. I wanted to stop and empty my shoes out but he wouldn't stop. He kept walking straight ahead and I was afraid of losing him in the dark so I just kept us as best I could. And we were completely silent the whole time. Never said a word to each other. We could barely see a foot in front of us, it was so dark. And these white owls kept swooping down out of nowhere, hunting for jackrabbits. Diving right past our heads, then disappearing. And we just kept walking silent like that for miles until we got to town. I could see the drive-in movie way off in the distance. That was the first thing I saw. Just square patches of color shifting. Then vague faces began to appear. And, as we got closer, I could recognize one of the faces. It was Spencer Tracy. Spencer Tracy moving his mouth. Speaking without words. Speaking to a woman in a red dress. Then we stopped at a liquor store and he made me wait outside in the parking lot while he bought a bottle. And there were all these Mexican migrant workers standing around a pick-up truck with red mud all over the tires. They were drinking beer and laughing and I remember being jealous of them and I didn't know why. And I remember seeing the old man through the glass door of the liquor store as he paid for the bottle. And I remember feeling sorry for him and I didn't know why. Then he came outside with the bottle wrapped in a brown paper sack and as soon as he came out, all the Mexican men stopped laughing. They just stared at us as we walked away.

(*During the course of the story the lights shift down very slowly into blues and greens—moonlight.*)

Eddie: And we walked right through town. Past the donut shop, past the miniature golf course, past the Chevron station. And he opened the bottle up and offered it to me. Before he even took a drink, he offered it to me first. And I took it and drank it and handed it back to him. And we just kept passing it back and forth like that as we walked until we drank the whole thing dry. And we never said a word the whole time. Then, finally, we reached this little white house with a red awning, on the far side of town. I'll never forget the red awning because it flapped in the night breeze and the porch light made it glow. It was a hot, desert breeze and the air smelled like new cut alfalfa. We walked right up to the front porch and I rang the bell and I remember getting real nervous because I wasn't expecting to visit anybody. I thought we were just out for a walk. And then this woman comes to the door. This real pretty woman with red hair. And she throws herself into his arms. And he starts crying. He just breaks down right there in front of me. And she's kissing him all over the face and holding him real tight and he's just crying like a baby. And then through the doorway, behind them both, I see this girl. (*The bathroom door very slowly and silently swings open revealing* MAY, *standing in the door frame back-lit with yellow light in her red dress. She just watches* EDDIE *as he keeps telling story. He and* MARTIN *are unaware of her presence.*) She just appears. She's just standing there, staring at me and I'm staring back at her and we can't take our eyes off each other. It was like we knew each other from somewhere but we couldn't place where. But the second we saw each other, that very second, we knew we'd never stop being in love.

MA RAINEY'S BLACK BOTTOM
by August Wilson

ACT I

Levee is a trumpet player in an all black pick-up band hired to play a recording session in a Chicago studio for Ma Rainey, a well-known black singer of the 1920's. Levee has written some songs and feels he has something new to say in music, but to record them he must have the approval of Mr. Sturdyvant, the white owner of the record company (who would rather be in a "respectable business" like textiles). The other musicians in the band make fun of Levee for his fawning and shuffling and prompt "yessir" whenever Mr. Sturdyvant talks to him. Levee tries to defend his actions. He claims he "studies the white man. I got him studied good." The others don't accept this and insist that the white man has him "spooked." Levee, exasperated, asserts again that the way he treats the white man is based on a plan, not on fear. The others try to calm him down, but they have touched a raw nerve and his rage won't be stilled.

Levee: Levee got to be Levee! And he don't need nobody messing with him about the white man—cause you don't know nothing about me. You don't know Levee. You don't know nothing about what kind of blood I got! What kind of heart I got beating here!

(*He pounds his chest.*)

I was eight years old when I watched a gang of white mens come into my daddy's house and have to do with my mama any way they wanted.

(*Pauses.*)

We was living in Jefferson County, about eighty miles outside of Natchez. My daddy's name was Memphis . . . Memphis Lee Green . . . had him near fifty acres of good farming land. I'm talking about good land! Grow anything you want! He done gone off of shares and bought this land from Mr. Hallie's widow woman after he done passed on. Folks called him an uppity nigger 'cause he done saved and borrowed to where he could buy this land and be independent.

(*Pauses.*)

It was coming on planting time and my daddy went into Natchez to get him some seed and fertilizer. Called me, say, "Levee you the man of the house now. Take care of your mama while I'm gone." I wasn't but a little boy, eight years old.

(*Pauses.*)

My mama was frying up some chicken when them mens come in that house. Must have been eight or nine of them.

She standing there frying that chicken and them mens come and took hold of her just like you take hold of a mule and make him do what you want.

(*Pauses.*)

There was my mama with a gang of white mens. She tried to fight them off, but I could see where it wasn't gonna do her any good, I didn't know what they were doing to her . . . but I figured whatever it was they may as well do to me too. My daddy had a knife that he kept around there for hunting and working and whatnot. I knew where he kept it and I went and got it.

I'm gonna show you how spooked up I was by the white man. I tried my damndest to cut one of them's throat! I hit him on the shoulder with it. He reached back and grabbed hold of that knife and whacked me across the chest with it.

(LEVEE *raises his shirt to show a long ugly scar.*)

That's what made them stop. They was scared I was gonna bleed to death. My mama wrapped a sheet around me and carried me two miles down to the Furlow place and they drove me up to Doc Albans. He was waiting on a calf to be born, and say he ain't had time to see me. They carried me up to Miss Etta, the midwife, and she fixed me up.

My daddy came back and acted like he done accepted the facts of what happened. But he got the names of them mens from mama. He found out who they was and then we announced we was moving out of that county. Said good-bye to everybody . . . all the neighbors. My daddy went and smiled in the face of one of them crackers who had been with my mama. Smiled in his face and sold him our land. We moved over with relations in Caldwell. He got us settled in and then he took off one day. I ain't never seen him since. He sneaked back, hiding up in the woods, laying to get them eight or nine men.

(*Pauses.*)

He got four of them before they got him. They tracked him down in the woods. Caught up with him and hung him and set him afire.

(*Pauses.*)

My daddy wasn't spooked up by the white man. Nosir!
And that taught me how to handle them. I seen my daddy
go up and grin in this cracker's face . . . smile in his face
and sell him his land. All the while he's planning how he's
gonna get him and what he's gonna do to him. That
taught me how to handle them. So you all just back up
and leave Levee alone about the white man. I can smile
and say yessir to whoever I please. I got time coming to
me. You all just leave Levee alone about the white man.

ANGELS FALL
by Lanford Wilson

ACT II

The setting is "a small and very plain adobe mission in
northwestern New Mexico." One June day a main road is
closed because of a possible accident at a nuclear power plant,
and cars are diverted through a barren stretch of terrain
where the mission is the only shelter. During the course of the
day various travelers and locals gather at the mission and, in
time, bare intimate details of their lives to each other. One of
the travelers is a young man named Salvatore Zappala, nick-
named Zappy. He is a professional tennis player and is traveling with a woman (somewhat older than himself) named
Marion Clay, an art dealer from Chicago, whose deceased
husband was a "regional painter" of the West.

In the moments just prior to Zappy's monologue, the mission priest had been trying to convince one of the group to
return to teaching, a profession that he believes one is "called"
to. Zappy interjects that he understands what it is like to be
called: "That 'call,' man, that's the moment, man. That's
magic. That's magic, that's magic . . . . that magic that happens and you know who you are, you know? Like, 'I'm a doctor, is what I do.' Or 'I teach kids.' . . . Or like when I found
out I was a tennis player. . . . No joke. I went to church and lit
a candle, man."

Zappy continues:

Zap: Really. I said my novenas, man, 'cause it had been like
a—not a miracle that anyone would know except just
me—but it had been like when those girls saw Our Lady
of Fatima up on that hill. It was really weird. I was like in
the fifth grade and I was watching these two hamburgers
on some practice court, and they took a break and one of
them hands me his racket. So I threw up a toss like I'd
seen them do and zap! Three inches over the net, two
inches inside the line. There wasn't nobody over there,
but that was an ace, man. You should have heard those
guys razz me. I mean, you know, they say, "Man, you
stink." And all those things you can't repeat in front of a
priest. They was really on my case. And I think that's the
first time anybody ever looked at me. I mean, I was
skinny, you've never seen—most of the girls in my home-
room had about twenty pounds on me. So this guy shows
me a backhand grip and he hits one to me and zap! You
mother! Backhand! Right down the line. And the thing
is, that's where I wanted it. I saw the ball come at me,
and I said I'm gonna backhand this sucker right down the
line, and I did.

   So then they took their ball back. Which I don't
blame them, 'cause no high school hotshot is gonna get off
on being showed up by this eleven-year-old creep that's
built like a parking meter, you know?

   But that was it. I hit that first ball and I said, "This is
me. This is what I do. What I do is tennis." And once you
know, then there's no way out. You've been showed something. Even if it's just tennis, you can't turn around and
say you wasn't showed that.

   So I went to church and said a novena for those meatballs 'cause they didn't know all the butterflies that was
in my stomach, that they'd been my angels. But, man, on
the way home, anybody had asked me what I did, right
there I'd have said, "I play tennis." Didn't know love from
lob, didn't matter. That's what I am. 'Cause once you
know what you are, the rest is just work.

ANTON CHEKHOV'S "THE DUEL"
adapted by Michael Schulman and Eva Mekler
from the translation by Ann Dunnigan

ACT III, SCENE 2

Ivan Layevsky and Nadyezhda Fyordorovna had been passionately in love. She left her husband for him and they fled St. Petersburg to lead a useful and meaningful life doing honest labor—something neither had ever done. They came to a seaside village on the Black Sea in the Caucasus and Layevsky took a job as an official in the Ministry of Finance. But they soon wearied of the place, the people, the interminable heat—and each other. They are unable to leave, though—neither has any money. Nadyezhda has no family to turn to, and Layevsky's mother, from an aristocratic family, will have nothing to do with them because of their adultery.

Last night, Nadyezhda, desperate for some excitement in her life, had a brief, unsatisfying affair that Layevsky discovered. Also last night, Layevsky got embroiled in an argument with Von Koren, a man who has been his constant enemy in the village and he rashly accepted Von Koren's challenge to duel with pistols. Layevsky knows that Von Koren is an expert marksman, and he realizes he will probably be killed.

His primary concern, though, is what will happen to Nadyezhda if he dies, how she will fare with no money. He feels that he is to blame for her seeking out another man—that he brought her to an arid place, then lost interest in her and, after that, either ignored or criticized her. It is late at night, just a short while before the duel is to take place. Layevsky is seated at a desk, writing a letter to his mother, asking her to take care of Nadyezhda.

(*For more information, see other scenes from this play in other sections of this book.*)

Layevsky: Dear Mother . . . Whether they kill me tomorrow or make a mockery of me—that is, leave me my life—I am ruined in any case. Whether this dishonored woman kills herself from shame and despair or drags out her pitiful existence, she is ruined in any case . . . I ask you in the name of a merciful God to give shelter and a little warmth and kindness to this unfortunate woman whom I have dishonored, and who is now alone and impoverished and weak; to forget and forgive everything . . . everything, and by your charity to atone, at least in part, for your son's terrible sin . . . (*Thunder is heard.*) A storm. (*He continues to write.*) It is storming now. I recall how as a child I always ran bareheaded into the garden when there was a storm, two fair-haired little girls with blue eyes chasing after me, and how we were drenched by the rain. The little girls would laugh with delight, but when there was a loud clap of thunder, they trustingly pressed close to me as I crossed myself and repeated Holy, Holy, Holy . . . Dear Mother, where have they gone, in what sea have they drowned, those early buds of fair, pure life? I no longer fear storms nor love nature; I have no God; all the trusting little girls I have ever known have been ruined by me and my contemporaries . . . In my entire life I have never planted one tree nor grown a single blade of grass in my own garden. Surrounded by living things, I have never saved so much as an insect, but have only destroyed, ruined, lied, and lied, and lied. Mother, I am not sure if you can understand all this or even if you really care . . . (*He stops writing and reading, and tears up letter on the line.*) What a fool!

SAVAGE IN LIMBO
by John Patrick Shanley

Tony Aronica lives in the Bronx. He is "a streamlined Italian stud with a streak of self-doubt and a yearning sweetness," and he wears leather pants. He has just told his girlfriend,

Linda, that he doesn't want to see her anymore. He says he only wants to see "ugly" women. Linda is very upset and very confused. Tony follows her to their neighborhood bar, Scales, to try to explain: "Hey, you think it was easy kissin off a fox like you? You don't know nothin," he tells her. He continues:

(For more information about this play, see other scenes from it in other sections of this book.)

Tony: I was in my car outside this place over the weekend. I hadda couple a drinks and I was a little fuzzy, so I was waitin till I cleared. It was dark. I was sittin there. And this unknown girl got in. She just got in the car. And she started talkin to me. She started rappin to me about the Soviet Union. Yeah. 'Bout their economy. Housin. How they feel about China bein right there. Everything. Everything about the Soviet Union. She musta talked for two hours. Russian paranoia. Tass. The Gulag. I'm sittin there an I'm takin this in. The Trans-Siberian Railroad. What kinda tanks they got in Eastern Europe. Why they need American wheat. And then she was finished. She'd told me everything she knew. So I took her in the back seat and I banged her. And do you know something? It was the best. It was the best I ever had. And it whadn't cause she knew a lotta tricks or like that. It was cause she'd told me about the Soviet Union. And then she left. Now here's the thing. She was very ugly. I don't even wanna talk about how she looked. Mucho ugly. I didn't think I could ever be with a woman like that. But it came about outta whatever, happenstance, and I was. And it turned out to be better than what I went after. Do you see what I mean? Do you see what I'm comin towards? I always went for the girl like you. And what finally fuckin come to me, what finally fuckin penetrated the wall here, was there was somethin else. Somethin I never even thought about, didn't have a clue about. When I talked to you, I called it ugly girls. I don't know what to call it. There's other people. Like in science fiction. Another dimension right there but you can't see it. I got into it for a minute by accident. Through a crack. I caught a flash. The dimension a ugly girls. I'm like onna those guys inna factory and they bring in all new machines. That's what I feel like. Like I gotta retrain or I'm gonna lose my place. Some girls you look at some girls you don't. I wanna see the things I didn't see before an let the stuff I was lookin at go by. I've done the fuckin thing we're in, Linda. I've been with you, I talked to you. I know what that is. That's what I meant when I said you didn't know nothin, but I whadn't sayin it right. You look at what I look at. You know what I know. I wanna look at somethin else. I wanna know somethin else. I'm thirty-two years old. I wanna change.

COMEDIANS
by Trevor Griffiths

ACT I

The setting is a night school in Manchester, England. Eddie Waters, a retired comic, teaches an adult education class for aspiring comedians. Waters takes comedy very seriously and stresses the ideals of the comedian: "A joke that feeds on ignorance starves the audience. We have the choice. We can say something or we can say nothing. Not everything true is funny, and not everything funny is true. Most comics *feed* prejudice and fear and blinkered vision, but the best ones, the best ones . . . illuminate them, make them clearer to see, easier to deal with. We've got to make people laugh till they cry. Cry. Till they find their pain and their beauty. Comedy is medicine. Not coloured sweeties to rot their teeth with."

Tonight the class members are excited because Waters has arranged for them to perform at a club. Waters is putting the class through some comedy "exercises" to warm them up when one of the comics, Price, makes up a sexual limerick that Waters calls "a joke that hates women." Waters then recites a litany of racial and ethnic slurs in order to shock the students into understanding why he finds the limerick so offensive. His message, though, is still not getting across. He tries to explain.

(To use as a monologue ignore McBrain's line.)

Waters: *(Driving home.)* If I've told you once I've told you a thousand times. We work *through* laughter, not *for* it. If all you're about is raising a laugh, OK, get on with it, good luck to you, but don't waste my time. There's plenty others as'll tek your money and do the necessary. Not Eddie Waters.

McBrain: *(Conciliatory, apologetic.)* So, a few crappy jokes, Mr. Waters . . .

Waters: It's not the jokes. It's not the jokes. It's what lies behind 'em. It's the attitude. A real comedian—that's a daring man. He *dares* to see what his listeners shy away from, fear to express. And what he sees is a sort of truth, about people, about their situation, about what hurts or terrifies them, about what's hard, above all, about what they *want*. A joke releases the tension, says the unsayable, any joke pretty well. But a true joke, a comedian's joke, has to do more than release tension, it has to *liberate* the will and the desire, it has to *change the situation*. *(Pause.)* There's very little won't take a joke. But when a joke bases itself upon a distortion—*(At* PRICE, *deliberately.)*—a "stereotype" perhaps—and gives the lie to the truth so as to win a laugh and stay in favour, we've moved away from a comic art and into the world of "entertainment" and slick success. *(Pause.)* You're better than that, damn you. And even if you're not, you should bloody well want to be.

END OF THE WORLD
by Arthur Kopit

ACT III

Playwright Michael Trent has been commissioned by a wealthy industrialist named Philip Stone to write a play about the destruction of the world through nuclear war. Stone gave Trent the outline and a lot of money *and* claimed that the production of this play could prevent the impending doom.

Trent became obsessed with understanding why Stone believes the world is doomed, and how a play can possibly prevent it. And he also needs to understand why Stone picked *him* to write it. Stone seems to indicate that nuclear war is inevitable because evil can be thrilling, that it can satisfy some kind of destructive curiosity. He also reminds Trent that they met once a long time ago, shortly after the birth of Trent's son. Trent realizes that he too knows something about the thrill of evil and that Stone once heard him describing how seductive that kind of experience can be. He describes his recollection to the audience.

Trent: Now I know where we met! . . . It was at *our* place, our apartment! We were living in the city then, and some friends came by to see our child, he'd just been born; obviously, one of them brought Stone, who? doesn't matter, Stone was there, I can see him, in a corner, *listening*, as I . . . tell. (*Pause.*) But *evil*? (*Long pause.*) Our son had just been born. We'd brought him home. He was what, five days old I guess. (*Pause.*) And then one day my wife went out . . . And I was left alone with him. And I was very excited. Because it was the first time I was alone with him. And I picked him up, this tiny thing, and started walking around the living room. We lived on a high floor, overlooking the river, the Hudson, light was streaming in, it was a lovely, lilting autumn day, cool, beautiful. And I looked down at this tiny creature, this tiny thing, and I realized . . . (*Pause.*) I realized I had never had anyone completely in my power before! . . . And I'd never known what that *meant*! never felt anything remotely like that before! And I saw I was standing near a window. And it was open. It was but a few feet away. And I thought, I could . . . *drop him out*! And I went *toward* the window, because I couldn't believe this thought had come into my head, *where had it come from*? Not one part of me felt anything for this boy but love, not one part! My wife and I had planned, we were both in love, there was no anger, no resentment, nothing dark in me toward him at all, no one could ever have been more in love with his child than

I, as much yes, but not more, not more, and I was thinking, I can throw him out of here! . . . and then he will be falling ten, twelve, fifteen, twenty stories down, and as he's falling I will be *unable to get him back*! . . . And I felt a *thrill*! I FELT A THRILL! IT WAS THERE! . . . And, of course, I resisted this. It wasn't hard to do, resisting wasn't hard . . . BUT I DIDN'T STAY BY THE WINDOW! . . . AND I CLOSED IT! I resisted by moving away, back into the room . . . And I sat down with him. (*Pause.*) Well there's not a chance I would have done it, not a chance! (*Pause.*) But I couldn't *take* a chance, it was very, very . . . seductive. (*Pause. He looks at* STONE.)

(*The lights come back a bit.* STONE *is sipping his tea, eyes on* TRENT.)

If doom comes, . . . it will come in *that* way.

LYDIE BREEZE
by John Guare

ACT II, SCENE 2

Jeremiah has come back to Nantucket after many years (the time is 1895). Now he is a successful young actor in England, where he has played Frankenstein's monster for five years. He has returned to confront Lydie Breeze, the woman who gave him syphilis when he was a boy. His father was having an affair with her when her husband, Joshua, caught them and killed his father. Later that same day, after her husband was taken to jail, Lydie approached the boy and seduced him. Now Jeremiah has returned to Lydie's home only to discover that she committed suicide years earlier. Jeremiah tells Joshua, "I've dreamed that some night, I'd see you in the audience and step down off the stage, strangle you in your seat and step back on the stage and they'd all think it was part of the play. . . . I came to kill you." But Jeremiah can't kill him. He reveals to Joshua what happened to him the day his father died.

(For more information see the introduction to another scene from this play in the section of the book, Scenes for Two Women.)

(To use the scene as a monologue omit Joshua's lines.)

Jere: I watched my father die. The police took you away. Amos went into town with you. The house was empty except for Lydie Breeze and me. I heard her footsteps coming up the stairs. Slow. Heavy. Her hair was down. She sat on the edge of my bed. She leaned over me. She held me. She had been weeping.

Joshua: Bam bam bam. Where have those hunters gone . . .

Jere: Her hair fell over me like a tent. Her hair smelled . . . Oriental. Omar Khayyam. *The Rubaiyat.* She whispered to me, Are you awake? Yes. I loved your father. I did too. She said, You fool, I loved him. And she began beating the walls and crickets were in them and began squawking. She was so angry. He betrayed me. How? You were all friends. I have something for you, she said. She reached under the sheet. Why were we whispering? Her hair made it all so quiet. And she began touching me I became frightened. What was happening? Oh yes, she said, you're his son. You're a man. And she rolled me onto her and I wanted to run away because I felt a power in me that had never existed in me before. I was thirteen. I did not know what that feeling was . . . She pushed me aside. And then she put her hair back and held me, all shaking, and began holding me like a mother. What have I done to you? What have I done to you? And she cried and she cried and she cried. At my father's funeral, she did not look at me. Then I was sent to England. Before I went, it began to hurt down there where she had taken me.

Joshua: Hurt?

Jere: I was afraid to tell anyone how much it hurt. I was afraid the people in England might send me back. Put me in jail. So I didn't tell anyone. The English relatives were so nice. The English school was so nice. Christ! I was even disappointed in the lack of horrors. The only horror was the pain coming out of me. And then the doctors diagnosed me and put me on medication of arsenic treatments which did not poison me but almost did. And I was told I could never have a normal life and must never touch a woman because of how infected I was and I began to live in that tent of hair and suffocate and dream only of Lydie Breeze who had poisoned me and I went with whores because I had to release this need in me. And then a series of murders began in London. Brutal murders. Prostitutes. Tarts. Useless bits of humanity. Murders on streets that I had been on . . . and I became terrified and to save myself and stop the bad dreams said I will become other people who are not afraid and I became an actor . . . and I had success . . . and now I want to face that woman and meet her as an equal. Because I am no longer afraid of her. I want myself back. I want to kill Lydie Breeze or make love to Lydie Breeze. But I come back and find she is dead. And there can be no—revenge? I don't want that. I want her to see her poison. I don't want to be this monster. I am sick of playing this monster and if I am asked to play it for the rest of my life I have to have a whole human being to come back to when the curtain comes down. A human being!

SPLIT SECOND
by Dennis McIntyre

ACT II, SCENE 4

Val is a black police officer. He shot and killed a white man whom he had caught trying to steal a car. The killing was unnecessary since the man was already handcuffed. Val lost control and drew his revolver in reaction to a string of ugly racial slurs that the man directed at him.

In his report, Val claimed the man came at him with a knife and he shot in self-defense. A departmental hearing is set up and Val's father, Rusty, a retired police officer, wants him to confess the truth about what happened. His wife wants him to maintain his lie. Val tries to defend himself to his father by inferring that he would have done the same thing if it had happened to him when he was an officer. The father retorts,

"I never let it happen! . . . You lost control, buster! You snapped! That's not why they gave you a badge!" Val tries to explain to his father what happened to him that led to the shooting.

(*For more information, see the scene from this play in the section of the book containing "Scenes for Two Men".*)

Val: That's right! I lost it! I finally lost my "cool." I snapped, and it was all out front. And do you want to know how long I've been waiting to do it? All my life. The "chip" just got too heavy, and I didn't want to carry it around anymore. One split second, that's all it took to knock it off, and that made him dead. No, it didn't happen to you. Not you. But let's say it did happen. One time, one night, when you'd finally heard it once too often. It was hot out. It was dark. You were alone. The scum of the earth, spitting it out at you. "Nigger!" "Coon!" "Shine!" "Jigaboo!" And you didn't want to take it anymore. You couldn't take it anymore. And then "click." Nobody heard the shot, and nobody saw him fall. Who was he, anyway? Who in the fuck was he?! What then? What would you have done? Thrown away Mom? Twenty-five years? Thrown away me? Thrown away your friends? Your job? Your reputation? Your weekends on the Allegheny teaching me how to fish? Your nights in the Poconos—after supper—teaching me how to ride? Is that what you would have done, Rusty? Just because some son of a bitch, the lowest of the low, finally screamed "nigger" at you once too often and once too loud?! Is it?!

SEA MARKS
by Gardner McKay

ACT II, SCENE 4

Colm is a fisherman from a small island off the coast of Ireland. He fell in love with Timothea, a "city woman" from Liverpool. He corresponded with her for over a year and then came to visit her. He cannot bring himself to leave her, although he dislikes Liverpool and longs to be home.

Timothea, who works for a publisher, found Colm's letters filled with poetry and, without telling him, had parts of them published as a book called *Sea Sonnets*. The newspapers are now fussing about him, calling him the Irish Robert Frost, and he has been invited by the Wednesday Afternoon Club to speak and read from his book. Colm is not comfortable with his new fame; nor does he like being described as a "primitive."

On the day he is to give his presentation he receives a letter that his closest friend, the man he fished with for years, has drowned—and that his body washed up on shore after ten days in the sea. The man, "the MacAfee," taught Colm fishing and was like a father to him. Colm feels responsible for the MacAfee's death because he wasn't by his side in their "curragh," or boat.

Later that day Colm keeps his appointment at the Wednesday Afternoon Club. He tells them about his "good father" who has "gone dark."

(For more information on this play, see additional notes in the "Monologues for Women" section of this book.)

Colm: I'll say a few words to you and then read you some marks that I made at a place as far away from this room as the other side of life. An island by the name of Cliffhorn Heads. In my language, the Irish, it would be called "Inish Shinderra." (*He pauses.*) Do any of you remember what a sunrise is like?

Sort of a gray meeting of the clouds at the east, and then a lightening of the sky, swiftening, lightening, swiftening, lightening until it is there?

Have any of you ever been out on the dark water, with not much sea running, and have known, really for true, that in a bit you'd be able to hold your hands out like this (*He holds his arms straight out at eye level, fingers stretched and raises them slightly.*) so that they could be warmed by the sun that is coming? For these elegances, you must become a fisherman. (*He pauses.*)

Fishing is, after all, a simple matter. You set your nets and you haul them in. You stay off the rocks at night and you anchor with care. And you look for signs that the sky is kind enough to provide. (*He pauses.*)

There are a number of people who do not understand the sea and I am among them. The sea is never simple—with its currents and strange habits—and bears watching. The sea is not a sentimental place to go—it is waiting for you to make a mistake. After all my years on it, I am kin to it, but I am not married to it—the sea is not a woman, after all. (*He pauses.*)

My partner is called the MacAfee.

From the time I could walk, I remember he had white hair, and a pipe growing out of his mouth. He'd smoke anything—I imagined—cow dung—just to keep his face lit. (*Pause.*)

There was never a man I loved more than the MacAfee. Men liked him every way there was to like a man. Ah, the eyes on him, like two candles burning. In one stroke of his eyes he could give you all the love you needed to last you a year. (*Pause.*)

I recall three ways I saw him.

The one was standing in the curragh, knee high in haddock—the first boat to fill—the hairs on his beard shiny from fish slime. And him calling out to me, just calling out to me.

The second, I see him at the Captain's with a black pint in front of him and another in his hand, drinking with us in front of the fire, older than us and smarter, too, but never letting on unless it was needed.

I see him then at Sunday breakfast. It would have been a crab or two with a thick buttered bannock and a pint.

He was a grand man. You should have known him.

Anyhow, there's an old fisherman drowned who'll live in me forever. (*Without meaning to,* COLM *has begun to see the MacAfee. Now, suddenly, he has put himself in the curragh with the MacAfee at the time of his drowning. Whatever* COLM *feels about it can be seen and heard in* COLM*'s momentary insanity.*)

When we would go to fish, we might carry a small sail on the curragh and set it right. Now if the seas were running high and the wind turning in sudden gusts, it would send us over the wave, and out, and down, into the vale between the waves. And my heart went down there, and my soul went along, too, if I had a soul at the time.

Oh, I knew we'd rise again, but it always seemed like tomorrow when we came above the wave, and then it was higher than before.

And we'd perch on the new wave a moment, the gale holding us balanced longer than ever, and then AAAAAAAAAAAAAAAAAAAAAAAAAAH—it was OUT and DOWN and into that dark place between the waves that want to hold you there. That place where the wind does not go. And again you be up, high, balanced. And then OUT and DOWN. All over again. (COLM *pauses a moment, stabilizing himself, relieved.*)

After a while of this, and when it looks like you might get home again and walk along a boreen, or duck under a laundry line, you begin to feel strong. And even though the wind is trying to tear your clothes away, you don't mind. You're grinning, and the wind is hissing in your ears, and you're sailing home!

But you should never feel as though you've conquered the sea. If you do, there's any number of words for the sort of fool you are. And the sea doesn't ever weary of making fools of us. For if it sends us home at night to light our fires, it's only because it wants us back to sport with us another time.

Don't ever think you had anything to do with it. Because you'll be mistaken.

Or maybe not. (*Pause.*)

When I was young, a wave so high swept across the low waist of our island and left the islandmen trembling with fear, and me among them. I will always have that feeling, but am now strong enough to visit the sea and live on it a while.

It has been my life good and bad.

And the sea provides.

The sea provides. (*Pause.*)

The oldies knit these pretty jerseys for us. The widows. They keen their yarn and knit this pattern into each one of them. Every town along both coasts has its own pattern and this is ours.

Would you like to know why they knit our jerseys at night? The sheep are asleep at night, and are content. They think the jerseys will be better for it. And so be the men inside them. (*Pause.*)

Now when a man floats into our harbor and the fish have taken out his eyes and nibbled off his lips, we can tell from his jersey where he might have come to us from. And so he gets brought home.

But the cleanest burial is when you slip away and are gone.

You should never be found by another man. You should make sure you go deep and not ever rise to the surface. Let the people remember you the way you were the morning you went out.

You shouldn't go floating down the coast looking for your harbor while the fish eat from you for days and wash up on the shore like that, putting frights into people and asking to be buried again, this time in the ground.

Anyhow; that's why we wear these very pretty jerseys. They settle the question of dress six days out of seven. But I was going to read you sonnets, wasn't I?, from this idiot book. I was going to tell you that the sea was a single great arm holding us all in our place, or some such nonsense. Instead, I'll tell you a short one.

We are now weavers, we are now caulkers,
We are now baiters, we are now young.

We are now rowers, we are now fishers,
We are now masters, we are now men.

We are now drinkers, we are now singers,
We are now mourners, we are now dead.

RAINDANCE
by M. Z. Ribalow

ACT I

John Wesley Hardin is a famous gunfighter in "the mystical American southwest." He is "a fine figure of a man . . . dignified . . . soft-spoken, proud . . . fearless . . . (and) at all times coiled, watchful (and) ready." He is "a killer." It is hot and dry and Hardin is drinking a whiskey in a saloon. He walks into a spotlight as the rest of the stage goes dark. He has something to tell the audience.

Hardin: I was in love with a woman once. Oh, I know I'm just John Wesley Hardin to you all: a little larger than life, the gunslinger in the ballads, the picture on the posters, the daydream in the dark of night. But even though you may not want to think so, I got a heart, I got lips, I got toes under these hand-tooled dusty boots.

Yeah, I was in love once too. She was no bigger'n a moonbeam and as pretty as an Arizona sunset; long yellow hair that reached down to her waist like a waterfall made out of spun gold. Her eyes were these great big purple pools of shimmering light that made me want to dive deep down into them like a tired dolphin.

You see what I mean? She had me talkin' just as bad as any harp-playing, pansy-assed, chickenshit faggot poet. I step aside for no living critter, but I just stopped cold whenever I saw her. I had faced down Ringo and the James boys, shot it out with twenty men at once and never had a scratch, gone hand to hand with a grizzly bear and once, when I ran out of bullets, killed four men with my spurs.

But I had no more chance with my golden Lily than

a shipwrecked sailor would with a mermaid. So one day I just told her: "There's a lump in my throat, and it's you." I never was much good at the talkin' part. But she just smiled at me, soft and easy, and she was my Lily from then on. Gave me something to live for. A reason to believe.

And don't you know, that was the trouble. For the first time, I began to taste fear. Fear I might lose her somehow, fear I might get shot down and leave her alone. Me, who never gave a damn. Nothing had ever made me hesitate the slightest split-second in drawing my six-gun and blowing someone to kingdom come.

But now there was sweat on my trigger finger.

If I'd left her, she would've grieved; and I loved her too much to hurt her. So I killed her. Couldn't bear the thought of putting a bullet into that pretty hide, so I waited till she was asleep and smiling one night and strangled her with her own hair. Long and yellow and soft; she couldn't have felt a thing.

That was all years ago now. Well, I had to, don't you see? I couldn't be loving her—I was John Wesley Hardin, the greatest gunfighter in the wild west. Love and death, fear and beer, all the same to me: I can take them or leave them, and I'll do plenty of both before you see the last of me. I'm John Wesley Hardin, damn it! John Wesley Hardin!

INDEX

ABOUT THE EDITORS

Having taught acting at the Lee Strasberg Theatre Institute and at the Actors Studio, MICHAEL SCHULMAN now teaches at his own workshop in New York City. He has also written and directed a number of plays for Off and Off-Off Broadway theatre. He is director of the British-American Acting Academy, a school with branches in New York and London, dedicated to the synthesis of the best of British and American techniques. He is also chairman of the theatre department of the Usdan Center for the Creative and Performing Acts. In addition to his theatrical career, he is a clinical and research psychologist who has held assistant professorships at Fordham and Rutgers universities. His Ph.D. is from the City University of New York.

EVA MEKLER is both a playwright and former actress who has performed on and Off Broadway. Trained in psychology, with a master's degree from New York University, she divides her time between her work as a clinician and writing. She is also editor of *The New Generation of Acting Teachers*.

Sam Shepard, Pulitzer Prize-Winning Playwright, Is:

"... PHENOMENAL ... THE BEST PRACTICING
AMERICAN PLAYWRIGHT."
—The New Republic

AND HIS PLAYS ARE AVAILABLE IN FINE
COLLECTIONS FROM BANTAM:

☐ *Sam Shepard: Seven Plays*
(34611 • $8.95)

Seven of his best plays with an Introduction by Richard Gilman

Buried Child   Curse of the Starving Class   Tongues
La Turista   The Tooth of Crime   Savage Love
True West

☐ *Fool for Love and Other Plays*
(34590 • $8.95)

FOOL FOR LOVE plus seven more
with an Introduction by Ross Wetzsteon

Angel City   Seduced   Action
Melodrama Play   Suicide in B♭   Cowboy Mouth
Geography of a Horse Dreamer

☐ *The Unseen Hand and*
Other Plays
(34263 • $8.95)

Fourteen plays from Shepard's backlist

The Unseen Hand   Forensic & The Navigators
Chicago   Holy Ghostly
Red Cross   Operation Sidewinder
4-H Club   Mad Dog Blues
Icarus's Mother   Black Bog Beast Bait
Fourteen Hundred Thousand Killers Head
Rock Garden   Cowboys #2

- -

Bantam Books, Dept. SS6, 414 East Golf Road, Des Plaines, IL 60016

Please send me the books checked above. I am enclosing $_____ (please
add $2.00 to cover postage and handling). Send check or money order—
no cash or C.O.D.s please.

Mr/Ms _____

Address _____

City/State _____ Zip _____

SS6—7/89

Please allow four to six weeks for delivery. This offer expires 1/90.
Prices and availability subject to change without notice.

Special Offer
Buy a Bantam Book
for only 50¢.

Now you can have Bantam's catalog filled with hundreds of titles plus take advantage of our unique and exciting bonus book offer. A special offer which gives you the opportunity to purchase a Bantam book for only 50¢. Here's how!

By ordering any five books at the regular price per order, you can also choose any other single book listed (up to a $5.95 value) for just 50¢. Some restrictions do apply, but for further details why not send for Bantam's catalog of titles today!

Just send us your name and address and we will send you a catalog!